Papers on the

ETHICS

of Administration

Papers on the

ETHICS

of Administration

EDITED BY

N. Dale Wright

Brigham Young University

Library of Congress Cataloging-in-Publication Data

Papers on the ethics of administration.

Includes index.
1. Business ethics. 2. Industrial management—Moral
and ethical aspects. 3. Political ethics. 4. Public
administration—Moral and ethical aspects. I. Wright,
N. Dale (Norman Dale), 1938–
HF5387.P365 1988   174′.4   88-16737
ISBN 0-88706-961-4c
ISBN 0-88706-962-2 (pbk.)

Brigham Young University, Provo, Utah 84602

Distributed by State University of New York Press,
State University Plaza, Albany, New York 12446-0001

Contents

Contents

Acknowledgments

W<small>E</small> thank Howard A. Christy, senior editor, and Louise E. Williams, assistant editor, of Scholary Publications at Brigham Young University, and Krista A. West, graduate assistant in the School of Management, for their diligence and skill in preparing this volume for publication. We also thank Paul H. Thompson, dean of the School of Management, and J. David Billeter, a member of the National Advisory Council of the School of Management, for their total support.

Introduction

N. Dale Wright and Stanford S. McConkie

THE recent well-publicized cases of unethical behavior on the part of top-level executives in business, as well as in government, have given impetus to an increasing national concern with organizational or administrative ethics. Universities have reflected this concern with a flurry of activity to introduce ethics courses into the management curriculum. Questions have been raised, from what and how to teach down to the question of whether a person can even be taught to be ethical.

In order to pursue this discussion, a group of scholars met at Brigham Young University in the spring of 1987. Each had been invited to write a paper about his or her own particular interest in the area of organizational ethics: there were no restrictions. They then met with other academicians, students, and interested practitioners to explore some of the dimensions of ethics in management and to test their thoughts in the rigors of academic debate. These essays resulted from that conference.

The evolution of the discussion gave rise to a comment by one of the participants that "we don't even agree on a common set of values upon which our organizational ethics can be based." To

N. Dale Wright is the director of the Institute of Public Management and Health Administration at Brigham Young University, and Stanford S. McConkie is an adjunct professor of organizational behavior at Brigham Young University and president of S and M Natural Resources, Inc.

1

begin a work on administrative ethics without some definition of the substance of the term would suggest, to the thoughtful student, that we know not of what we speak. To attempt some definition would only confirm the suspicion. It may well be that the single most significant aspect of this collection of essays is not in what is said but in what is left unsaid. We search for ethical paradigms to guide our teachings and practice, yet we avoid the hard questions as to the nature and ends of the society that our paradigms will create. Our decision-making models are of more interest to the philosophical taxonomist than to the administrative practitioner. We make declarations as to the modes of behavior that ought to be expected of, and followed by, our disciples without equivalent consideration of the means for transmitting the expectation from generation to generation. In our individual self-confidence, each remains unsure that his or her personal value commitments are shared by colleagues as the basis for the renovation of administrative theory and practice. Yet, as this particular conference progressed, more agreement than disagreement was generated.

To begin, the *significance* of organizational ethics is a major point of agreement. We work, study, pray, play, travel, and sometimes eat and sleep in organizations. Organizations amplify the impact of administrators in all our lives. Decisions with ethical implications are especially magnified. Regardless of the claims made by others, administration is, in one form or another, the world's oldest profession. It is an essential part of coordinating any commonly pursued activity and is especially important in conducting the affairs of the government and the economy. As societies have grown and developed, administrative activities have increasingly become more complex.

Administrative ethics are the formal and informal restraints that give legitimacy to the actions of an administrator. From classical times, writings treating the teaching of administrative ethics have been found in political philosophy, political economy, and theology. Political writings dealt with the broad sweeps of governmental theory, including efforts to define "the good life," questions of "who should rule" and "how is power to be controlled." Early writing in political economy established the "proper" or "non-socially responsible" role of the economic endeavor, as well as the questions of how wealth was to be shared and the proper relations between employee and employer. While such writings have had profound influence among the well-educated at the highest levels of administrative organization, they have had but little conscious impact among the rank and file, for the philosophies of the economists and the political scientists were imposed through societal organizations without individual participation by the common person. The churches provided the arena in which values were taught directly to the average person, enabling her or him to internalize an ethical framework.

As a practical matter for most, popular theology has been and remains the most important source of ethical training in a society. Unlike political theory and economics, which searches for answers by human intellect, religions authoritatively declare the answers by divine revelation. Where philosophical writings are "understood" by the intellectual elite, religion is taught by and becomes part of the emotions of average individuals. By intellect, only a few can understand the standards of ethical behavior; through religion, all can know standards of right and wrong. Operating by intellect alone, the motivation toward ethical behavior may be little more than the subjective probability of being caught. In most religious teachings, there are no odds of getting away with it; the day of judgement will come. This is but one of the snags in the thicket of administrative ethics deserving reflection and exploration.

As the *Papers on the Science of Administration*,[1] published some fifty years ago, represented the apex of the "Principles of Administration" era, we hope that this collection will make a significant contribution to the search for ethics and to the birth of a new era in which we return the ancient and difficult questions of the ends of society and the role of the individual in pursuing those ends. It is on the answers to these questions that the search for ethical guidance must begin.

Administrative Heritage

In this introductory essay we discuss the value context of the development of management thought. The earliest discourses of administrative ethics we title "Organizational Ethics of God's Order." Under this rubric are included the political theorists, many of whom wore the cleric cloak, who developed the concepts of the divine right of kings. These concepts gave legitimacy to the exercise of power for the maintenance of social order at almost any sacrifice of individual dignity of the common individual. Rulers of all types occupying the thrones of monarchies of Christian Europe quickly transformed this into what could be termed the "divine right of rulers." Basically, these concepts pronounced that "monarchs," whether enthroned by inheritance, election, or armed revolt, fulfilled a position in the grand order of deity. They could do no wrong for they, their representatives, and their actions were sanctified by God.

It was against the philosophy of the divine right of rulers, accepted for generations, that the Framers of the Declaration of Independence and the Constitution fought. For they postulated a form of government based on inherent rights of each individual bestowed by the same God who, it had been said, endowed kings solely with divine rights. The Founders espoused a philosophy stating that, ideally, governance must be based on ethical character of the individual governors. Because many of the Founders held concerns that the common man may not fulfill the idealistic view of man, they also developed governing structures that prevented bad character from dominating. We title this "Organizational Ethics of Good Character." This view of organizational ethics enjoyed a relatively brief life span of less than a century and, in some ways, may have been a fortuitous aberration in the development of organizational values.

The captains of industry and commerce during the industrial revolution crept under the skirts of the divine right of kings and set up a new throne in the kingdoms of Christianity—the Seat of Merchants. They tied the new throne carefully into the Ethics of God's Order. Commerce and Christianity became one in their eyes and in their propaganda. The immoral use of power with its unconscionable imposition of suffering was imposed in the name of a commerce sanctified by Christianity.

The Ethics of God's Order eventually changed in tandem with societal changes brought about by the acceptance of the science of the period, wherein the value questions of organizational life became answerable by the scientific method. We label this period the "Ethics of Empirical Order." The early proponents were typified by Jeremy Bentham.[2] The Protestant Ethic was replaced with a utilitarian precursor to social Darwinism. A transition was made from "one is wealthy because one is righteous" to "one is wealthy because one is strong." Both of these viewpoints were desirable to the proponents of the day because the world was explained as being either in God's order or in the compelling order of social nature. Social Darwinism was actually preferable because one did not need to rationalize one's mistreatment of his fellow by attributing it to the order of God. One could say that the mistreatment of others was an inherent good because that is the way society operated and the strongest, and perhaps the meanest, should occupy positions of power regardless of how they got there or how they were abusing the position.

From the pseudoscience of social Darwinism the ethical trail leads to the empiricism of both the administrative and behavioral sciences. This occurred in the late 1800s and early 1900s. The acceptance of the scientific method led to either the abandonment of traditional values or at best their relegation to an insignificant position in management thought. We lost the societal view posited by the "Ethics of God's Order" as well as the concern for the individual pursued by the Founders. These were replaced with an ultimate value of impersonal efficiency.

Society in general, following the Korean War, became uneasy with the new efficiency deity which gave sanctification to all forms of administrative excesses. These ranged from an organizationally controlled society which trampled individual rights to a lack of concern with the ends of the same society. We label this period the "Organizational Ethics of Social Unrest." It is a period of concern with the social responsibility of organizations. An attempt was made to create organizational systems that would either create good people or control the excesses of bad people.

An underlying theme in many of the sessions of the BYU conference was the necessity to be concerned with the ethics of the individual within the organization. There seemed to be a call to return to the Organizational Ethics of Good Character.

We cannot explore all of these eras of organizational ethics in this brief essay, albeit they deserve honest, deep pondering. We can highlight only a few of the overlapping and perhaps conflicting values in the colorful plaid of administrative thought.

In the final chapter of the *Papers on the Science of Administration*, Luther Gulick wrote: "In the science of administration whether public or private, the basic 'good' is efficiency. The fundamental objective of the science of administration is the accomplishment of the work in hand with the least expenditure of man-power and materials. Efficiency is thus axiom number one in the value scale of administration."[3] This statement summarizes fairly the role of values in the management thought of the era. This is not to say that all of the writers of the period accepted the view that human beings were valued only as appendages to machines, whether mechanical or organizational. Gulick and his colleagues addressed themselves to the administration chaos that typified the extant conduct of administrators—at all levels. Thus, they espoused a narrower view of administration that centered on such aspects as formal organization, coordination, and delegation of authority, with efficiency as the locus. In short, they sought a "science" of administration.

They had accepted for public administration the dichotomy between politics and administration urged by Woodrow Wilson.[4] Wilson had argued that policy (or value) issues were the proper task of politics and political debate and that administration should center on the efficiency of implementation. Wilson believed that American business administration, on the other hand, was based upon laissez-faire markets, in which the ultimate value of efficiency found a comfortable lodging. Therefore, he urged public administration to follow the lead of business administration and get out of the policy-making trap. Efficiency was the magical cure. Because the "market" set the value parameters, business administrators could ignore sticky value problems and concentrate on administrative efficiency. Gulick and his colleagues brought that movement to its apex in the late 1930s. Interestingly, their ideas were nearly as influential in business administration as they were in public administration.

MODERN PUBLIC ADMINISTRATION

But with the rise of the science of administration, the ignored ethical issues of administration began to be troublesome. It is instructive to look at the development of *public* administration to get at the problem. The early development of public administration in the United States emerged from the political philosophy that was espoused during the founding years. It is commonplace to argue that the Constitution was written, in part, to bridle the powers of the political executive and its bureaucracy. It is less clearly understood that the Founders were also deeply concerned with the exercise of tyranny by the masses, through elections and legislatures.

This leads us to an essential point in this argument. The Founders were, for the most part, intellectuals who were undaunted by the philosophic works of the ages. They used them easily and well. But the moral instruction of the people was shaped more by popular religion than it was by the writings of philosophers and politicians. Their judgments were made from the framework of the "right" and "wrong" of religious thought. Therefore, the ethical criteria that the people brought to the processes of government, especially through the selection and election of politicians, were religious criteria—and this caused real concern on the part of the Founders. They were clearly aware of the dangers inherent in the fusion of church and state, and they had made the separation clear in the Declaration of Independence.

But they had to face it again in the constitutional years,

7

although in a different guise. To explain, government becomes most personal to people through the actions of public administrators, and the people judge the moral worth of public policy, at that level, using the ethical criteria with which they are most familiar. Those popular criteria were largely forged by religion and later admixed with the political ideas espoused by the various political parties, candidates, and elected officials. The problem of public administration in the days of the founding was not so much one of efficiency as it was one of ethical bias. The Founders stressed the importance of *general* religious commitment, as it shaped moral character, but worried about the undue influence of *specific* religious movements.

Judged in context of the writings of the Founding Fathers, the separation of church and state was not only to prevent the government from creating a state religion, but also to prevent the various religions from dominating government. However, religions, independent of government, created the ethical atmosphere that shaped the government, because popular religion laid the ethical foundations for the rank and file.

It was in this context that American public administration was born. With the establishment of the Constitution and the government that flowed therefrom, George Washington was given a rare opportunity. He was able to establish an administrative structure, as well as the criteria of selection and standards of behavior for public servants. He resolved the ethical dilemma of undue influence by *specific* religious movements by arguing that the primary criterion for service was "fitness of character." This first era of constitutional government has come to be known as an era of "Government by Gentlemen."[5]

For Washington, it was clear that national policy had to rest on principles of private morality. To the first Congress he declared: "The foundation of our national policy will be laid in the pure and immutable principles of private morality. . . . The propitious smiles of Heaven can never be expected on a nation that disregards the eternal rules of order and right which Heaven itself has ordained."[6] In his Farewell Address, after two terms in office, he warned again:

> Of all the dispositions and habits, which lead to political prosper-
> ity, Religion and Morality are indispensable supports. In vain
> would that man claim the tribute of Patriotism, who should labor
> to subvert these great pillars of human happiness, these firmest
> props of the duties of Men and Citizens. . . . And let us with
> caution indulge the supposition, that morality can be maintained
> without religion. Whatever may be conceded to the influence of
> refined education on minds of peculiar structure, reason and
> experience both forbid us to expect, that national morality can
> prevail in exclusion of religious principle.[7]

Carrying the theme further, Thomas Jefferson described the
character of those who administer the affairs of state as needing
to be

> enlightened by a benign religion, professed, indeed, and prac-
> ticed in various forms, yet all of them including honesty, truth,
> temperance, gratitude, and the love of man; acknowledging and
> adoring an overruling Providence, which by all its dispensations
> proves that it delights in the happiness of man here and his
> greater happiness hereafter—with these blessings, what more is
> necessary to make us a happy and prosperous people?[8]

In other words, general religious principles of ethical conduct
were not only acceptable, they were necessary. But the religious
codes of *specific* religions introduced an unacceptable fusion of
church and state.

Thus, with the birth of this nation came the idea that good
government was the result of the moral character of those who
governed. As Leonard D. White concluded in his classic study
of American public administration: "Fitness did not mean to
him [Washington] technical competence (except in legal and a
very few scientific appointments), nor can it be said that in
Washington's time technical competence was recognized generally as a prerequisite for selection."[9] Fitness of character as a
standard for appointment centered on personal integrity and
standing in the community.

These standards, as typified by Washington, were adopted
and followed by his immediate successors, Federalist and Republican alike. It was not until the establishment of Jacksonian
Democracy that we find the rapid and devastating decline in the

desirability of government by gentlemen, which resulted in the governmental reform movements of the late 1800s—and the birth of public administration as a discipline.

But the change came slowly. As a developing discipline, public administration became a subject of serious academic study only toward the end of the century. The "classical" essays of Woodrow Wilson (1887)[10] and Frank Goodnow (1900)[11] set the intellectual tone into which modern public administration as a discipline was born. They also set the tone for a very subtle movement away from the ethical constructs the Founding Fathers so deliberately sought to include in both the Constitution and the system of government which flowed from it.[12]

Wilson, and later Goodnow, argued that the "science of administration"—and note that it was to be a "science"—was desperately needed in administering the Constitution. Harmonious with the developing scientific management of the time, Wilson posited the existence of a major distinction between politics and administration. "Politics," for Wilson, embraced the policy-making function, while "administration" was the execution of that policy. The point then was to have civil servants who neither made policy nor evaluated its morality. The politics/administration dichotomy was designed to free public administrators of the responsibility of making moral or ethical determinations. They were to be value neutral—a position very different from that of the Founding Fathers, who saw government occurring as a consequence of moral individuals administering its needs. This "secular spirit" of the politics/administration dichotomy became the consuming spirit from which public administration as a discipline emerged. Indeed, so far did this secular spirit

> advance from the old belief that the problem of good government is the problem of moral men that they [i.e., those of the Wilson, Goodnow vintage] arrived at the opposite position: that morality is irrelevant, that proper institutions and expert personnel are determining. The new amorality became almost a requisite for professional respect.[13]

To use the language of business administration, well-designed systems made the *character* of the administrator irrelevant; all that was relevant was functional expertise. Organizations would no longer be dependent upon the uncontrollable and unpredictable qualities of moral character. Like good machines, they would run in spite of the machine tenders.

This new amorality also became a Trojan horse, concealing a thousand hostile elements. When Wilson argued that we could imitate a murderer's method and skill in sharpening his knife without copying his intention to commit murder with it, he failed to recognize that the means shape and distort the ends.[14] By 1933, the notion of a politics/administration dichotomy had begun to collapse. In that year, Luther Gulick publicly acknowledged the obvious fact that administrators did indeed create policy—and thus were involved in politics.[15] What he failed to do was to discuss where these policy-making administrations received their ethical instruction.

The final blows to the idea of a value-free public administration came shortly after World War II. Many political scientists, having served in governmental agencies during the war, were returning to the classroom with a whole new set of ideas. Versed in the actual experience of administration, they rejected the myths of value neutrality in public administration. Some disturbing new questions came to the fore. The Founders believed that the moral character of the governors was the central issue in good government. They were clear on their beliefs as to what constituted good character. But, in the post–World War II years, those verities had been so diluted that there was virtually no ethical consensus from which to argue for organizational ethics. The values so eloquently expressed by the Founders had been battered almost beyond repair by the blows of "scientific method" and "cultural relativism."

As it became clearer and clearer that administration was deeply involved in ethical and moral decision making, students of administration avoided the issue; indeed at times they turned and ran. The great exception was Dwight Waldo, who met the problem head on in his now-classic book *The Administrative State*.[16] During a 1968 conference on the "Theory and Practice of Public Administration," he called for the rethinking of the implications of administrative theory and practice. Waldo had observed that administrators were facing "a bewildering array of value problems," including questions as to the "nature and ends of government."[17]

Among the value questions raised by Waldo were:

- "Problems of personal ethics in and related to administration"
- "Problems of politics and power"
- "Problems of constitutional status, law, and jurisprudence"
- "Problems of public policy"
- "Problems of political theory and philosophy"

In sum, Waldo concluded:

> It is disturbing because, by widespread agreement, ours is an organizational, an "administered," civilization, and if it is to survive and flourish, then we need the most serious attention possible to the connection between what used to be called the "ends of the State" and the organizational-administrative apparatus (in and out of formal government) which helps both to define and to realize these ends.[18]

Even as Waldo wrote, administrators in both the public and private sectors were buffeted by the social unrest of the 1960s and 1970s. Cities were being burned by angry mobs, the war protests were in full swing, and in the White House amoral administrative aides brought on the Watergate scandal, an event that strangled the legitimate affairs of the federal government for months and ushered in an era of increased skepticism and cynicism among the electorate. While social unrest clarified for many students of administration the need for positive involvement in solving social problems, we believe it was Watergate and its aftermath that made the need for heightened attention to ethics a major issue for both public and private administrators.

MODERN BUSINESS ADMINISTRATION

Business administration in the United States underwent a different philosophical development than public administration.

There were some concerns with the impact of the laissez-faire mentality developed in the middle 1700s and early 1800s. This corresponded with the sprawling, booming industrialization of England, which began in the middle of the eighteenth century. The history of industrialization is quite familiar. Suffice it to say, the industrial successes were purchased at the cost of decency in the lives of the workers, who were given over into a new, mechanical slavery. One cotton manufacturer wrote: "Bad and unwise as American slavery is . . . the white slavery in the manufactories of England was at this unrestricted period far worse than that of the house-slaves whom I afterward saw in the West Indies and in the United States."[19]

Unfortunately, such expressions of compassion were not typical of the mainstream of thought of the industrial leaders of England, who had "the conviction that industrial aims were intertwined with the very purposes of Deity."[20] Many of these wealthy industrialists retired from industry to become "preachers," as it were, of their view of the new laissez-faire doctrines both in England and on the Continent. One of them, Richard Cobden, who was particularly active (and ultimately obtained a seat in Parliament) wrote: "We advocate nothing but what is agreeable to the highest behests of Christianity—to buy in the cheapest market and sell in the dearest."[21] In other words, God was a laissez-faire economist who was trotted out as the primary justification of the industrial status quo. And, where God wouldn't fit, Herbert Spencer and the doctrine of "survival of the fittest" would fill the gaps.[22] This was particularly apparent during the late 1800s as industrialists built massive fortunes.

Some American writers in the early 1900s were concerned with the excesses and lack of humanity which they saw in American business. They were also concerned with the socialistic responses to similar excesses they saw in Great Britain and Europe and, later on, in Russia. As one writer stated:

> It seems probable that the demand for government ownership of capital and government management business is due very largely to beliefs in social abuses, which, it has been thought, can be lessened better through the government than otherwise.

The distribution of the product of industry among the different classes of producers has been considered by many most unjust. The rise of the railways and the development of other forms of public utilities afford numerous examples of abuse.

As these abuses became known, remedies were naturally sought; and in the excited state of public opinion, mistakes were frequently made from the effect of which we are only gradually recovering at the present day. The good intention of the people to remedy abuses and raise the standards of business morals cannot, however, be questioned.[23]

H. L. Gantt, a colleague of Frederick W. Taylor, wrote a fascinating book in 1910, especially when one considers the time in which it was published. He wrote:

It is thus clearly seen that the maintenance of our modern civilization is dependent absolutely upon the service it gets from the industrial and business system.

This system as developed throughout the world had its origin in the service it could and did render the community in which it originated. . . .

. . . [T]he idea that the profits of a business were justified only on account of the service it rendered was rapidly giving way to one in which profits took the first place and service the second. This idea has grown so rapidly and has become so firmly imbedded in the mind of the business man of today, that it is inconceivable to many leaders of big business that it is possible to operate a business system on the lines along which our present system grew up; namely, that its first aim should be to render service.

. . . *The community needs service first, regardless of who gets the profits, because its life depends upon the service it gets.* The business man says profits are more important to him than the service he renders; that the wheels of business shall not turn, whether the community needs the service or not, unless he can have his measure of profit. *He has forgotten that his business system had its foundation in service, and as far as the community is concerned has no reason for existence except the service it can render.* A clash between these two ideals will ultimately bring a deadlock between the business system and the community. The "laissez faire" process in which we all seem to have so much faith, does not promise any other result.

. . . *We all realize that any reward or profit that business arbitrarily takes over and above that to which it is justly entitled for service rendered, is just as much the exercise of autocratic power and a menace to the industrial peace of the world, as the autocratic military power of the Kaiser was a menace to international peace. This applies to Bolshevists as well as to Bankers.*[24]

Gantt's notion that service to the community should be the ultimate value of business appears to be a rather enlightened view and provides a basis for additional philosophical thought concerning the ethics of business.

A SEARCH FOR ETHICS

Without much more than a fleeting acknowledgment in a footnote of critics of unbridled laissez-faire, the philosophical development of business thought in the United States continued along its hereditary English path, at least until the post–World War II years. Business administration had preceded public administration by decades to a similar philosophical position at the turn of the century. Both had accepted amoral scientific management as the central value. Whereas public administration had thrown aside Washington's notion of virtuous administrators in its embrace of amoral scientific administration, business administration had never been so cloaked. But the social unrest of the 1960s raised the difficult issues of the social responsibility of business. The public became concerned with the goals and activities of large organizations. This concern was reflected in the curriculum of both business and public administration programs.

Administrative science born out of the optimism of nineteenth-century positivism lacked any firm guidance in ethical matters. Worse yet, it had reduced the status of classical moral teachings, if taught at all, to merely giving a cursory overview. In Waldo's words, "The old curriculum of moral philosophy and allied studies became transmuted into a series of courses on the history of political theory, courses without widely accepted rationale and tolerated only as a 'cultural' gloss upon a professional education."[25] One could add empirical theories of human behavior and decision making as well.

15

The literature of business and public administration has provided a variety of views related to ethical and moral concerns. They are, in the vast majority of cases, based on what William G. Scott, one of the essayists in this volume, has referred to as the "Management Orthodoxy." This paradigm represents the rejection of the possibility of knowing, if not the very existence of, fundamental or absolute moral truths. It is a combination of both positivism and historicism. Positivism is exemplified by the methods of science, and has interest only in those truths that are demonstratable by empirical observation. That which is unprovable by the methods of science is classed as metaphysics, and generally considered unknowable or unworthy of being known. Historicism in its various forms sees the world in a constant state of change, which leads to contingency views of ethics. As Eugene F. Miller describes the teaching:

> Knowledge was now conceived in terms of creation rather than discovery. Worldviews and theories were seen as individual or social creations, which are shaped decisively by subrational forces. It was denied that the human mind can grasp the character of "reality" or "nature" in any final, objective, or absolute way. [26]

In the context of these teachings, there was little need for students of administration to concern themselves with unknowable questions of ethics and morals. Yet, as social circumstance forced the issue, the hunt for ethics began.

Efforts to discover ethical guidance for administrators have taken a variety of forms. Some, such as Krislov's *Representative Bureaucracy*,[27] attempted to insure ethical administration through institutional arrangements. Others have suggested desired ends based on current intellectual moods, such as Dvorin and Simmons's *From Amoral to Humane Bureaucracy*.[28] Other efforts have been aimed at creating theoretical bases for reform, the most sophisticated of these being John Rawls's *Theory of Justice*[29] and David Norton's *Personal Destinies*.[30] Finally, some have suggested that pragmatic reasons alone should justify the adoption of a code of ethics. After all, we live in a litigious age, and who wants to go to jail?

Typical of professional organization is the adoption of a procedural code of ethics. If you cross the t's and dot the i's you are ethical regardless of the results. Such codes would be typified by the American Bar Association's "Canon of Legal Ethics." This approach is common to organizations that rely strictly on legal interpretation to define their conduct.

University courses in organizational ethics seem to be based mainly on the case-study approach, with a corresponding lack of attention to the classic books on moral thought. In this approach a dilemma is presented and the students are encouraged to discuss the issue in order to clarify their personal standards. In context of the historicism of the day, no suggestion is made as to a possible right or wrong answer nor is an ethical standard suggested. An instructor would be considered unethical if he or she suggested such, because a belief in the rightness or wrongness of an action is at best an attachment to social custom and at worst it is an unknowable proposition. Thus, while we recognize the need for ethical standards we are unable or unwilling to accept or reject any ethical paradigm. Typically then, our formal teaching has, in fact, been nihilism, which leaves students in a more precarious ethical position than when they came to us.

None of these approaches satisfactorily addresses the questions: Must we be ethical as individuals in order to have an ethical society? Do good systems produce good people or do good people produce good systems? and, Are there absolute ethical standards to which we as individuals must adhere?

What Goes Around, Comes Around

It seems to us that we have now come full course, or, in the parlance of youth, that which goes around, comes around. The Founders understood the primary problem of good government to be a problem of the good moral character of the individuals within government. For many reasons, and under many influences, the science of administration abandoned that position.

But today, faced with exploding crises of administrative morality in both the public and the private sectors, we are turning again to the conclusion that the primary problems of good government, as well as good business, are essentially problems of good moral character.

This conference was convened to give a group of scholars the freedom to attack the issues of organizational ethics in ways that they thought most important. Interestingly, most all the essays in this volume return to the familiar theme: organizational ethics is dependent upon personal ethics. In other words, we must become better people if we are to have better organizational governance. Good systems do not produce good people: rather, good people produce good systems.

The essays in this collection describe a variety of ideas about how contemporary management can incorporate ideas like personal integrity, mutual trust, and true concern for others as the basis of organizational life. In particular, they acknowledge that ethics, as a discipline, is changing. As David Norton observes, there is a growing rejection of the attempt to justify all in terms of some version of science, with a corresponding return to the "systematic formulation in the thought of Socrates, Plato, and Aristotle" and to the thought that "generally prevailed through the late Middle Ages." We will find our answers where our Founders did: in the classic struggles with the eternal issues of human morality in action as we return to the search for Organizational Ethics of Good Character.

Notes

1. Luther Gulick and Lyndall Urwick, eds., *Papers on the Science of Administration* (New York: Institute of Public Administration, 1937).

2. W. Stork, ed., *Jeremy Bentham's Economic Writing*, 3 vols. (London: George Allen & Urwin, 1952–54).

3. Gulick and Urwick, *Papers on the Science of Administration*, 192.

4. Woodrow Wilson, "The Study of Administration," *Political Science Quarterly* 2 (June 1887): 197–222.

5. Frederick C. Mosher, *Democracy and the Public Service* (New York: Oxford University Press, 1968), 55.

6. James D. Richardson, *A Compilation of the Messages and Papers of the Presidents 1789–1897*, 10 vols. (Washington D.C.: Government Printing Office, 1896), 1:52–53.

7. Ibid., 220.

8. Ibid., 322 (emphasis added). To stress our contention that the Founders believed a general religious commitment, as regards qualities of character, to be necessary to good government, but rejected specific religious domination, note the observations about Calvinism made by Jefferson to John Adams in his letter of 11 April 1823, in Thomas Jefferson,*Writings*, ed. M. Peterson (New York: Library of America, 1984), 1466–69.

9. Leonard D. White, *The Federalists: A Study in Administrative History* (New York: Macmillan, 1948), 259.

10. Wilson, "Study of Administration."

11. Frank J. Goodnow, *Politics and Administration* (1900; reprint, New York: Russell and Russell, 1967).

12. Note John A. Rohr's devastating attack on Wilson and Goodnow in his book *To Run a Constitution* (Lawrence: University Press of Kansas, 1986).

13. Dwight Waldo, *The Administrative State* (New York: Ronand Press, 1948), 23.

14. Wilson, "Study of Administration."

15. Luther Gulick, "Politics and Administration and the New Deal," *The Annals of the American Academy of Political and Social Science* 169 (September 1933): 55–56.

16. Waldo, *Administrative State*, 23.

17. Dwight Waldo, "Scope and Theory of Public Administration," in

James C. Charlesworth, ed., *Theory and Practice of Public Administration: Scope, Objectives, and Methods*, special edition volume of *The Annals of the American Academy of Political and Social Science*, October 1968, 1–26.

18. Ibid., 16.

19. As quoted by Miriam Beard, *History of the Business Man* (New York: Macmillan, 1938), 582.

20. Ibid., 594.

21. Ibid., 595.

22. For instance, see Richard Hofstadter, *Social Darwinism in American Thought* (Boston: Beacon Press, 1944), esp. chap. 2, "The Vogue of Spencer," and Daniel T. Rodgers, *The Work Ethic in Industrial America: 1850-1920* (Chicago: University of Chicago Press, 1978).

23. Jeremiah W. Jenks, *Business and the Government*, in *Modern Business*, ed. Joseph French Johnson, 24 vols. (New York: Alexander Hamilton Institute, 1918), 24:322–23.

24. H. L. Gantt, *Organizing for Work* (New York: Harcourt, Brace and Howe, 1919), 3–5, 8.

25. Waldo, "Scope and Theory," 23.

26. Eugene F. Miller, "Positivism, Historicism, and Political Inquiry," *American Political Science Review* 66 (September 1972): 796.

27. Samuel Krislov, *Representative Bureaucracy* (Englewood Cliffs, N.J.: Prentice-Hall, 1974).

28. Eugene P. Dvorin and Robert H. Simmons, *From Amoral to Humane Bureaucracy* (San Francisco: Canfield Press, 1972).

29. John Rawls, *A Theory of Justice* (Cambridge: Harvard University Press, Belknap Press, 1971).

30. David L. Norton, *Personal Destinies* (Princeton: Princeton University Press, 1976).

CHAPTER ONE

The Concentric Circles of Management Thought

William G. Scott

INTRODUCTION

A MERICAN management has lost its soul. Corrupt and barbaric managerial practices reported in the press and on television have eroded the public's confidence in management leadership legitimacy.[1] In academic theories, organizational culture, values, and social realities are thought to be "enacted" by management without regard for objective content.[2] Such theories legitimize manipulative practices and trivialize work life in modern organizations. In research, behavioral scientists are tempted to do either methodologically safe projects on nano-issues or sell their technical research skills to practicing managers. Succumbing to this temptation for publication or money compromises the integrity of their research.[3]

This assessment of the status of the field is the opposite of the one Lyndall Urwick made in 1937 in *Papers on the Science of Administration*.[4] Then, and it might as well have been light-years ago, Urwick argued that the main problems of organization were technical since he thought that all the *principles* of organization

William G. Scott is Affiliate Program Professor of Management, University of Washington.

needed to solve them had been discovered. Urwick dreamed of a rational science of management; but, more importantly, he as well as the other contributors to the 1937 *Papers* had an optimistic vision of management's future. They believed it would be built on science and enlightened theory and practice. This optimism is difficult to recapture in this essay fifty years later.

The difficulty lies not so much in the failure of science and theory (although it plays a part); mostly my lack of optimism stems from a moral failure of the field that involves the unwitting complicity of those in practice and scholarship in a web of pathological values. The purposes of this essay are to document these charges and to suggest a reform project for management scholarship. The next part of this essay describes the present state of affairs in management and how it got to be the way it is. Buried in this description are the inherent flaws and paradoxes of the field which will be ferreted out and examined. The last part of the essay goes beyond criticism to recommend fundamental changes in the zeitgeist of management scholarship.

THE SEEMING PARADOX OF MANAGEMENT THOUGHT: PRELUDES TO THE BARBARISMS OF POWER

The paradox of management thought is rooted in its orthodoxy—an orthodoxy that has been refined for over fifty years. It has three major elements: markets, positive science, and myth. Each element has been central to the field since the 1930s, and taken together they comprise the orthodox triad.

The Orthodox Triad

The first element in the triad is markets. The management orthodoxy stresses markets because they are objective; they are capable of rigorous analysis; and they provide managers with guides for resource allocation. Markets are, therefore, the quintessential economic criteria for managerial decision making. Peter Drucker wrote, "The first definition of management is . . . that it is an economic organ, indeed the specifically economic organ of an industrial society. Every act, every decision, every

Figure 1
Management's Triad of Orthodoxy

Markets:

1. Analyzable
2. Predictable
3. Reliable guides for resource allocation

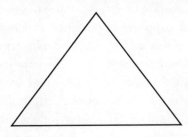

Positive Science:

1. Instrumental
2. Objective
3. Factual

Myths:

1. Substantive
2. Nonobjective
3. Fictional

deliberation of management has as its first dimension an economic dimension."[5]

Positive science is the second element of the orthodoxy. Empirical research in management is desired because it is objective, instrumental, and factual. The close link between positive science and markets is easily discerned, since knowledge about market behavior and human behavior in them can be acquired by methods of rational analysis and quantification. However, there is another aspect of positive science that needs to be noted. One of Herbert Simon's main contributions to the field was to convince management of the value of an empirical research agenda that would increase the verifiability of administrative facts and concepts. Relative to organizational concepts, he observed that "these concepts, to be scientifically useful must be operational; that is, their meanings must correspond to empirically observable facts or situations."[6] This operational vision of positive science has been thoroughly integrated into the orthodoxy of the field.

Myth is the third element of the triad of orthodoxy and it refers to management's efforts to shape, mold, and otherwise condition the attitudes, values, motives, and norms of individuals and small groups in organizations. It symbolizes management's efforts to influence those circumstances in the life of organizations not readily amenable to control by conventional standards of market analysis or the rigors of positive science.

Management's responsibility to influence employee motives and morals was of supreme importance in Chester I. Barnard's and Herbert Simon's construction of management thought. Barnard wrote that managers must alter "the conditions of behavior, including a conditioning of the individual by training, by the inculcation of attitudes, by the construction of incentives."[7] Simon's position was similar: "The behavior of a rational person can be controlled . . . if the value and factual premises upon which he bases his decisions are specified for him."[8] While this interpretation of managerial influence has taken many forms in the last fifty years, its present currency, expressed as control of organization culture, has been given weight by such popular books as *In Search of Excellence*.[9] Myth, viewed through the lens of managerial control, is indispensable to the orthodoxy of the field.

Each element in the orthodox triad offers an answer to the question, What is the truth in this or that administrative situation? Thus, truth could be what markets determine it to be; or truth could be what positive science reveals by strict induction; or truth could be what management says it is because it has the mythopoeic power to impose cultures by fiat. Truth seeking within the boundaries of the orthodox triad has defined the mission of the field which we will examine in terms of the circles of management thought.

The Inner, Middle, and Outer Circles of Management Thought

The circles of management thought (figure 2) describe how the elements of the orthodox triad are translated into the work of the field. While many examples could illustrate this point (the curric-

Figure 2
The Inner and Outer Circles of Management Thought

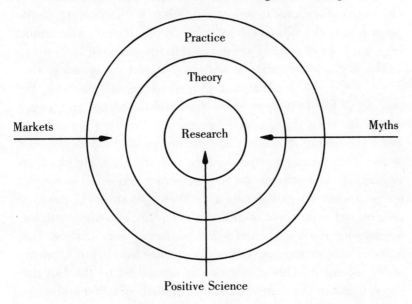

Positive Science

ula of business schools, the content of management textbooks, the socialization of MBA students in the ways of practice), there are few clearer cases than the publication program of the Academy of Management. *The Academy of Management Journal* publishes empirical research studies, which apply the methods of positive science to instrumental administrative problems, much as Simon wished. *The Academy of Management Review* publishes theoretical pieces at the level of frameworks, model building, and analytical schemes. Many of these articles discuss substantive administrative issues that are not susceptible to treatment by positive science. Barnard would have approved. The Academy has started a third journal which is aimed at practice. Whether it will fulfill Peter Drucker's vision of a market-driven management practice remains to be seen, but the probabilities are high that it will not disappoint him.

Too fine a point should not be put on this division of labor since in many instances research, theory, and practice in management are intermingled. Nevertheless, what the Academy publishes under its various rubrics does give us a rough approximation of the scope of the field. But this approximation leaves two major questions unanswered. What is the content of the published work? Which circle, if any, is preeminent in determining what lines of activity are pursued in the other circles?

The first question can be answered in just the broadest way. Since 1980 the *Journal* has published about two-thirds the number of full-scale articles as the *Review*. *Journal* articles are longer because the *Journal* places high editorial priority on extensive literature reviews and the methodological aspects of a study. They average sixteen pages per article in length. Conversely, *Review* articles are more abstract and brief, averaging ten pages per article. Between 1980 and 1986, 4,711 pages of the *Journal* were spent on mainline empirical research articles, whereas the *Review* devoted 4,391 pages to theory articles. This space allocation suggests a positive science bias in the Academy of Management. This conclusion is reinforced by the fact that the *Journal* in the same years also published 1,000 additional pages of empirical-type "research notes" that averaged eight pages per note.[10]

But there is a qualitative difference. The *Journal* deals in objectified facts; the *Review* often deals in deobjectified fictions. Some may not agree with this assessment, since it suggests that frameworks, models, and conceptual schemes are phenomenological constructions. However, there is strong philosophical support for this point of view. Vaihinger argued persuasively for it in 1924,[11] and it is now the centerpiece of theoretical thinking in public administration. Business management is just beginning to catch on if the numerous articles in the *Review* since mid-1983 on organizational culture, myths, and enacted social realities are any gauge of popularity.

The second question of what is influencing what among the three circles is crucial. The official orthodox position, stated by Fred Luthans in his presidential speech to the Academy in 1986, is that the Academy's work is exemplified by its publications and by its meetings. They have had, according to him, a profound impact by creating knowledge that is translated by popular writers and consultants into terms that influence practicing executives. Luthans stressed that this chain of causality in the influence of managers begins with "Academy members, Academy journals, Academy meetings."[12] Luthans does admit that gaps exist in our knowledge about management because the academic side does not know much about what practicing managers do. Therefore, he calls for empirical research on "real" managers.

As canonical as Luthans's views are, they do faithfully represent the scholarly mission of the field as it is seen from the summit of the Academy, namely:

A. Academic management is the center of the universe orbited by journalists, consultants, and practitioners.
B. Gaps in academic management knowledge can be filled by doing positive normal science.

The alternative view is not this spirit:

A. Academic management is not central in the management universe.
B. Positive normal science excludes more valid knowledge than it creates.

The Paradox and the Paradox Tentatively Reconciled

The paradox in management thought springs from the orthodox triad (figure 1) and from the division of work in the field (figure 2). It is simply this: On the one hand management objectifies instrumental problems through the rigorous application of positive science (the inner circle). On the other hand, management deobjectifies many other matters that are beyond the reach of hard-core empiricism (the middle circle).

Modern management scholarship works within these two circles, and this division of labor has created something of a muddle: a concrete world of empirically verifiable facts embedded in an insubstantial theoretical world of myth and fiction.

This is a paradoxical vision for a field of scholarship that makes pretenses about analytical rigor and scientific method.

Chester I. Barnard and Herbert Simon successfully propagated a vision of management that based empirical fact-finding in frameworks that accepted the objective reality of administrative and organizational concepts. In terms of our circles, Barnard had one foot in the theory circle and the other in the practice circle. He constantly compared his theory development to his organizational reality. Simon, building in considerable part on Barnardian theory, introduced an agenda of empirical research that captured the imagination of scholars after World War II. Simon also spanned two circles—the circle of theory building and the circle of empirical verification.

The significant result for management was neither Barnard's nor Simon's unique circle-spanning contribution. Rather it was the combination of both scholars' efforts that created an essential continuity of viewpoint that integrated practice, theory, and research. By around 1950 the field came about as close as it had before or has since to a legitimate paradigm of thought, because of Barnard's and Simon's seminal work *taken together*.[13]

This was the Barnard-Simon legacy. How was it used?—1987-style management has corrupted this vision and has taken a direction that does not represent progress. The objectification-deobjectification paradox suggests that the domains of theory and research are spinning off into separate orbits with only the most tenuous connections between them. For the objectivity of theory, based on the premise that there are "real things" in organizations being theorized about, there is a deobjectification of such phenomena as culture, ethics, and values. For important empirical observations about management concepts and bodies of data, there is "misplaced concreteness" in overelaborate research designs and methodologies for addressing trivial questions.

Our paradox describes a world view wherein management facts and management fictions are *seemingly* irreconcilable. However, the word *seemingly* is emphasized for a reason. The circles of research and theory are enclosed by a third circle: practice. This circle represents the power of practice to reconcile what is apparently irreconcilable. Thoughtful practitioners have known this since the 1920s and have supported and used the theoretical and research production of academic management whenever and wherever it has seemed pertinent to the practical solution of instrumental problems. In short, the outer ring of managerial power, the power of practice, drives academic management scholarship and reduces its professoriate to being servants of this power. Loren Baritz wrote, "The position . . . social scientists have taken regarding the ethics and politics of power obtrudes as a red thread in the otherwise pallid canvas on which they have labored. . . . Almost all industrial social scientists have either backed away from the political and ethical implications of their work or have faced these considerations from the point of view of management."[14]

This reconciliation is opposite to the official orthodox description of how the management universe works—opposite because it posits that management theory and research are the captives of practice. It rejects the point of view that management scholarship is the cause of practicing management enlightenment. One might be generous and allow that scholarship and practice have an interactive relationship, each situationally and differentially influencing the other. But this generosity is misplaced because it obscures the *realpolitik* of the power of practice.

The Administrative State and the Realpolitik of Paradox Reconciliation

The administrative state is a twentieth-century governance artifact and the source of managerial power. In the second and third decades of this century its institutional incarnations ranged from Italian fascism to American New Dealism. They represented alternative social orders and theories of how such orders were maintained. However, despite national differences the overriding purpose of the administrative state was to provide systems of national resource mobilization and coordination required by the autarkic motives of national power, the demands for mass production and consumption in mass societies, the

advancement of technology, the growing complexity of organization, and rapid population growth. For these reasons as well as
the equally important social, political, economic, and ideological crises of the times, corporatism emerged as the realpolitik of
administrative statecraft. It provided a rational form of centralized resource management, based on a social order in which
national policy goals were decided and implemented by a cooper-
ating government, business, labor, and university management
elite.

In its earlier versions, corporatism established primary functional work groups (workers, technicians, professionals, government regulators, manufacturers, service providers, etc.) organized into industry syndicates (automobile makers, airlines,
movie producers, food processors, banking, etc.). The whole
was presided over by a small management elite who ran things
because they were thought to be the only class that understood
the broad issues that affected the whole society. Thus, work
roles determined status in the administrative state, and the
elite's leadership status was *the* critical role. [15]

Barnard pointed out that this elite's responsibility was to
"maintain" the social order. To do so they had to rely on three
operational principles: hierarchy (authoritative communication),
uniformity (equality in the exchange process), and planning
(organizational decision making and strategy). [16] However, the
overwhelming fact was that the administrative state made it
possible for managers to control vast economic resources and to
make virtually unaccountable allocation decisions. As Barnard
saw it, exercising this unprecedented power was the only way
management could meet its "maintenance" responsibilities.

A highly articulated management practice and theory evolved
from the administrative state and its corporative apparatus. The
two most important developments in this evolution were a "self-
aware" managerial elite in the public and private sectors, and a
single-set value orthodoxy that informed this elite across these
organizational sectors.

Dwight Waldo documented the rise of self-awareness in both
public and private administration. He held that it pertained to

administration as a unique objective activity—"a 'mutation' in human culture"—which could be studied, taught, improved, and communicated.[17] But there was also a subjective aspect to self-awareness that he did not capture so succinctly. Administrators become aware that they were a class apart from other classes with a mission and a legitimacy peculiar to their status and expertise.

Hand in hand with a self-aware administration came a value orthodoxy that began, according to Waldo, with Towne's speech to the American Society of Mechanical Engineers[18] and Wilson's famous essay on public administration.[19] Towne and Wilson established the value framework for administration in an elementary form—Towne for business management, Wilson for public administration. However, the central elements of these frameworks were the same. Both authors valued a rational administration informed by science and economics. These values are still present in the orthodoxy of modern administration.

With the rudimentary administrative values and a dawning managerial self-awareness in place by the turn of the century, all that American management practice and theory needed was an appropriate environment in which to flower. This environment appeared in the 1930s in the form of the crises mentioned above. The American response to these crises was an Americanized version of the administrative state, starting with the New Deal in 1933.

Management scholarship was particularly influenced by these events in the 1930s, and in some respects from that time to the present it has been a measure of the scope of this social transition. Management theory spawned a "heroic" utopian literature with lionized gurus, such as Chester I. Barnard, Herbert Simon, Peter Drucker, and Thomas Peters and H. Waterman, Jr., whose work reinforced orthodox values and heightened managerial self-awareness. Furthermore, professional academic graduate programs in public and business administration emerged to socialize students for their elitist and functional roles in the administrative state. And finally a dedicated professoriate in administration, itself inculcated by the values of administrative statecraft, transmitted those values to students as well as imparting to them vocational skills. In short, a practice-inspired orthodoxy became preeminent in management scholarship.

Since the morality of contemporary management practice is now under attack with growing frequency, some management scholars must wonder what responsibility management education bears for the managerial incivilities that are being documented. We scholars must ask what we can do to put right what has gone wrong in the administrative state. For if we do not ask this fundamental question, then, in Paulo Freire's words, we will be "unable to perceive critically the themes of [our] time, and thus to intervene actively in reality."[20] Management scholarship otherwise is simply carried along in the wake of change.

THE OBLIGATIONS OF MANAGEMENT SCHOLARSHIP: PRELUDES TO THE REFORM OF EDUCATION IN THE ADMINISTRATIVE STATE

The dilemma of professional education in management is posed by two questions. Is the purpose of scholarship to prepare students for jobs and to seek instrumental, puzzle-solving information useful for practice? Is the purpose of scholarship to build students' moral character and to seek wisdom regardless of its usefulness?

While most hold that scholarship must address both questions, academic management has drifted into an emphasis on the voc/tech dimension in education and instrumentalism in research and theory building. At the same time, it has all but abandoned a commitment to civility and wisdom. For these reasons management scholarship is not fulfilling its obligation to attend to the moral health of the field. To do so it must reorder its priorities.

Obligations of Scholarship

The purpose of scholarship is to heighten an individual's plane of consciousness through the use of reason. As there are four planes of consciousness there are also four levels of reason on which this may be done (figure 3): the mimetic (the realm of influence), the empiric (the realm of positive science), the mythopoeic (the realm of social interpretation and belief), and the noetic (the realm of intellect).[21] Each of these levels has a purpose and a mode of inquiry: respectively, imitation of exemplars through role modeling and opinion shaping, generation and dissemination of information through communicative scholarship, creation and maintenance of collective orthodox beliefs through theory building, and a quest for wisdom through disclosive scholarship. As demonstrated in the preceding section, management scholarship has fixed itself on those modes of inquiry (the inner and middle circles of management thought) that produce information and maintain orthodox beliefs.

The empiric and the mythopoeic

The second plane of consciousness (figure 3) is the empiric aspect of management scholarship. Scholars who are "craft competent" create and communicate information to students and peers who want to be "craft literate" in various management specializations. Since the market determines the value of these competencies and literacies, the worth of specific crafts is always fluid, varying with time, place, and fashion. Thus, the second plane is a relatively low form of consciousness. Being almost entirely reactive to external influences, it precludes much critical thinking, judgment, and moral development.

The third, or mythopoeic, plane (figure 3) is a higher form of consciousness. However, it must take much of the same criticism as the second plane. The single-set value orthodoxy to which management scholarship is wedded is a cultural pattern of accepted collective beliefs that define management. The main liability of this orthodoxy is that it inhibits the development of alternative values and perspectives on the field, thereby limiting the freedom of choice for those engaged in scholarship and practice.

The sheer amount of effort that management expends on the maintenance of its orthodoxy is a demonstration of Thomas

33

Kuhn's observations about the remarkable power of a paradigm to bring discipline and conformity to a field of study.[22] Nevertheless, it is true that management scholarship does have obligations to meet in both the empiric and mythopoeic aspects of its professional work. This entails creating and communicating information as well as maintaining the accepted collective beliefs about the nature of the field. In short, management scholarship must live in the world it claims to represent. *It must be a part of the fray.*

The mimetic and the noetic

Plane 1 (figure 3) is the lowest level of consciousness, yet scholarship has a specific and absolute obligation to influence and to develop the opinion of students and professional colleagues. This obligation is clear with respect to doctoral students who look toward their major professors for examples of

Figure 3
Planes of Consciousness and the Obligations of Scholarship

Levels of Reason	Purposes	Modes of Inquiry
4. Noetic (realm of intellect)	4. Seek wisdom	4. Disclosive scholarship a. moral reflection b. moral discourse
3. Mythopoeic (realm of societal self-interpretation)	3. Create and maintain orthodox collective beliefs (ref. Figure 1)	3. Theoretical scholarship: Frameworks and model building (ref. Figure 2, the middle circle)
2. Empiric (realm of positive science)	2. Generate and disseminate information	2. Communicative scholarship: craft literacy and competency (ref. Figure 2, the inner circle)
1. Mimetic (realm of influence)	1. Imitate exemplars	1. Role modeling, opinion shaping

34

craft expertise, strong research methods, commitment to the values of the field, and professional conduct and demeanor. The norms for such role modeling are drawn from the inner and middle circles of management thought, and they are translated into academic criteria for such decisions as degree granting, promotion, tenure, merit, and hiring.

The development of young scholars must be imitative to some extent, and the certification of their passage from one stage of their career to another is done according to the standards implicit in planes 2 and 3. This is by and large how the established scholarship in the field has interpreted its obligation to its juniors: mimic our empirical research methods, mimic our theory building, mimic our values. However, the penalty for this unbalanced interpretation of the mimetic plane has been the neglect of scholarship's obligation to encourage the intellect's quest for wisdom through disclosive learning. Where does one find these exemplars to imitate in schools of management? Disclosive learning has been the victim of management's rush to indulge in instrumentalism, market relevancy, and self-preservation.

Noetic reason pertains to the realm of the mind. It seeks wisdom through intellect and thus represents the highest plane of consciousness. Noetic reason requires concentration, continuity, articulate precision, and self-awareness in the search for knowledge for its own sake.

Thus, the mode of inquiry on this plane of consciousness demands moral reflection and moral discourse. As Jacques Barzun wrote, noetic reason needs "the congregation of talents spurring one another to higher achievements by the right degree of proximity . . . ; it needs the language and the conversation that maintains its unity . . . ; it needs precision to dispel the blinding fogs of folly or stupidity; it needs self-awareness to enjoy its own sport and keep itself from vainglory."[23]

The *sine qua non* of the scholarly obligation is a commitment to the noetic plane of reason. This in turn requires that scholars provide the young with examples of community, language and conversation, precision of thought, and playfulness with ideas. These obligations demand a new zeitgeist.

A New Zeitgeist for Management Scholarship in the Administrative State

I mentioned that management scholarship had to be a part of the fray to meet its obligations on the second and third planes of consciousness. It has been precisely on these planes that it has made most of its contributions to the administrative state. But, as also mentioned, management scholarship has another obligation on the fourth plane that it is not meeting. We therefore ought to consider a new zeitgeist to redress the imbalance between the empiric and the mythopoeic aspects of scholarship on the one hand and the noetic aspects on the other hand.

Our deliberations should begin with a reformulation of a previously stated dictum, which is that, while management scholarship must be a part of the fray, *it must, at the same time, occupy a moral high ground above it.* Nothing short of a *moral order of scholarship* can begin to satisfy this revised zeitgeist, and it has two essential ideas: the idea of a calling and the idea of an enclave.

The idea of a calling

A calling is often used to characterize the divine summons to a religious life. It need not be so narrowly construed. Alternatively, calling also has been used to describe a commitment to any job. This generalized usage seems to rob the idea of special meaning. (Are people "called" to be supermarket managers?) Because of the nature of their telos, there are, between these extremes, certain other occupations to which the idea of calling applies. In addition to the ministry, one could argue that people are called to a life of politics, military service, and scholarship.

What is it about *these* occupations that permits us to say that people are called to them, and upon entering them they are set apart from most other people in the world? Part of the answer to this question is that the telos of these occupations transcend the mundane. The telos of the ministry is intercession with God; the telos of politics is statecraft elevated to a level of "civil theology";[24] the telos of the military is obedient and honorable service as an instrument of diplomacy in state policy;[25] the telos of scholarship is the quest for wisdom and truth. By necessity those who practice these professions must have a moral vision guiding them. The tactics they use in the fray are informed by this vision of the world.[26]

Virtually every culture has exalted these telos and has honored those who practice the occupations associated with them: the politicians, the warriors, the priests and mystics, and the scholars. No other professions have had as long-standing a status in human affairs. But with this respect and approval have come social expectations that those who pursued these telos had to live a life that was palpably different from the way that the overwhelming majority of people lived. This was a life of total commitment, dedicated and consuming. It did not accommodate itself easily or comfortably to the normal interpersonal experiences of the majority. The life often was lonely, solitary, and self-contained. But it was also a life where probity, devotion to duty, self-discipline, and trustworthy friendship often were counted as the higher virtues. When one was called to such a telos one accepted a vocation.

Just because management scholarship is intimately connected with professional practice in the administrative state, it is not released from the obligations of its calling. However, it does make these obligations more difficult to meet. Accepting this, the hard fact of a scholar's life is the effort that he or she must make to minimize those outside influences that interfere with the calling. For the scholar, the usual human arrangements and worldly diversions that are thought to lead to personal gratification are often dysfunctional to the pursuit of telos.

To what arrangements and diversions do we refer?

- Emotionally intense interpersonal relationships
- The quest for power from administrative academic jobs or positions in the hierarchy of professional associations
- The money gained from consulting or rendering other services to practice

37

- Instrumentalism that diverts energy from disclosive learning to lower forms of scholarship that have more immediate payoffs
- Inertia that makes abandoning ideals easier when confronted with injustice

This list could be made longer, of course. To paraphrase the title of an article in *The Christian Century*,[27] American management scholarship has lost its soul because it has no sense of calling. For the management scholars to be fit to occupy a moral high ground demands that the individual professor discover the calling and engage in those acts of moral courage necessary to follow the telos of scholarship.

The idea of enclave

An enclave is an order of self-aware, like-minded people who share a calling to one of the aforementioned telos. Self-awareness implies a collective sense of moral tradition and moral community that joins people in an enclave that is capable of action in the world.

Moral tradition means that the members of an enclave are aware that they have a legacy of moral values that is unique, persistent, and continuous. *Moral tradition transcends time.* Moral community is an existential awareness of likeness with others who participate in the same calling. It is the sense of being in the same moral space with them. *Moral community transcends place.* One is "called" to a moral tradition; one "lives" that tradition in a moral community.

The idea of enclave is alien to mainstream American culture.[28] Indeed, three of its modern advocates are French, English, and Brazilian.[29] Furthermore, Solidarity, as an active example of an enclave, is healthy today in Poland, not as a formal organization, but as a moral community under whose aegis meetings are held to discuss everything from poetry to philosophy.

This brings me to the point: enclaves often thrive in adversity. Other people, particularly Europeans, have a long history of barbaric threats to civilization. Their strategy—in fact the only possible response to the overwhelming power of barbarism—has been to gather in enclaves and protect the good that is worth preserving in the old culture. Then, when the dark age passed this good would be there to pass on to future generations. Levy, MacIntyre, and Ramos hold this view, and they are among the contemporary scholars who are writing about enclaves.

Both Bernard-Henri Levy and Alasdair MacIntyre stress the barbarian assault on civilization. Levy, who represents the modern French school of philosophic pessimism, asks the questions posed by Nietzsche's "Mandarin of Königsberg." What can I know? What am I permitted to hope? What, finally, should I do? These questions reflect Levy's main concern: Who resists the barbaric threat? He answers that it is the intellectuals, whose

> way is indeed harsh and strait is the gate. If it is true that we are neither the bureaucrats nor the leaven of history, that the king doesn't give a damn for the wise man and that the wise man is not a king, that the masses don't give a damn for enlightenment and the enlightened abuse the masses, then this and simply this is left for us: that we are that species which the West names Intellectuals, that we have to spell out that name and take on that status, that it is urgent to accept it and to resign ourselves to its misery.[30]

Who then are of this enclave of intellectuals? Levy names three sorts of people: the metaphysicians, because they consider the ontological possibility of revolution; the artists, because in affirming life they affirm civilization against the death instinct of barbarism; and the *moralistes*, because they affirm myths about "a morality of courage and duty confronting the dismal cowardice of submission to facts."[31] Without these mythopoeic virtues of the *moralistes*, civilization quickly is drawn into "the whirlpool of fascism."

The "stock characters" in the drama of modern life represent to the English philosopher, Alasdair MacIntyre, the spawn of the barbarian assault on civilization. These characters—the bureaucratic manager, the consuming aesthete, the psychotherapist, and the celebrity protester, rally about the slogan "the expertise of the few and of the moral agency of everyone."[32] The moral dismemberment of modern society has resulted from this ethos and with it the destruction of moral community, the discounting of moral tradition, and the degeneration of civility.

MacIntyre does not say who should ask the Mandarin's questions, although one suspects he would agree with Levy. The intellectual and the scholar are not in the stock cast, nor do they necessarily depend on the barbarians to affirm their essences. They could be apart from the modern drama, if they had the courage so to choose. However, MacIntyre was clear about what might be done by "men and women of good will" to survive the ages of barbarism and darkness.

> If the account of our moral condition is correct, we ought also to conclude that for some time now we too have reached that turning point. What matters at this stage is the construction of local forms of community within which civility and the intellectual and moral life can be sustained through the new dark ages which are already upon us. And if the tradition of the virtues was able to survive the horrors of the last dark ages, we are not entirely without grounds for hope. This time however the barbarians are not waiting beyond the frontiers; they have already been governing us for quite some time. And it is our lack of consciousness of this that constitutes part of our predicament. We are waiting not for a Godot, but for another—doubtless very different—St. Benedict.[33]

The Brazilian organization theorist A. G. Ramos addressed MacIntyre's theme of local forms of community. To Ramos the present moral issue is the suppression of diversity in market-dominated managerial societies. But more importantly, the organizations that mobilize the resources of the administrative state were to Ramos the main threat to civilization because they create the unidimensionalization of modern life.

Ramos's alternative is found in his principle of delimitation. It is similar to the ideas of federalism and subsidiarity: In good societies larger social units leave to the smaller ones activities that they (the smaller) can best perform. On the one hand, the delimitation of social enclaves emphasizes positive values such as self-help, local self-determination, community building, group and individual creativity, and protection of small groups and individuals from large organizations. Ramos observed, "Organizational delimitation is . . . a systematic attempt to overcome the continuous process of unidimensionalization of individual and collective life."[34]

On the other hand, Ramos noted that delimitation heightens an individual's personal tensions by participating in enclaves that often have competing cultures and values. But Ramos argued that such conflict and tension was an essential part of moral development—that life posed many dialectical problems which, while unresolvable, enhanced the moral character of an individual when lived through in a substantive way.

But who asks the Mandarin's questions in Ramos's scheme? He identified them far more directly than either MacIntyre or Levy: the *management scholar*. In his most provocative chapter, entitled "Cognitive Politics," Ramos excoriated Chester Barnard and Herbert Simon for their treatment of the dual personality of organizational employees, observing that undue organizational loyalty leads to "hideous existential outcomes."[35] He referred to Barnard's approval of the telephone operator who watched her house burn down with her invalid mother in it, noting that she did not move from the switchboard because she was driven by the "moral necessity of uninterrupted service."[36]

This perversion of moral priorities has turned some ordinary individuals into agents for moral corruption who have accepted Nazi extermination camps, or Watergate, or the Iran-Contra affair as normal facts of state life. Similarly, the revelations of the "Mayflower Madam,"[37] insider Wall Street trading, greenmail, and leveraged buyouts are secretly admired by others as smart management practices.

The management scholar therefore asks the Mandarin's questions. The management scholar has the obligation to resist corrupt values. And the management scholar has the right to hope that disclosive learning within the scholarly enclave will enhance the moral character of those within its sphere of influence. Such an image of the scholarly enclave is a reminder of the old guild system in the sense that the morality and ethics of management scholarship cannot be woven out of the social fabric. The scholarly enclave must follow its calling with an eye on the welfare of the commonweal.

CONCLUSION

And so as management scholars in an administrative state, where do we stand in this fiftieth year marking the publication of the *Papers on the Science of Administration?* A story by Franz Kafka summarizes our plight. It is called *The Helmsman.*[38]

> "Am I not the helmsman here?" I called out. "You?" asked a tall, dark man and passed his hands over his eyes as though to banish a dream. I had been standing at the helm in the dark night, a feeble lantern burning over my head, and now this man had come and tried to push me aside. And as I would not yield, he put his foot on my chest and slowly crushed me while I still clung to the hub of the helm, wrenching it around in falling. But the man seized it, pulled it back in place, and pushed me away. I soon collected myself, however, ran to the hatchway which gave on to the mess quarters and cried out: "Men! Comrades! Come here, quick! A stranger has driven me away from the helm!" Slowly they came up, climbing the companion ladder, tired, swaying, powerful figures. "Am I the helmsman?" I asked. They nodded, but they had eyes only for the stranger, stood around him in a semicircle, and when, in a commanding voice, he said: "Don't disturb me!" they gathered together, nodded at me, and withdrew down the companion ladder. What kind of people are these? Do they ever think, or do they only shuffle pointlessly over the earth?

One cannot help but be struck by the similarities between Kafka's parable and management scholarship. We scholars are at once like the crew and the displaced helmsman, shuffling id-like across the face of the earth, ego-involved in our specializations, but all the time mindlessly accepting the barbaric values imposed by the superegos of those in power—the managerial helmsman of the administrative state.

All of this imparts for management scholars a certain urgency to the Mandarin's third question: "What, finally, should I do?" The answer for us, in Levy's words, is "harsh and strait." We must find our souls as scholars in the company with other scholars who are active in the world but who have morally transcended it. Odd as it may read, management scholarship can be a strong point in a defense system of civilization. Pertinent to the instrumental interests of our field we must be, but not at the cost of surrendering the high ground that is our privileged legacy from history. The face of the enemy is clear along our entire front. Do we have the moral courage to defend our heights from attack?

Notes

1. Seymour Martin Lipset and William Schneider, *The Confidence Gap: Business, Labor, and Government in the Public Mind* (New York: Free Press, 1983).

2. William G. Scott and Terence R. Mitchell, "Markets and Morals in Management Education," *Selections: The Magazine of the Graduate Management Admission Council* 3 (Autumn 1986): 3–8.

3. Loren Baritz, *Servants of Power* (Middletown, Conn.: Wesleyan University Press, 1960).

4. Lyndall Urwick, "Organization as a Technical Problem," in *Papers on the Science of Administration,* ed. Luther Gulick and Lyndall Urwick (New York: Institute of Public Administration, 1937), 49.

5. Peter F. Drucker, *The Practice of Management* (New York: Harper and Row, 1954), 8.

6. Herbert A. Simon, *Administrative Behavior* (1947; reprint, New York: Macmillan, 1954), 37.

7. Chester I. Barnard, *The Functions of the Executive* (Cambridge: Harvard University Press, 1938), 15.

8. Simon, *Administrative Behavior,* 223.

9. Thomas J. Peters and Robert H. Waterman, Jr., *In Search of Excellence* (New York: Harper and Row, 1982), 75, 82, 260, 282.

10. These numbers are based on a content analysis of the Academy publications done by the author and his research assistant T. Paluchowski.

11. H. Vaihinger, *The Philosophy of "As If"* (London: Routledge and Kegan Paul, 1924).

12. Fred Luthans, "Fifty Years Later: What Do We Really Know about Managers and Managing?" Academy of Management *Newsletter* 16 (October 1986): 3.

13. Terence R. Mitchell and William G. Scott, "The Barnard-Simon Contribution: A Vanished Legacy," forthcoming in *Public Administration Quarterly.*

14. Baritz, *Servants of Power,* 198–99.

15. This is Mayo's main point in the last two chapters of his influential book. See Elton Mayo, *The Human Problems of an Industrial Civilization* (New York: Macmillan, 1933), 138–80.

16. William G. Scott and Terence R. Mitchell, "The Universal Barnard: His Macro Theories of Organization," *Public Administration Quarterly* 11 (Spring 1987): 34–58.

17. Dwight Waldo, *The Enterprise of Public Administration* (Novato, Calif.: Chandler and Sharp Publishers, 1980), 10-12.

18. Henry R. Towne, "The Engineer as Economist," *Transactions of the American Society of Mechanical Engineers* 7 (1886): 428–32.

19. Woodrow Wilson, "The Study of Administration," *Political Science Quarterly* 2 (June 1887): 197–222.

20. Paulo Freire, *Education for Critical Consciousness* (New York: Seabury Press, 1973), 7.

21. Suggested by Eric Voegelin, *Order and History* (Baton Rouge: Louisiana State University Press, 1956), and *The New Science of Politics* (Chicago: University of Chicago Press, 1952).

22. Thomas S. Kuhn, *The Structure of Scientific Revolutions* (Chicago: University of Chicago Press, 1962), 10-34.

23. Jacques Barzun, *The House of Intellect* (New York: Harper and Brothers, 1959), 261.

24. See Eric Voegelin, "Industrial Society in Search of Reason," in *Technology and Human Destiny*, ed. R. Aron (Ann Arbor: University of Michigan Press, 1963), 36.

25. See John Keegan, *The Face of Battle* (New York: Viking Press, 1976), 191–92.

26. I confess that I have idealized these telos; maybe I have even romanticized them as some of my critics might say. However, humanity does on occasion rise out of the slime and shows characteristics of sterling nobility. I am thinking here of the remarkable combination of religious and scholarly commitment of a number of eighteenth-century English and Scottish moral philosophers, and of the honor of the English army officer at Waterloo as well as the Athenian practice of democracy in its forum during the golden age.

27. Robert S. Bachelder, "The Lost Soul of American Business," *The Christian Century*, 24–31 December 1986, p. 1171.

28. The American concept of voluntarism provided the underpinnings for enclave-like thinking and action (it was a central premise in Samuel Gomper's labor movement strategy). Arising from American voluntaristic principles were many enclaves that protected or advanced ethnic, religious, and economic interests. However, these voluntary associations seem to have been significantly different from those suggested in the main line of my argument.

The cutting edge between the two perhaps is this. Voluntary groups in America have tended to be self-interested, issue-specific, pragmatic, and instrumental. They have often demonstrated their concerns by either economic action or special interest politics from the ward to the national levels of government. By contrast, the enclaves that have formed around the ideas of moral tradition and moral community have been substantive, global in outlook, less tangible in time and space, and have had a greater concern for broad moral issues that bear on the welfare of the commonweal.

In this respect, the words of Edmund L. Pincoffs and David L. Norton are helpful. Typical American voluntary associations are focused on problem-solving "quandary ethics" while the enclaves in my thoughts are focused on moral development or "character ethics." See Edmund L. Pincoffs, *Quandaries and Virtues* (Lawrence: University Press of Kansas, 1986), and David L. Norton, essay in this volume.

29. Julius Stone is a notable exception to this observation. While Stone, as an American, acknowledged the buffering role played by voluntary associations between the individual and state intervention, he concluded his monumental book with an opinion about enclaves that is similar to mine: that they are bastions of defense against "ever-resurgent barbarism." He wrote, "We have humbly to conclude that it would be wrong for those who hold these enclaves to surrender them again to the wilderness, and a dereliction no less grave to shirk their defence, or to flinch from the duty to extend them as we can." Julius Stone, *Social Dimensions of Law and Justice* (Stanford: Stanford University Press, 1966), 798.

30. Bernard-Henri Levy. *Barbarism with a Human Face* (New York: Harper and Row, 1979), 194–95.

31. Ibid., 197.

32. Alasdair MacIntyre, *After Virtue: A Study in Moral Theory* (Notre Dame: University of Notre Dame Press, 1981), 239.

33. Ibid., 244–45.

34. Alberto Guerreiro Ramos, *The New Science of Organizations* (Toronto: University of Toronto Press, 1981), 123.

35. Ibid., 96.

36. Barnard, *Functions of the Executive*, 269.

37. Sidney Biddle Barrows, *Mayflower Madam* (New York: Viking Press, 1986).

38. Franz Kafka, *Franz Kafka: The Complete Stories*, ed. Nahum N. Glatzer (New York: Schocken Books, 1971), 443–44. Reprinted by permission of Schocken Books, Inc.

CHAPTER TWO

"Character Ethics" and Organizational Life

David L. Norton

M Y most useful role in this essay, as I see it, is as a bearer of news from the field of moral philosophy. The news that I bear may not be such to some readers, but I think most of us can profitably explore some of its implications together. Others may regard the very idea of "news" from moral philosophy as incongruous, by virtue of philosophy's traditional devotion to eternal verities. But philosophers dispute the question of which direction leads to the enduring truths, and just at present there are signs— by no means conclusive, but unquestionably significant—that moral philosophy may be undergoing a sea-change in this respect. I want first to consider the kind of change of which there are today intimations, and then suggest certain of its broader implications for organizational theory, organizational life, and organizational management.

The sea-change of which there are significant intimations amounts to the displacement of the dominant modern mode of moral philosophy by the ancient or "classical" mode associated with Hellenic Greece and Republican Rome. Thus the "new" moral philosophy is in fact quite old, and what is new is the

David L. Norton is a professor of philosophy in the Department of Philosophy, University of Delaware.

revival of interest in it. It first found systematic formulation in the thought of Socrates, Plato, and Aristotle, and it generally prevailed through the late Middle Ages. It was not gently displaced in the modern era but decisively routed by such of the "new men" (in Bacon's term) as Machiavelli, Bacon, and Hobbes, who laid the foundation for the mode of moral philosophy that has since prevailed. As with all reforms, in the beginnings of modernity it was the deficiencies of the ancient mode and the advantages of the modern mode that captivated the attention. The four hundred years of subsequent history have uncovered the deficiencies in the modern mode of moral philosophy, and what strikes some moral philosophers today is that the classical mode makes good these deficiencies.

Alasdair MacIntyre calls the modern mode "Nietzschean," and the classical mode "Aristotelian"; Richard Taylor terms the modern mode "ethics of duty" and the classical mode "ethics of aspiration"; Edmund L. Pincoffs speaks of the modern mode as "quandary ethics" and the classical mode as "ethics of virtue."[1] Each of these pairings has indicative force, but to suggest the features I want to identify I will name the modern mode "ethics of rules" and the classical mode "ethics of character."

Before attempting characterization of the two, I must offer a caveat. As for MacIntyre, Taylor, and Pincoffs, so for me, the modern/classical dichotomy must be understood not as "hard" but as "soft," and in two senses. In the first place the difference between the modern and the classical mode does not constitute mutual exclusion but is in the nature of a significant difference in emphasis. Thus, modern "rules ethics" does not altogether ignore the problem of character but gives less attention to it and attends to it in the light in which it appears when rules are the paramount concern. Conversely, "character ethics" does not altogether neglect rules but subordinates them to the development of moral character and views them instrumentally with reference to that end. Secondly, the dichotomy is "soft" and not "hard" in the sense that historical exceptions are to be recognized: there are "character" ethicists in modernity, but they are a distinct minority and relatively lacking in influence; and "rules" ethics was not unknown in the ancient world but was, so to speak, the moribund residue of ethics of character.

I begin my characterization by observing that "rules ethics" and "character ethics" address different primary questions. For modern moral philosophy the primary question is "What is the right thing to do in particular (moral) situations?" and it is answered by finding the rule that applies to the given situation and acting in accordance with it. Thus, if I am driving my car and collide with another vehicle, I am obligated by law to describe the event, and morality holds me to the rule, "Always tell the truth." This is an example of the many situations for which the covering rule is established and uncontroversial. On the other hand, what we refer to as "contemporary moral problems"—abortion, euthanasia, and compensatory preferential hiring are examples, as are most problems in the field of "business ethics"—are problems for which the covering rules are unsettled and in dispute. The point, however, is the unquestioned assumption that such problems are to be solved by discovering (or inventing and contractually agreeing upon) the covering rule.

The accepted agenda of ethics in modernity is to formulate a supreme and universally applicable moral principle—Hobbes's natural right of self-preservation, Kant's categorical imperative, Bentham's "greatest happiness of the greatest number," and Rawls's two principles of justice are famous examples—together with criteria for distinguishing moral from nonmoral situations, criteria for recognizing relevantly different kinds of moral situations, and as far as practicable, a complete list of rules amounting to the application of the supreme principle to all types of moral situations. Then moral conduct at bottom is obedience to the appropriate rules in the appropriate situations.

By contrast, classical morality begins with the question, "What is a good life for a human being?" It is led straightaway to the problem of the development of moral character, because any adequate description of a good life will be sure to include attributes that are not manifest in persons in the beginning of their lives but are developmental outcomes. Central examples are the classic moral virtues of wisdom, courage, temperance, and justice—none of which we expect of children, but only of persons in later life. In the classical understanding the virtues are excellences of character that are objective goods, of worth to others as well as to the virtues-bearer. Secondly, the manifestation of virtue is held to be the actualization of what was theretofore a potentiality. In other words, to be a human being is to be capable of manifesting virtues; and the problem of moral development is the problem of discovering the conditions for the actualization of these qualities that are from the beginning within persons as potentialities. While overly simple, it is nevertheless indicative to say that by the predominant moral mode of modernity it is the appropriate rule that tells a person what the right thing to do in a given situation is, while in classical ethics it is the developed moral character of the individual. To be sure, classical ethics requires rules, in the first instance to guide persons whose moral character is insufficiently developed. But the priority given to character development means that such rules must contribute to, or at any rate not obstruct, such development. And modern morality cannot wholly ignore the problem of character development, attending to it especially in children; but the centrality it gives to rules tends to limit its concern for character to the virtue Pincoffs terms "conscientiousness," that is, the disposition to live in accordance with established rules.[2]

It is important for our purposes to notice that by contrast to classical ethics, the modern mode is "minimalist" in at least two important senses. First, it makes minimal demands on the intelligence and developed moral character of persons; and second, it delimits the arena of moral choice to but a small sector of human experience.

Regarding the first: Modern ethics is founded on what can be called the Hobbesian truism that in the absence of recognized rules and generally rule-abiding conduct, life would be unbearable. Social order requires the observance by (almost) everyone of rules acknowledged and understood by (almost) everyone. For this to be the case, the rules must be very simple and straightforward conceptually, and acting in accordance with them must require very little in the way of developed moral character. This accounts for the tendency of modern modes of normative moral philosophy—contractarianism, deontology, rule utilitarianism, ideal observer theory, agent theory—to move toward rules of the sort as "Do not lie" and "Do not steal," and to introduce exceptions and complications very reluctantly. An effect of this reduction has been to shift much that was central to classical moral life to the category of the supererogatory, or to banish it from moral consideration altogether.

A consequence of conceiving of morality in terms of the need for social order is that morality becomes only problematically distinguishable from law; moral rules are directed to the same basic purpose as civil and criminal statutes and have the same form, and moral judgments are modeled on judicial decisions in terms of impartiality and impersonality. This puts an end, for example, to the classical principle of noblesse oblige—the principle that privilege and advantage carry larger obligations, and especially that more is to be expected of persons of higher moral development, who demonstrate their higher moral development by expecting more of themselves. I cannot here discuss the extreme resorts of ingenuity to which modern ethical philosophers have been put to try to distinguish morality from law, but the end result of holding both morality and law responsible for social order was a foregone conclusion. Matters of conduct deemed essential to social order are regulated by law, and morality is left to manage the less essential interstices and penumbra. Notice that today, when we reach consensus on a "contemporary moral problem," we typically write it into the law.

The effect of moral minimalism is that the moral minimum is taken to be the moral life: everything else is relegated to the category of the supererogatory, about which modern moral philosophy has little more to say. (In modern moral philosophy the supererogatory typifies what C. I. Lewis termed a "scrapbasket" category.)[3] One effect of this is that persons who fulfill minimal moral requirements are freed to direct their ample leftover energies and aspirations elsewhere. Another effect is that persons who

51

perceive a well-lived life to involve much more than minimal "rules responsibility" (in Pincoffs's expression),[4] are left without help or encouragement by ethics and moral philosophy.

But I must show the relevance of the large picture I have been painting to organizational life, organizational theory, and organizational management. The implications are formidable, and they will begin to emerge as I describe the second respect in which modern moral theory is minimalist in comparison to classical moral theory.

Recalling the respective central questions of the two moral modes: classical morality centers on the question, "What is a worthy life?" while modern morality centers on the question, "What is the right thing to do in particular moral situations?" The difference I want to highlight can be expressed in terms of the expression, "the moral situation." For classical morality "the moral situation" is the life of each person in its entirety (including, of course, but not confined to, interactions among persons). For modern morality "moral situations" are distinguished from "nonmoral situations"; they are partitioned off as a part of life. Much of life is nonmoral in the modern understanding, in the sense that moral considerations are inapplicable, and to endeavor to apply them is the type of logical error that Gilbert Ryle termed a "category mistake."[5] By contrast, from the classical point of view nothing in life is without its moral meaning.

An example of a situation that is adjudged nonmoral by the modern ethics is the situation of vocational choice. Suppose, for example, that my supreme moral principle is Kant's categorical imperative of universalizability, and I decide to become an engineer. It is obvious that I cannot will that everyone in my situation, that is, the situation of vocational choice, choose to become an engineer, and it is equally obvious that this choice may be the right choice for me. There is more than one way that this problem might be handled, but the typical modern mode of resolution is the simple expedient of agreeing to regard vocational choice as nonmoral. Then to say that my choice is the "right" choice for me is to use the term "right" in one of its nonmoral senses.

The same categorical distinction expels from the domain of the moral countless other choices human beings characteristically make: for example, what friends to cultivate, what avocations to pursue, what books to read. Indeed, John Stuart Mill on his utilitarian side (he had another side that related him closely to classical morality) says that "ninety-nine hundredths of all our actions are done from other [than moral] motives, and rightly so done if the rule of duty does not condemn them."[6] He is thus obliged to delimit the workings of the utilitarian principle in order to preserve any vestige of individual autonomy under utilitarianism. Were we always called upon to produce the greatest happiness of the greatest number (with its correlative rule on diminishing pain), we would be morally culpable in reading a book, writing a poem, or attending to the needs of our children, for in such cases there are many things we might do instead that would serve better to alleviate human misery in the world.

The point I will return to in a moment is that if moral situations can be marked off from nonmoral situations, the opportunity exists for any human being—or, indeed, whole institutions, practices, vocations, and disciplines—to set up shop on nonmoral turf. But it deserves note beforehand that the partitioning of life into moral and nonmoral domains has proceeded not just objectively (by distinguishing moral from nonmoral situations), but also subjectively, by identifying morality as a special point of view. Thus, Kurt Baier and others speak of "the moral point of view," John Rawls describes the ground of morality as the "original position," and R. M. Hare offers what he takes to be the obligatory logic of moral language.[7] What is immediately evident is that "the moral point of view" is one viewpoint among others, the "original position" is one position among others, and "moral language" is one vernacular among others. As in the case of the delimited moral situation, this affords to persons and institutions the opportunity to pitch camp outside the point of view or position, and no argument has been successful at compelling them to move to moral ground; nor, I think, can there be a compelling argument, for all such arguments are inevitably circular, resting on premises that the outlander finds oneself under no obligation to accept.

Modern history displays two campouts beyond the moral perimeter that are of such importance as to enable us to say with only a little exaggeration that they *are* modern history. One of them is business and economics, and the other is science. Modern science gained its freedom on the ground of what modernity has represented as the logical gulf between "is" and "ought," or description and prescription. This is sometimes termed "Hume's law," expressed in the form, "No 'ought' from an 'is.' " In its orthodox meaning, it says that descriptions of fact cannot imply anything but other descriptions of fact, and prescriptions (including moral prescriptions) cannot be derived from anything but other prescriptions. The effect of this is to divorce fact from value, with the consequence that people and disciplines are granted leave to devote themselves to matters of fact and declare themselves immune to moral considerations, claiming to be "value-free."

This resort was not available to business and economics at the beginning of the modern period, for the very good reason that economic values are by any yardstick unquestionably *values*. What happened here will be familiar, thanks to any number of sound historical accounts. Business incentives, including the very avarice that classical morality and medieval theology had condemned, were moralized on the argument of "Private Vices, Publick Benefits" (Bernard Mandeville), and the "invisible hand" of Adam Smith and others.[8] This *moral* endorsement has been abetted by the propensity to regard economic values as the supreme values (most concrete, most universally sought after, most reliable, etc.), and even to judge all other values in economic terms, as, for example, Bentham does when after listing many kinds of happiness he says that all are subject to the common measure of money.[9] What has happened in the last hundred years, of course, is that business has sought for itself the prestige, as well as the added exemption of science, through its connection to the social sciences on the bridge of economics. In this period, business management, public administration, and bureaucratic organization theory have gained a measure of recognition as applied social sciences, bound externally only by the market imperative to maximize economic values, and internally by the "my station and its duties" rules that no social organization can be without. I refer here to what William G. Scott and Terence R. Mitchell term the "orthodox single-set value system of present management practice and management education.[10] If such nefarious affairs as typified by E. F. Hutton, Ivan Boesky, and Kidder, Peabody put the question, "What has happened to moral character?"—I propose that the answer must begin with the recognition that modern rules morality does the best it can to ignore the problem of the development of moral character.

The modern rise to predominance of both science and business appears to be accounted for on the basis of powerful *a priori* human incentives—the love of truth on one side and the desire for material gain on the other. But to this I believe the following consideration should be added. Both the love of truth and the desire for gain are expressions of a more general trait that any conception of humankind must include, namely *aspiration*. The effect of modern moral minimalism is to afford modern moral life little room for aspiration; it is a small room with a low ceiling and not much of a view. An important consequence of this, I believe, has been to redirect human aspirations away from the confines of morality and toward the apparently limitless horizons afforded by the laboratory and the market. Needless to say, the recently mushrooming interest in "business ethics" will do nothing to open up prevailing conceptions of moral theory and practice to larger human aspirations, since it is but the application to business situations of minimalist rules morality.

By contrast to modern ethics, classical ethics is an ethics not of rules but of ideals, and it is characteristic of ideals that they make large demands on human aspiration. But the point that I want to focus on is classical morality's premise that morality is coterminous with human life itself, affording no nonmoral domain of refuge. This is because to be a human being is to possess potential excellence, excellence that it is one's inalienable moral responsibility to discover and progressively actualize in the world. And it will be immediately obvious that vocations, friends, avocations, and books (to cite previous examples) are relevant to the development of character. On the matter of vocation, for example: If it is the fundamental moral responsibility of every person to discover and progressively actualize his or her potential worth in the world, then vocational choice is clearly one of the important means for such actualization, and vocation has thematic moral meaning beneath the periodic "moral situations" that arise in it. This is why, for example, Socrates, Plato, and Aristotle refused to categorically divorce vocational skills from moral virtues (and not, as many modern commentators have hastily conjectured, because they lacked the analytical skills by which to recognize the difference). Indeed, classical thought integrates the vocation and the life of the individual by regarding the true work of the individual as his or her total life, to which vocation and every other dimension should be contributory. In our "jobs" in the workaday sense, as well as in the other dimensions of our lives, we are to offer the very best of which we are capable. Because this best is an objective good or goods, it is of worth to others no less than ourselves, and thus we are led to the classical conception of both one's well-performed work and one's well-lived life as the foundational form of generosity, consisting in giving the best of oneself to others. When Emerson says, "Your own gift you can present every moment,"[11] he is a modern spokesman for the classical mode and is contrasting ceremonial and occasional gift giving and "philanthropy" with the foundational generosity of the well-lived life.

Similarly, friendship is inseparable from the moral work of self-discovery and self-actualization, and the long section given to it by Aristotle in the *Nichomachean Ethics* is not, as modern moral philosophers have supposed, a diversionary ramble. According to Socrates in the *Lysis* and Aristotle in the *Nichomachean Ethics*, true friends, willing the best for one another, furnish reciprocal aid toward worthy living. Socrates says that friends, to be of such use to one another, must be alike in pursuing the good but different and complementary in the kind of good that each pursues, each contributing to the other what the other cannot self-supply. It is cautionary advice to modernity when Socrates, at the beginning of the *Lysis*, insistently distinguishes friendship from flattery and warns of the dangers of the latter. Friends must assist one another in the attainment to self-knowledge (including knowledge of limitations), while flattery, by its indiscriminate praise, misleads unwary and often all-too-eager recipients into mistaking themselves for persons of other sorts than they are, thus diverting them from their true courses.

The limitation of space prevents me from pursuing further the ineradicable moral dimension of the distinguishable aspects of life—our distinguishable sociological roles, our distinguishable psychological faculties, our distinguishable life-shaping choices. But on this matter there is a pronounced difference of reference between modern and classical modes of moral philosophy that requires brief comment for its bearing on organizational theory and management. Heralded by Descartes, modern philosophy has equipped itself with analytical methods and has judged success to be the arrival at clear conceptual distinctions. By contrast, the classical mode regards experience as beginning in a multiplicity of disparate and conflicting factors that require to be knit together into harmonious wholes. The *locus classicus* of the ancient view in respect to the individual is Plato's image *(Phaedrus)* of the human soul as chariot, charioteer, and two contrary-minded horses. Shall we ignore the logical and historical connections between the modern favor for analysis, and what many social critics regard as the present fragmentation of the lives of individuals into disconnected roles, competing psychological faculties, and conflicting life-shaping choices? This outcome would not have surprised the ancients, who recognized *integration* as the first problem of worthy living, so much so that among the virtues they gave priority to integrity even over wisdom, courage, temperance, and justice.

What this means for organizational life is, on one hand, that the integrity of the organization is a paramount responsibility of management. And it also means that the integrity of workers must be respected, which is to say that job performance cannot be judged in terms that disregard such dimensions of life as family, avocations, place of residence, and civic and religious commitments. Such familiar modern figures as the person who does superior work but at the expense of family relations, or the timeserver who works solely for the paycheck, are not acceptable by classical parameters.

If morality is coterminous with human life and unrestrictedly pervasive within it, then no human institution, practice, or discipline can claim exemption from its ultimate concern—the good life for human beings. Plato expresses this for state government when he says, in his *Republic*, "Can anything be better for a commonwealth than to produce in it men and women of the best possible type?"[12] Mill is a modern spokesman for this classical view when he says, "the most important point of excellence which any form of government can possess is to promote the virtue and intelligence of the people themselves."[13] And John Dewey puts the same principle by saying, "Democracy has many meanings, but if it has a moral meaning, it is found in resolving that the supreme test of all political institutions and industrial arrangements shall be the contribution they make to the all-around growth of every member of society."[14] These are three expressions—two modern and one ancient—of the classical principle of all social organization. We can best find its central imperative for organizational theory and management in its philosophical source, which is to say in Plato's *Republic*.

An immediate obstacle, to be sure, is that the *Republic* has latterly been discredited—in good measure by Karl Popper in *The Open Society and Its Enemies*[15]—as a nest of authoritarian-totalitarian atrocities. The trouble with this wholesale condemnation is that it buries enduring truths that the *Republic* contains. Plato indeed makes an important mistake in the dialogue, both in his own terms and in ours; but it has to do, not with the ends of social organization, but with the means by which the ends can best be achieved. It is on the ends of social organization that I believe we do well to consult him. What he holds to follow from his thesis on the purpose of social organization (noted above) is that the primary problem of social organization is the proper placement of persons within the organization. If the major support industry devoted to job placement today makes this advisement seem a truism for modern management, I think this supposition will be overturned by looking to what classical theory understood placement to entail.

In the first place, in classical belief "work" is not an unpleasant necessity that all people would avoid if they could. Persons are by nature active and seek to be productively so, unless and until this innate incentive is ruined by bad work experience. Their keenest satisfaction lies in productive activity that is for them the right kind of activity, and the right kind of activity is "self-fulfilling" in the sense that it is both intrinsically rewarding and productive of value for (some) other persons. To this must be added the proposition (put by Socrates as the starting point of the central portion of the *Republic*) that human beings innately differ from one another in significant ways. What this means with respect to the organization of work is that human beings are innately diversified with respect to the kind or kinds of productive activity that each will find intrinsically rewarding.

In support of this, I think that if each of us looks to his or her own case, we find that there are many kinds of entirely useful work that we as the individual we are would experience no intrinsic rewards at performing—indeed, we might even hate it—while there are a few kinds that we either know from experience, or believe, would afford us deep satisfaction. I have sometimes surveyed classes of a hundred students on this point. I begin by asking them what kinds of work they would hate to do; it is an easy question for them, and I fill many blackboards with their answers (my own profession of college teaching is always cited by several students as singularly abhorrent). Then I ask them to indicate kinds of work at which they know or think that they would experience significant intrinsic rewards, and with few exceptions their answers are already chalked up; it is the matching of persons to blackboard entries that is rearranged.

When I have followed this by the question, "What career are you preparing yourself for?" the correlation with the "intrinsically rewarding" list has been abysmal. From the classical viewpoint, here is our malaise in a nutshell; and it is deeply corrosive both of society and of the lives of individuals. An added factor is that students will typically have had little practical experience of the work they cite as likely to be intrinsically rewarding and next to none in the careers for which they are preparing themselves, nor will they have troubled to think out correlations and implications of the types of work they find (or believe they would find) distasteful. I conclude from this that the crucial questions concerning individual well-being and social organization from the classical viewpoint can be said scarcely to arise in our social setting.

The mistake that Plato made was in supposing that a group of qualified professionals—his Guardians—can determine right placement of the individuals of a society while those individuals are still in their childhood. According to modern developmental knowledge, such determination cannot except in the rarest of cases occur before adolescence. And if it is to occur in adolescence, then the new-found autonomy that characterizes adolescence must be respected, which means that placement and the exploration and experimentation that necessarily precede it must be largely the responsibility of individuals themselves. The social responsibility is to provide practical recognition of the importance of this enterprise by removing obstacles and constructing social supports and a conducive social setting.

I believe that we should uproot our conventional expectation of schooling as sixteen-years-at-one-sitting and generalize the "work-study" format, combining practical learning with formal learning in the interest of acquiring knowledge of the world and self-knowledge. I am also in favor of a large-scale voluntary National Youth Service, including international exchange of tens of thousands of young people, affording exposure to diverse life-styles, once again in the interest of better life-shaping choices. (Incidentally, the round-robin exchange by many nations of 50,000 of their youth might reasonably be expected to have some dampening effect upon the belligerence of nations; but on the other hand such exchanges would require built-in safeguards against wholesale hostage-taking.)

Regarding social advantages, the classical thesis is that persons who are engaged at the work that is right for them will identify with it and invest themselves in it, giving their best to it. If this thesis is correct, then it is possible that we have in our hands a corrective to our country's falling productivity together with the soaring wages and other costs of production that have priced our country's goods out of both foreign markets and our domestic market. Indeed, in classical perspective our support industry at manufacturing artificial work incentives, as well as work-reform movements under such of the publicized headings as "job enrichment," "humanizing the workplace," and "workplace democracy," do not go deep enough and are therefore little more than temporary palliatives.

By the Platonic conception of the purpose of social organization, the state and every social organization within a society are responsible for providing to persons whatever conditions persons cannot self-provide, conditions that enable them to position themselves rightly, in the right organizations, and to function at their best in these positions. Given the centrality of individual initiative in personal growth, those of its conditions that can be self-provided should be self-provided. But the limits of the individual capacity for self-provision delegate important responsibilities to the state and to organizational management. As noted earlier, the state, for example, is responsible for provision of the kind of public education that conduces to self-knowledge.

By the same criterion, what business management must provide can be divided into utilities and coordination. On coordination, I think our everyday experience bears out Plato's contention that there is a significant distinction between thinking in behalf of the whole and thinking in behalf of one's place within the whole, and this is so notwithstanding the fact that the well-being of the whole entails the well-being of all parts of the whole. To be a good college dean, for example, is to perceive the college in a way that is significantly different from the way it

61

is perceived by good department chairpersons and good faculty; and the same holds for managers and workers. If this is so, then managers are needed to secure harmonious productive relations among workers and their diverse kinds of work. The principle of such relations is complementarity, such that the excellence of each part does not detract from but contributes to the excellence of other parts. The excellence of each part is to be judged partly in terms of standard production criteria, but not exclusively. The reason is that the well-being of the whole depends upon the well-being of each part; and we have seen that by classical criteria the well-being of each worker is grounded in the integration of the aspects of his or her life, such that distinguishable roles and faculties interrelate, once again, in complementary fashion. This does not mean that companies should seek to exercise authority in every dimension of the lives of workers, as did George Pullman, for example, in his creation of the paternalistic company town of Pullman, Illinois, toward the end of the last century. It means that management must respect the moral responsibility of workers to achieve integrity in their own lives, where "respect" entails nonobstruction, together with provision of supporting conditions. I think this entails, for example, that every company or factory that employs women must provide day care for their infants and small children on the premises, together with the opportunity for mothers to visit the facilities occasionally. I think it also entails released time granted to employees who seek further formal education, perhaps with tuition payment. It may entail something like "sabbatical leave" for purposes of personal enrichment, and it entails company participation in programs contributing to civic welfare.

In the matter of utilities, workers are normally to be supplied the tools, materials, and training that their work requires. Each of these calls for detailed treatment, but I will confine myself to two or three observations. Tools and materials must be such as to conduce to work of the highest quality. Training must include acquaintance with the place of one's role in the organization as a whole, and the place of one's particular work in the total product. In addition, the work is to be taught as a practice—that is, as a mini-tradition with its intrinsic standards of excellence and honor; and it is to be taught only by master practitioners who honor the practice and take satisfaction in the excellence they have achieved in their performance. It is another matter of utilities that companies maintain apprenticeship programs, dovetailed with the work-study pattern of education, and that apprenticeship not be understood to entail commitment to the company by apprentices. As we are now speaking of it, apprenticeship serves the purpose of exploration by young people in the interest of sound later vocational choice, and the benefits to a given company are not the immediate ones of employee training, but the deeper, long-term ones of helping to insure that most of the employees of every company are where they want to be, doing what they want to do.

Does good management entail workplace democracy? I think it does, but democratizing the workplace will not produce the results of which it is capable until the groundwork is done to obtain as far as possible the situation in which employees (including managers of course) are so positioned as to experience intrinsic—and not merely monetary—rewards in their work. To be sure, decision making itself has a measure of intrinsic reward for many people; but most people find little reward in helping to decide matters about which they are at bottom indifferent.

The self-responsibility of workers as workers and as human beings precludes the "scientific" ambition of management to totally control the way work is done; and preservation of intrinsic rewards in work precludes the subdivision of work into tasks so limited that they can be fulfilling to no one.

My thoughts on management as offered here are meant merely as suggestive; and persons who know more about the field will, I am sure, better perceive managerial implications of the classical perspective if they choose to experiment with it. In the end, the very best application of the theory is sure to leave some kinds of work undersubscribed, and some persons under the best conditions will not find the course of life or the work that affords them adequate intrinsic rewards. Michael Walzer in *Spheres of Justice* offers a useful categorization of types of work that are likely to be undersubscribed, namely "hard work," "dangerous work," "grueling work," and "dirty work"[16]—to which I would add "gruesome work": for example, cleaning up after airline disasters, tornadoes, and traffic accidents; and work in hospital emergency rooms and mortuaries. His suggested handling is also mine, and admittedly ad hoc: eliminate what we can eliminate; automate what we can automate; compensate some of it with more pay and shortened hours; divide up the rest. I think there is no discredit to the viewpoint I have been sketching in recognizing that it cannot be expected to work perfectly. My argument is that by resolutely and resourcefully endeavoring to increase the amount of meaningful work and meaningful living in our society, we have reason to expect a significant measure of success, and that this measure is worth striving for.

Notes

1. Alasdair MacIntyre, *After Virtue: A Study in Moral Theory* (Notre Dame: University of Notre Dame Press, 1981), chap. 9; Richard Taylor, *Ethics, Faith, and Reason* (Englewood Cliffs, N.J.: Prentice-Hall, 1985), chap. 2; Edmund L. Pincoffs, *Quandaries and Virtues: Against Reductivism in Ethics* (Lawrence: University Press of Kansas, 1986), e.g., 28–29.

2. Pincoffs, *Quandaries and Virtues*, 28–29.

3. Clarence Irving Lewis, *Mind and the World-Order* (New York: Dover Publications, 1956), 350.

4. Pincoffs, *Quandaries and Virtues*, 29–31.

5. Gilbert Ryle, *The Concept of Mind* (London: Hutchinson, 1949), 15–16.

6. John Stuart Mill, *Utilitarianism*, ed. Oskar Piest (1863; reprint, Indianapolis: Bobbs-Merrill, 1957), 23.

7. Kurt Baier, *The Moral Point of View: A Rational Basis of Ethics* (Ithaca, N.Y.: Cornell University Press, 1958); John Rawls, *A Theory of Justice* (Cambridge: Harvard University Press, Belknap Press, 1971), chap. 1, pt. 4; R. M. Hare, *Moral Thinking: Its Levels, Method, and Point* (Oxford: Oxford University Press, 1981), notably chap. 6.

8. The process is insightfully described by Albert O. Hirschman, *The Passions and the Interests: Political Arguments for Capitalism before its Triumph* (Princeton: Princeton University Press, 1977), pt. 1.

9. Jeremy Bentham, *The Theory of Legislation*, ed. C. K. Ogden (London: Routledge and Kegan Paul, 1931), chap. 6, 103.

10. William G. Scott and Terence R. Mitchell, "Markets and Morals in Management Education," *Selections: The Magazine of the Graduate Management Admission Council* 3 (Autumn 1986): 3–8.

11. Ralph Waldo Emerson, *Self-Reliance* (Mount Vernon, N.Y.: Peter Pauper Press, 1967), 51.

12. Plato, *Republic*, trans. Francis MacDonald Cornford (New York: Oxford University Press, 1945), 154.

13. John Stuart Mill, *Considerations on Representative Government*, ed. Currin V. Shields (1861; reprint, Indianapolis: Bobbs-Merrill, 1958), 25.

14. John Dewey, *Reconstruction in Philosophy*, enlarged ed. (Boston: Beacon Press, 1957), 186.

15. Karl R. Popper, *The Open Society and Its Enemies*, 2 vols. (London: George Routledge and Sons, 1945), esp. chap. 6.

16. Michael Walzer, *Spheres of Justice: A Defense of Pluralism and Equality* (New York: Basic Books, 1983), chap. 6, 165–83.

CHAPTER THREE

The Sympathetic Organization

David K. Hart

It was also fashionable in Butler's time to deny the possibility of disinterested action. This doctrine, which was a speculative principle with Hobbes, has always had a certain vogue. . . . As a psychological theory it was killed by Butler; but it still flourishes, I believe, among bookmakers and smart young business men whose claim to know the world is based on an intimate acquaintance with the shadier side of it. . . . Still, all good fallacies go to America when they die, and rise again as the latest discoveries of the local professors.

—C. D. Broad, *Five Types of Ethical Theory*

THE fundamental question of management theory is: What links individuals together in cooperative endeavor?[1] The answer, according to the contemporary management orthodoxy, is self-interest—the raw egoism of Hobbes and Mandeville, refurbished in chic, modern, linguistic garb. Such self-interest

David K. Hart is the J. Fish Smith Professor of Free Enterprise Studies in the Institute of Public Management in the School of Management, Brigham Young University. Professor Hart acknowledges the invaluable aid of his research assistant, Krista West, in the preparation of this essay.

is assumed to be the primordial motive for all human behavior and, as such, is the metaphysical ground for management theory. All organizational behavior is summarized in the inelegant phrase, "What's in it for me?"

"Not so!" counter the proponents of the various versions of Theory Y management. They cite, most often, Douglas MacGregor and his spiritual progeny as exemplars of a more compassionate mode of management. Granted, it is more compassionate, but that compassion works out to be a nicer form of self-interest, but self-interest just the same.[2] When one gets past the facade, MacGregorian management is as dominated by self-interest as the work of Frederick W. Taylor.

But there is good reason to doubt the validity of that assumption about human nature. As C. D. Broad argues, the preeminence of self-interest was effectively unhinged in the eighteenth century. Nonetheless, the theory of predominant self-interest did indeed migrate to America, where it has been canonized as an unquestionable (and unquestioned) "scientific" law. As Bishop Joseph Butler observed about the egoist creed of his day: "No creature whatever can possibly act but merely from self-love; and every action and every affection whatever is to be resolved up into this one principle."[3] Unfortunately, our vast organizational society rests on the assumption that human nature is solely self-interested.

Yet some philosophers of the eighteenth century argued, with considerable perspicuity, that human nature had not one, but two, primordial aspects: the need to love self (self-love) and the need to love others (benevolence). The "benevolists"[4] mounted a powerful, even conclusive, counterattack against the psychological egoists but, sadly, they lost the war and egoism carried the day. The purpose of this essay is to argue that the benevolists were correct and that benevolence is as fundamental to human nature as self-interest. The loss of benevolence, both in theory and in practice, is the cause of the malaise of our organizational, alienated society. The parameters of the argument are best set with Adam Smith (1723–1790) and Bishop Joseph Butler (1692–1752).

To begin, Adam Smith has been particularly ill-used by those who claim him, for they have perverted his economic analysis into a moral justification of the acquisitive egoism he detested. We must rid ourselves of the popular misconception that contorts him into a post-Hobbes, pre-Bentham egoist. This confusion is partially the result of giving too much attention to his most well-known book, *The Wealth of Nations* (1776),[5] to the neglect of his more important first book, *The Theory of Moral Sentiments* (1759).[6] Smith intended that his economic and political arguments would be interpreted in the light of the moral philosophy developed in his first book.[7]

We can get past the misinterpretations by taking seriously Smith's distinction between the optimal society, resulting from the free expression of the true moral nature of the individual, and a suboptimal society, resulting from a "violation of human nature."[8] The first society was the result of the conduct of all affairs—social, economic, and political—with the love of others in mind:

> It is thus that man, who can subsist only in society, was fitted by nature to that situation for which he was made. All the members of human society stand in need of each other's assistance, and are likewise exposed to mutual injuries. Where the necessary assistance is reciprocally afforded from love, from gratitude, from friendship, and esteem, the society flourishes and is happy. All the different members of it are bound together by the agreeable bands of love and affection, and are, as it were, drawn to one common centre of mutual good offices.[9]

That was the optimal human condition. Adam Smith used the word "sympathy"[10] to refer to a more modest version of benevolence: thus, I term his ideal the "sympathetic society," guided by the sympathetic value paradigm.

But humans often fail to act on that innate sympathy and the result is a suboptimal society:

> But though the necessary assistance should not be afforded from such generous and disinterested motives, though among the different members of the society there should be no mutual love and affection, the society, though less happy and agreeable, will

not necessarily be dissolved. Society may subsist among different men, as among different merchants, from a sense of its utility, without any mutual love or affection; and though no man in it should owe any obligation, or be bound in gratitude to any other, it may still be upheld by a mercenary exchange of good offices according to an agreed valuation.[11]

Such a society can be termed the "mercenary society," based on the mercenary value paradigm. The mercenary society is accurately epitomized in Bernard Mandeville's phrase: "private vices, publick benefits."[12]

As in so many other things, Adam Smith anticipates future scholars. The distinction just made is quite close to the distinction made between the "gemeinschaft" and the "gesellschaft" by Ferdinand Tönnies.[13] The identification of the gemeinschaft with the sympathetic society is a bit problematic, because Smith—differing a bit from Tönnies—allowed that a gemeinschaft could be achieved through intention. But the mercenary society compares well with a gesellschaft:

> Individuals who enter a *Gesellschaft* do so with only a fraction of their being, that is, with that part of their existence which corresponds to the specific purpose of the organization. . . . In the *Gemeinschaft* unity prevails, in spite of occasional separation; in the *Gesellschaft* separation prevails, in spite of occasional unity.[14]

The key notion is that in a mercenary (or gesellschaft) organization, individuals are reduced to the single function congruent with the ends of the organization. In the mercenary society, the dominant conception of human nature is based on self-interest and self-interest alone: all are reduced to a single dimension. That vision determines the nature of organizational life. Accordingly, all exchanges among individuals within such organizations are given a mercenary valuation and all human relationships are determined by a calculus of personal felicity. Here Smith anticipates Karl Marx, with the conversion of human relationships into "commodity exchanges." Paradoxically, the classical economists often come close to the same view. The gemeinschaft cannot exist in such a utilitarian environment.

The disappearance of benevolence,[15] both in theory and in practice, would only be of interest to intellectual historians were it not for the nagging suspicion that maybe the eighteenth-century benevolists were correct. Perhaps Butler and Smith knew what they were about and that humans did need to love one another. If they were correct, then the absence of benevolence from management theory and practice would create major problems, for it looses alienation into our organizational society:

> It is not only the moral or practical benefits accruing to the agent or the recipient of benevolent action which are important; the amount of benevolence encountered in society serves as a barometer of man's concern for others, and where benevolence prevails human alienation diminishes.[16]

"ALIENATION LEADS TO THE PERVERSION OF ALL VALUES"

In the eighteenth century, alienation was understood as the separation of individuals from what was rightfully theirs. "To alienate," said Dr. Samuel Johnson, is "to withdraw the heart or the affections," and the supporting quotations make it clear that alienation involves the separation from things central to human fulfillment.[17] With the inclusion of the intangibles of the human spirit, Johnson anticipated modern interpretations of the term. Alienation results when an individual is separated from something *essential* to the development of his or her full human potential. It is not, then, just a minor psychological dyspepsia, but rather the spiritual sickness that comes with the ruination of one's life possibilities. Our modern age experiences it through the soul-destroying entanglements of modern organizational life:

> As a concept that is concerned with the inner life and involves a moral critique of the mechanization and spiritual isolation of modern society, alienation is particularly suited to the present-day mood. . . . Today, most social scientists would say that alienation is . . . a consequence . . . of employment in the large-scale organizations and impersonal bureaucracies that pervade all industrial societies.[18]

Adam Smith early on described the unique form of alienation that would afflict the workers in an industrial society. In a famous passage he indicted the dehumanizing effects of the division of labor:

> In the progress of the division of labour, the employment of the far greater part of those who live by labour, that is, of the great body of the people, comes to be confined to a few very simple operations; frequently to one or two. But the understandings of the greater part of men are necessarily formed by their ordinary employments. The man whose whole life is spent in performing a few simple operations, of which the effects too are, perhaps, always the same, or very nearly the same, has no occasion to exert his understanding, or to exercise his invention in finding out expedients from removing difficulties which never occur. He naturally loses, therefore, the habit of such exertion, and generally becomes as stupid and ignorant as it is possible for a human creature to become. . . . His dexterity at his own particular trade seems, in this manner, to be acquired at the expence of his intellectual, social, and martial virtues. But in every improved and civilized society this is the state into which the labouring poor, that is, the great body of the people, must necessarily fall, unless government takes some pains to prevent it. [19]

Smith's concern was, as always, for the quality of the lives of individuals over and above any systemic efficiencies. Puzzled, he touched on alienation, knowing that humans were intended for more but unclear as to what that entailed within an industrial society.

While de Tocqueville shared Smith's concerns, [20] and Hegel developed the philosophic aspects of alienation, it received its major development from Karl Marx. [21] Noting with irony the popular misconceptions of Marx's intentions, Erich Fromm neatly summarized contemporary society:

> The majority of people are motivated by a wish for greater material gain, for comfort and gadgets, and this wish is restricted only by the desire for security and the avoidance of risks. They are increasingly satisfied with a life regulated and manipulated, both in the sphere of production and of consumption, by the state and the big corporations and their respective bureaucracies; they have

reached a degree of conformity which has wiped out individuality to a remarkable extent. They are, to use Marx's term, impotent "commodity men" serving virile machines. [22]

He describes an alienated society, for these are not people who are fulfilling themselves. Rather, they are but adjuncts to their machines and inefficient ones at that. To make matters worse, they are alienated. One need not accept Marxian economics, nor his vision of the destination of history, to appreciate the acuity of his description of alienation.

There are flaws in that conception, of course. He could not anticipate the development and significance of modern organization, based on the behavioral sciences, that was just then coming into being:

> Marx did not foresee the extent to which alienation was to become the fate of the vast majority of people, especially of the ever-increasing segment of the population which manipulate symbols and men, rather than machines. If anything, the clerk, the salesman, the executive, are even more alienated today than the skilled manual worker. [23]

Because management, as a discipline, was not known, Marx could not understand the alienation of the "brain workers."[24] Yet he came close. Managers and managees alike are caught in the uniquely depersonalized processes of management that, according to Fromm, are even more alienating than manual labor. They require managers to adjust their personalities to the rhythms of managerial work,[25] where the manual worker has only to adjust the body and focus the mind. The brain worker is the creation of the managerial elite:

> A being does not regard himself as independent unless he is his own master, and he is only his own master when he owes his existence to himself. A man who lives by the favor of another considers himself a dependent being. But I live completely by another person's favor when I owe to him not only the continuance of my life but also *its* creation; when he is its *source*. [26]

The other problem is more significant, for it contains the concept vital to the solution of the problem of alienation: Marx's failure to consider benevolence as fundamental to human nature. While he writes often and powerfully about affectionate relationships among workers, he does not develop the concept of benevolence as a central feature in the depersonalization of modern society.

There is not space to recount the development and elaboration of the concept of alienation from the time of Marx to the present day.[27] Suffice it to say, the neglect of benevolence is a primary source of the alienation that is the most significant problem of our time. Nowhere is that neglect more destructive than in management theory and practice. The contemporary management orthodoxy is just a more sophisticated version of Adam Smith's mercenary paradigm, the offspring of the egoism of the seventeenth and eighteenth centuries, within which the possibilities of both benevolence and moral noblesse oblige were excluded. Refurbished by the organizational "scientists" of the nineteenth century and honed to a fine edge in the twentieth century, the modern incarnation of exclusive self-interest is found in the assumptions of the most influential contributors to the management orthodoxy: from Chester I. Barnard and Herbert A. Simon to Milton Friedman and B. F. Skinner.

But the philosophy of exclusive self-interest was given a subversive twist by the organizational theorists of this century. Self-interest only had meaning *within* the structures of modern organization, since such organizations were the essential condition for human happiness. This meant that one's primary self-interest was the health and survival of the network of modern organizations. "Individualism" had to be molded to fit the requirements of that reality. Thus, the management orthodoxy, as Wolin wrote about Durkheim, is "developed with surprising overtones of hostility towards individualism."[28]

This is the stuff of alienation, the gesellschaft writ large, for it requires a mutilation of the essence of the individual. The mutilation comes from the rending of benevolence from human nature and the reduction of the individual down to his or her organizational function. The orthodoxy states that human nature is entirely encompassed in a self-interest which is subordinate to organizational survival. By now, the doctrine of exclusive self-interest has been warped beyond the recognition of the philosophers of the seventeenth and eighteenth centuries who made it central to the new societies emerging. The addition of the paternalistic role of the modern organization has led to a philosophy of *instructed* self-interest. This is made clear by Simon, who argues that those self-interested individuals do not have the wits to maximize their self-interest.[29] Thus, the organization becomes essential to the individual because, through cooperative endeavor, it provides a collective maximization: "Man could accomplish great things without himself becoming great, without developing uncommon skills or moral excellence."[30] If that is the case, then, obviously individuals must shape themselves to the organizational requirements, rather than vice versa. As Urwick wrote:

> The idea that organizations should be built up round and adjusted to individual idiosyncrasies, rather than that individuals should be adapted to the requirements of sound principles of organization, is as foolish as attempting to design an engine to accord with the whimsies of one's maiden aunt rather than with the laws of mechanical science.[31]

Organizational personnel must grant management the right to shape their personalities to fit organizational needs. All actions and thoughts must be supportive of the organization, which is identified (by management, of course) as the most intelligent form of self-interest. This is precisely the condition that produces alienation.

This means that for organizations to run well, individuals must be de-complicated and rendered homogenous in all things. In that way, they will be predictable and fit into the planning schemes of organizations. Pappenheim indicts this compulsion to make everything predictable, especially people:

> Therefore individuals must be stripped of their individuality and treated as materials . . . [and] the association between em-

ployer and laborer is dominated by a basic indifference to human beings, by an attitude which considers man as nothing and the product as everything.[32]

This strips individuals of all that makes them human, thus alienating them from their work and from each other. What has this to do with benevolence? Basically, if one must consider oneself as a function, then one must also consider others as functions. If all relationships are as "function-to-function," then benevolence—or even friendship—is quite unnecessary, even harmful. Functions require neither love nor friendship, just a prior agreed valuation for performance. Every action, including those described as "moral," is evaluated in terms of a cost-benefit formula for an individual's well-being. Thus, one is kind to another because the other may be in the position of being kind to oneself. Benevolence is reduced to an insurance policy:

> In such societies individuals have become so separated and isolated that they establish contact only when they can use each other as means to *particular* ends: bonds between human beings are supplanted by useful associations, not of whole persons, but of particularized individuals.[33]

I contend that the most severe problems of alienation in our organizational society are the result of the neglect of benevolence—the trivialization of the imperative need to love others. Benevolence is not directly concerned with the nature and substance of work as a product. If we define work as the need of the individual to leave the stamp of the unique self upon the products of endeavor, then it is easy to see how individuals in our organizational society are alienated from the products of their work. How few individuals ever have the opportunity to leave the stamp of their uniqueness on anything.

But the real impact of that alienation is felt in the atomization of individuals from each other:

> A direct consequence of the alienation of man from the product of his labor, from his life activity and from his species life is that *man* is *alienated* from other *men*. When man confronts himself he also confronts *other* men. What is true of man's relationship

to his work, to the product of his work and to himself, is also true of his relationship to other men, to their labor and to the objects of their labor.[34]

Benevolence, as both the need to love and to be loved by others, comes into play whenever human relationships are involved. Management is entirely about human relations, as it brings together individuals, technologies, and materials into collective endeavor.

But in modern organizations, individuals are linked to other individuals in artificial relationships defined solely by the organizational mission. They are trained to think only in organizationally eufunctional ways. Management cuts away any *enduring* affectionate links among individuals because they may impede the realization of organizational goals. As Pappenheim observed about Marx and Tönnies: "Both thinkers come to recognize the separation between man and man as the basic characteristic of modern society."[35]

Wolin is correct when he writes that we live "in an organizational age which longs for community."[36] But community requires a correct understanding of, and belief in, the entailments of benevolence. Community, within organizations, must be built on affection of one for another, rather than on a mercenary exchange of services—even if the exchange is made cordially. No small part of the alienation of our organizational society is the result of the corruption of the soul that comes from the violation of human nature, which requires "a peculiar inward dishonesty."[37]

> There is not anything, relating to men and characters, more surprising and unaccountable, than this partiality to themselves which is observable in many; as there is nothing of more melancholy reflection, respecting morality, virtue and religion. Hence it is that many men seem perfect strangers to their own characters.[38]

The denial was then, as it is now, a rejection of the irrepressible spark of benevolence in human nature that presses for realization in both spirit and action.

The management orthodoxy provides us with a fatally diminished vision of humanity—as much as the systems of Hobbes, Mandeville, or Bentham—which denies and even mocks the possibilities of noninstrumental human generosity one to another. In such atrophied societies, individuals cannot become fully human because both structure and ideology deny them the opportunities to love one another—except actions as such might be useful to self:

> Marx . . . like Tönnies after him . . . envisaged contemporary man as living in a society without human community, in a world in which he is barred from human fulfillment.[39]

Those arguments for exclusive self-interest were, I believe, demolished by the philosophers of benevolence, from Shaftesbury and Butler to Hutcheson, Hume, and Smith. Their more expansive vision of human nature put the love of others on an equal footing with the love of self. Unfortunately, there are almost no benevolist philosophers on the contemporary scene and certainly none in management theory. The mercenary paradigm flourishes unopposed. To counter it, we must return to the eighteenth century for the arguments to use against the cosmetically enhanced, but still unalloyed, egoism of the management orthodoxy.

Bishop Butler and "Our Obligation to the Practice of Virtue"

The close of the seventeenth and the first half of the eighteenth century were not the best of times for those of a humane disposition. Egoism was the "state-of-the-art" theory, Deism was mauling institutional Christianity, and cynicism was triumphant over idealism.[40] The spirit of the age was personified by Mandeville's mocking, acerbic satire. But, out of all this, those of a more idealistic bent managed to give benevolence its finest defense and its clearest explication.

Samuel Johnson defined benevolence as the "disposition to do good; kindness; charity; good will," and the definition hasn't changed much down to our time.[41] The important point for the benevolists was the nature of that "disposition." They believed benevolence to be a fundamental characteristic of innate human nature, the capacity for a disinterested, noninstrumental love of others. As Adam Smith wrote about sympathy, so also it can be said about benevolence:

> How selfish soever man may be supposed, there are evidently some principles in his nature, which interest him in the fortune of others, and render their happiness necessary to him, though he derives nothing from it except the pleasure of seeing it.[42]

This does not mean that the benevolists neglected self-love.[43] To the contrary, as Roberts observed: "There are several affections or feelings which can motivate action, but self-love and benevolence are the most important."[44] Generally, they put benevolence on a par, and synergistic, with self-love. Thus, to ignore benevolence was to ignore that aspect of human nature that was the saving principle for all individuals within all organizations—whether social, economic, or political.[45] The neglect of benevolence produced self-estrangement and social isolation. While the philosophers of the Scottish Enlightenment are usually identified as the most outspoken friends of benevolence, the benevolist movement actually began with an English peer, Lord Ashley Douglas, the third Earl of Shaftesbury.[46] The Scottish connection resulted from the influence of his writings on a young pastor, Francis Hutcheson, who later occupied the chair of moral philosophy at the University of Glasgow. His friend, David Hume, and his student, Adam Smith, also accepted the reality of benevolence, with modifications.[47] But the clearest argument for benevolence was preached and written by the Sassenach prelate, Bishop Joseph Butler.

As noted, Christianity was in bad repair, both theologically and organizationally, in the early eighteenth century. Butler, a man of good religious conviction, exemplary character, and keen mind, was a key figure in the attempts at reform.[48] A man of affairs more than a sequestered divine and a student of the New Science, he wished to ground morality in the realities of a common human nature, rather than in the elegance of a postulated *a priori.* If the psychological egoists were to be defeated, it was essential that they be bested on the field of their own choosing—the sensible world of ordinary life. It was to that end that his *Fifteen Sermons* (1726) were dedicated.[49]

"Man Is Born to Virtue"

Butler's conception of innate human nature is happy: all of the various "passions, appetites and affections"[50] are implanted in humans for good purposes. Some are related to our animal nature, as hunger or fear; others to our human nature, as inventiveness and the appreciation of beauty. They all have strengths appropriate to the realization of the "real" nature[51] of man, although on occasion one or another might overwhelm the others—a condition that compromises true happiness in favor of momentary gratification. If the imbalance continues, however, it could destroy the possibility of true happiness.

The problem is to keep them all in balance, which means there is a hierarchy of propensities—some are obviously superior to others. As Broad writes:

> So the essential thing about man as a moral being is that he is a complex whole of various propensities arranged in a hierarchy . . . and . . . we must distinguish between the actual relative strength of our various propensities and that which they ought to have. The latter may be called their "moral *authority.*"[52]

The key fact for Butler is that the knowledge of the good is accessible to each individual: *"Every man is naturally a law to himself,* that *everyone may find within himself the rule of right, and obligations to follow it."*[53] To act according to those obligations is "natural" and to act against them is "unnatural,"[54] following the Stoic creed that "virtue is natural and vice is unnatural." Ideally, all of that complexity will be meshed into a functionally harmonious psychology, wherein all propensities—in their proper order—work synergistically for the optimal human life.

Additionally, none of the propensities is evil. Evil is good run amok, the intemperate obsession to gratify one propensity to the neglect of others. Such intemperance is condemned by nature, through conscience; and to pursue the false course requires a destructive self-deceit. This implies, of course, that one has a sense of the ideal moral person one should become—that we know our home.[55] Butler's approach to human nature is teleological and, thus, "He says that we do not fully understand it till we know what it is for and what are the various functions and relations of the various principles and propensities."[56] Butler argues that all individuals can know their natural destination and so writes:

> Our province is virtue and religion, life and manners; the science of improving the temper, and making the heart better. This is the field assigned us to cultivate: how much it has lain neglected is indeed astonishing. Virtue is demonstrably the happiness of man: it consists in good actions, proceeding from a good principle, temper or heart.[57]

For Butler and the benevolists, humans are intended by nature for happiness and happiness comes only from virtue—thus, "man is born to virtue." Happiness includes much more than the sum of the pleasures associated with the gratification of particular propensities—a quantitative principle of happiness. Happiness comes from fidelity to one's true nature and is the result of the harmony produced when all propensities are functioning as nature intended. This entails the recognition of the fact that in the hierarchy of propensities, the most important are self-love and benevolence. All of the particular propensities, while possessing pleasure in and of themselves, hold the additional pleasure of contributing to the progressive realization of self-love and benevolence. This requires the exercise of extensive reason in balancing and harmonizing them in the service of the higher propensities.

Butler presents a strong brief for the general affection of self-love, which "in its due degree is as just and morally good as any affection whatever."[58] However, he puts self-love in the perspective of an entire lifetime, rather than in the constricted time of immediate gratification, and this requires all particular propensities to be marshalled to enhance that lifetime. To those who trumpet the exclusive supremacy of self-love, he calmly points out just how often we violate its demands, succumbing knowingly to ruinous overindulgence in particular gratifications.

For instance, does the alcoholic serve her self-interest when she continues to drink, or does the salesman with a fiery temper serve his self-interest when he explodes at a customer? But egoists claim that whatever persons do is what they want to do and, thus, is in their self-interest. That is obviously wrong, but it enables them to escape the problems of the criteria for moral judgment. Immediate gratification serves as the prime criterion and the only external moral criterion is that one's actions must not impede any other person's right to their immediate gratification. For Butler, this was anathema, for self-love has to be considered through a lifetime and must be judged by specific moral ideals.

Thus, correctly understood, self-love is as important for the good of all as is benevolence, because it means that all individuals will develop their talents and virtues to the maximum. This is the meaning behind Broad's observation that

> Butler makes the profoundly true remark that there is far too little self-love in the world; what we need is not *less self-love* but *more benevolence*.[59]

Because individual happiness can only be achieved within society, the good of society must be a major aim of each individual. This is the domain of benevolence, which Butler defines broadly:

> And if there be in mankind any disposition to friendship; if there be any such thing as compassion, for compassion is momentary love; if there be any such thing as the paternal or filial affections; if there be any affection in human nature, the object and end of which is the good of another; this is itself benevolence or the love of another.[60]

Benevolence and self-love are not separated, but must work in conjunction, as Roberts observed:

> The general affection of self-love must be aroused by the perception or awareness of the condition of the self as a whole, and the general affection of benevolence must be caused by the perception of the state of a certain individual or a group of individuals taken as a whole.[61]

In defense of the actuality of the general affection of benevolence, Butler points to the obvious historical manifestations of the predisposition of individuals to love one another. If the egoists could point to empirical evidence for their claim, so also could the benevolists:

> From this review and comparison of the nature of man as respecting self, and as respecting society, it will plainly appear, that *there are as real and the same kind of indications in human nature, that we were made for society and to do good to our fellow-creatures; as that we were intended to take care of our own life and health and private good:* and *that the same objections lie against one of these assertions, as against the other.*[62]

However, if historical evidence is insufficient, an even more powerful confirmation can be obtained introspectively:

> [Butler] remarks that the question of whether benevolence is part of the natural constitution of mankind is "a question of fact or natural history." Like other such faculties, its existence is proved by appeal to the external senses, inward perceptions, and by the testimony of mankind.[63]

Knowledge about the reality of benevolence is available to all. Butler goes further, arguing that our greatest happiness comes from benevolence,[64] because it contains all virtue:

> Thus benevolence includes in it the sum of all virtues when, in striving to achieve the good of others, it is guided by reason, thus forming a "settled reasonable principle of benevolence" in a man.[65]

It is a more refined happiness, requiring the employment of imagination to consider the feelings of the recipients of our actions. Butler never quite extricates himself from the utilitarian snare: if love of others should be disinterested, but acts of benevolence bring us happiness, then can our benevolence ever be said to be disinterested? The answer lies, of course, in the *motive* for the benevolent act: it is done for the other and not for the self.

To conclude, the two general affections of self-love and benevolence are both equal and the basis for all moral action.[66] One does not derive from the other; they work against each other and each in its sphere is necessary. Thus, benevolence, "whose primary use and intention is the security and good of society," matches with self-love, "whose primary intention and design is the security and good of the individual,"[67] for a decent society is impossible without both.

Conscience

Butler is neither naive nor "enthusiastic." Virtue, realized through self-love and benevolence acting in harmony, is the natural condition of humanity, but it must be nurtured and developed. Unfortunately, "there is a manifest negligence in men of their real happiness or interest in the present world."[68] The route to that real happiness is monitored by conscience:

> In "real human nature" there exists a harmony between the different principles and propensities so that action motivated by passion, affection or appetite is always subservient to the superior and supreme principle of conscience.[69]

One of the most distinctive features of Butler's moral philosophy is the absolute sovereignty he gives to conscience, the moral faculty:

> It is by this faculty, natural to man, that he is a moral agent, that he is a law to himself: but this faculty, I say, is not to be considered merely as a principle in his heart, which is to have

some influence as well as others; but considered as a faculty in kind and in nature supreme over all others, and which bears its own authority of being so.[70]

Conscience is the superior facility, presiding over both self-love and benevolence, along with all the lesser propensities, balancing and directing them in the service of the life of virtue. He acknowledges that, at various times, various passions may come to have undue influence. But conscience has "judgment, direction, superintendency" and, if heeded, will bring any rogue propensities into their appropriate relationship. "Had it strength, as it has right: had it power, as it has manifest authority; it would absolutely govern the world."[71]

For Butler, conscience is the key to human progress, because its dictates are clear and they require moral action. Conscience may speak and we may not comprehend how the decision benefits anyone; but given its moral authority, one must always follow conscience:

> The dictates of conscience are often quite clear. Thus we can be far more certain about what is right than what is to our own ultimate interest; and therefore, in an apparent conflict between the two, conscience should be followed since we cannot be sure that this is not really to our own interest.[72]

To ignore conscience is to guarantee an existential alienation.

It is conscience which most distinguishes humans from animals, because it requires individuals to exercise moral agency, or moral voluntarism. After setting the metaphor of a watch, Butler concludes:

> A machine is inanimate and passive: but we are agents. Our constitution is put in our own power. We are charged with it; and therefore are accountable for any disorder or violation of it.[73]

With all of the benevolists, Butler accepts the rule that for any moral act to have meaning for the actor, it must be voluntary, freely chosen and not compelled. Conscience is the imperative force behind that voluntarism. Since moral agency is necessary to virtue, it is obvious that Butler would agree to nothing that would limit such agency. It is here that the implications for organizational theory and practice become apparent.

The Sympathetic Organization

We live in the mercenary society of Adam Smith. Because it is an organizational society, its metaphysical ground and moral justification is embodied in a management orthodoxy based upon a crude self-interest, defined by organizational eufunctionality. Because that society has been so successful in ministering to the material desires of its members, the defenders of the mercenary paradigm have adjudged it history's success and denounce criticisms as caviling.

But it is also a society that, by its very nature, alienates its citizens from the inherent satisfactions of their work and from affectionate relationships with organizational others. With respect to our organizational life—which is to say, most of our life—gesellschaft has replaced gemeinschaft, as Tönnies glumly predicted. Those under the sway of the management orthodoxy are estranged from themselves because their organizations deny them the realization of the most important characteristics of their moral nature: self-love and benevolence. In particular, benevolence has been the major casualty.

The defenders of the mercenary paradigm have long argued that benevolence is a chimera and that, even if it wasn't, it can not coexist with self-love: the two are mutually exclusive. Butler encountered the same argument:

> And since further, there is generally thought to be some peculiar kind of contrariety between self-love and the love of our neighbour, between the pursuit of public and of private good; insomuch that when you are recommending one of these, you are supposed to be speaking against the other; and from hence arises a secret prejudice against, and frequently open scorn of, all talk of public spirit, and real good-will to our fellow-creatures. [74]

For him, there was no contradiction between the two; for neither functions well without the other and both are necessary for the sympathetic organization:

> I must however remind you that though benevolence and self-love are different; though the former tends most directly to public good, and the latter to private: yet they are so perfectly coincident, that the greatest satisfactions to ourselves depend upon our having benevolence in a due degree; and that self-love is one chief security of our right behaviour towards society. It may be added, that their mutual coinciding, so that we can scarce promote one without the other, is equally a proof that we were made for both. [75]

Benevolence is the key to the creation of any humane organization, however. If we take Butler's argument seriously, then the management orthodoxy is not only incorrect but unendurable. Based upon a mutilated version of the whole self, the orthodoxy reduces individuals to their organizational functions and estranges them from the rewards of their work. Work is devalued into an instrumental activity valuable only for what it contributes to organizational goals. It has no intrinsic meaning. The individual's labor is a commodity and this makes the individual a commodity also, as Chamberlain noted:

> Employees are being paid to produce, not to make themselves into better people. Corporations are purchasing employee time to make a return on it, not investing in employees to enrich their lives. Employees are human capital, and when capital is hired or leased the objective is not to embellish it for its own sake but to use it for financial advantage. But somewhere in this philosophy there is an inconsistency with the notion of a society of self-governing individuals. The large corporation has become an organizer of people, a *user* of people, a molder of identities, according to criteria that it has evolved, without regard to the effect on those people except as this is registered on the balance sheet. [76]

This arbitrary and unwarranted atrophy of human nature renders a full third of the individual's life—the time on the job—as irrelevant to anything but organizational goals. Large salaries only ease, but do not prevent, the psychic damage.

The management orthodoxy emphatically eliminates benevolence as it strikes at the affectionate bonds between workers. Organizationally speaking, love of others is not only extraneous to organizational purposes, it is downright dysfunctional. Others are valuable only insofar as they assist in the achievement of organizational goals. To love organizational others interferes with the flexibility of management.

If alienation is to be overcome, then a new management theory must be created, incorporating the intentional love of others, along with self-love, as its primary moral ground. The key is benevolence, for the acceptance of its reality automatically prohibits the reduction of individuals to self-interestedness in the service of organizational eufunction. Furthermore, it requires the intentional creation of community—the gemeinschaft—within the organization. Following Adam Smith and Butler, we must create the "sympathetic organization." Butler argues that this ideal can be achieved in the actual world of everyday actions and leaves us with an inducement:

> Virtue is demonstrably the happiness of man: it consists in good actions, proceeding from a good principle, temper or heart. Overt-acts are entirely in our power. What remains is, that we learn to *keep our heart*. . . . He, who should find out one rule to assist us in this work, would deserve infinitely better of mankind, than all the improvers of other knowledge put together.[77]

Obviously the new paradigm involves some large problems. The demands of organizational life are too intense to allow time for leisurely friendly association; the movement of personnel is too frequent; and the geography is wrong (we do not live where we work). But that does not mean the ideal cannot be achieved. The philosopher, John Kekes, recommends a form of civil friendship for society and his scheme makes a great deal of sense for the sympathetic organization.[78]

Basing his proposal on Aristotle and Hume, he begins with the recognition that, in a good society, people treat one another decently. Kekes is more concerned with casual acquaintances, work mates and strangers, than he is with intimate friends. He describes this form of friendly association as

> a mixture of spontaneous good will, casual friendliness, a spirit of mutual helpfulness. It is an attitude citizens have toward each other and friendly visitors. It assumes no intimacy; in fact, it holds between passing acquaintances and strangers who have nothing more in common than the mutual recognition that they belong to the same group. It does not involve deep feelings; it is not personal, for anyone may be its beneficiary; it is spontaneous, but hostility, rudeness, or abuse may destroy it. . . . I shall call this attitude *civility*. [79]

Such civility serves self-interest, for it does make the society (or the organization) more pleasant. It equally serves benevolence, for it requires a genuine regard for the happiness of others. It requires no rules, for "the conduct of civic friends is not governed by any rules, but by mutual benevolence." [80] The life within a society such as Kekes describes is comparable to the life within the sympathetic society described by Adam Smith. With the modest improvements recommended by Kekes, the sympathetic organization is entirely within our reach.

But why should we go to all the effort to revamp organizations? Hopefully, the answer is self-evident: it is required by both self-love and benevolence. Adam Smith's vision of capitalism—which means people organized to achieve specific goals—requires individuals that epitomize happiness. West describes that happy, unalienated individual:

> In Adam Smith's case the man who is *unalienated* (in the self-fulfilment sense of the term) is simply the one who finds a Hellenic type of happiness. Happiness is found not in isolation but in the society of one's fellows and only in a dynamic, creative, and forward-looking environment wherein the individual is absorbed in the pursuit of new excellence, new knowledge, and new invention (or to use Smith's terms: Wonder, Surprise, and Admiration). [81]

A life of virtue requires a medium and the organizations of our lives can provide that medium. A life of virtue requires action and organizations are all about action. The goal is to instruct that action with a vision of happiness that comes from a fully realized self-love and love of others. This will only happen when we make the love of self and the love of others central to management theory and practice and teach our students accordingly:

> A man's heart must be formed to humanity and benevolence, he must *love mercy*, otherwise he will not act mercifully in any settled course of behaviour. . . . So to get our heart and temper formed to a love and liking of what is good is absolutely necessary in order to our behaving rightly in the familiar and daily intercourses amongst mankind.[82]

The end of all this would be a society of self-fulfilled individuals, who act and interact in the completeness of their true moral nature, within organizations sympathetic to that nature. It would be, in other words, the sympathetic society of Adam Smith.

Notes

1. William G. Scott argues that since the essential aspect of any organization is coordinated human action and that such action necessarily entails management, the term "management theory" is the most appropriate general classification. The phrase "management orthodoxy" also comes from Scott.

2. David K. Hart, "Management and Benevolence: The Fatal Flaw in Theory Y," in *Organizations and Ethical Individualism*, ed. Konstantin Kolenda, (New York: Praeger, 1988). A stronger case can be made for the organizational prescriptions of A. H. Maslow and Carl R. Rogers. However, note the critique in Michael Maccoby, *The Gamesman* (New York: Simon and Schuster, 1976), chap. 8, "The Psychology of 'Development.' "

3. Joseph Butler, *Fifteen Sermons Preached at the Rolls Chapel*, ed. Rev. W. R. Matthews (1729; reprint, London: G. Bell and Sons, 1914), Sermon XI., para. 7, 168.

4. I will use the older terms "benevolism" and "benevolist" to refer to the philosophy and philosophers of benevolence.

5. Adam Smith, *The Theory of Moral Sentiments*, ed. D. D. Raphaela and A. L. Macfie, 6th ed. (1790; reprint, Indianapolis: Liberty Classics, 1982) (hereafter cited as *TMS*).

6. Adam Smith, *An Inquiry into the Nature and Causes of the Wealth of Nations*, ed. R. H. Campbell and A. S. Skinner (1776; reprint, Indianapolis: Liberty Classics, 1981) (hereafter cited as *WN*).

7. A. L. Macfie, "Adam Smith's *Moral Sentiments* as Foundation for His *Wealth of Nations*," in his book *The Individual in Society* (London: George Allen and Urwin, 1967), 59–81. The *TMS*, first published in 1759, went through six editions and was Smith's last effort before his death. On the other hand, the *WN* was not substantially revised after its publication in 1776. The apparent contradiction between the morality of the first book and the self-interest of his second book has been effectively resolved in favor of Smith's moral philosophy. See Glenn R. Morrow, *The Ethical and Economic Theories of Adam Smith* (1923; reprint, Clifton, N.J.: Augustus M. Kelley, 1969).

8. T. A. Roberts, *The Concept of Benevolence: Aspects of Eighteenth Century Moral Philosophy* (London: Macmillan, 1973), 32.

9. *TMS*, II.ii.3.1, 85.

10. The first chapter of *TMS* is entitled "Of Sympathy" and opens with the

observation: "How selfish soever man may be supposed, there are evidently some principles in his nature, which interest him in the fortune of others, and render their happiness necessary to him, though he derives nothing from it except the pleasure of seeing it." I.i.1.1, 9. He goes on to identify those "principles" as sympathy.

11. *TMS*, II.ii.3.2, 85–86.

12. Bernard Mandeville, *The Fable of the Bees: or, Private Vices, Publick Benefits*, 2 vols. (1732; reprint, Oxford: Clarendon Press, 1924). See also M. M. Goldsmith, *Private Vices, Public Benefits* (London: Cambridge University Press, 1985); Thomas A. Horne, *The Social Thought of Bernard Mandeville* (New York: Columbia University Press, 1978).

13. Ferdinand Tönnies, *Community and Society*, trans. Charles P. Loomis (1887; reprint, New York: Harper and Row, 1957).

14. Fritz Pappenheim, *The Alienation of Modern Man* (New York: Modern Reader Paperbacks, 1959), 66, 67.

15. There have been some ineffective attempts to incorporate benevolence into utilitarianism. See, for example: Richard B. Brandt, "The Psychology of Benevolence and Its Implications for Philosophy," *Journal of Philosophy* 73 (August 1976): 429–53; and J. J. C. Smart, "Utilitarianism and Generalized Benevolence," *Pacific Philosophical Quarterly* 61 (January–April 1980): 115–21.

16. A. Koutsouvilis, "On Benevolence," *Mind* 85 (July 1976): 428.

17. Samuel Johnson, *A Dictionary of the English Language* (1755; reprint, London: Times Books, 1979). The above subhead is quoted from Erich Fromm, *Marx's Concept of Man*, with a translation from Karl Marx's *Economic and Philosophical Manuscripts* (New York: Frederick Ungar, 1961), 54.

18. Robert Blauner, *Alienation and Freedom* (Chicago: University of Chicago Press, 1964), 2–3.

19. *WN*, V.i.f. 50, 781–82.

20. See Alexis de Tocqueville's similar comments in *Democracy in America*, ed. Phillips Bradley, 2 vols. (1840; reprint, New York: Vintage Books, 1945), chap. 20, "On a Theory of Manufactures," 2:168–71.

21. An excellent source is David McLellan, *Karl Marx: His Life and Thought* (New York: Harper and Row, 1973) and the bibliography therein. See also E. G. West, "The Political Economy of Alienation: Karl Marx and Adam Smith," *Oxford Economic Papers* 21 (March 1969): 1–23.

22. Fromm, *Marx*, 4.

23. Ibid., 56–57. For the rise of modern organization, see William G. Scott and David K. Hart, *Organizational America* (Boston: Houghton Mifflin, 1979).

24. Maccoby, *Gamesman*, 173.

25. Ibid.

26. Karl Marx, *Economic and Philosophical Manuscripts*, in Fromm, *Marx*, 138.

27. See Richard Schacht, *Alienation* (Garden City, N.Y.: Doubleday, Anchor Books, 1970) and the references therein.

28. Sheldon S. Wolin, *Politics and Vision* (Boston: Little, Brown, 1960), 387.

29. "Administrative theory is peculiarly the theory of intended and bounded rationality—of the behavior of human beings who *satisfice* because they have not the wits to *maximize*." Herbert A. Simon, *Administrative Behavior*, 2d ed. (New York: Free Press, 1957), xxiv.

30. Wolin, *Politics and Vision*, 380.

31. Lyndall Urwick, "Organization as a Technical Problem," in *Papers on the Science of Administration*, ed. Luther Gulick and Lyndall Urwick (New York: Institute of Public Administration, 1937), 85.

32. Pappenheim, *Alienation of Modern Man*, 42, 89.

33. Ibid., 81.

34. Marx, *Economics and Philosophical Manuscripts*, in Fromm, *Marx*, 103.

35. Pappenheim, *Alienation of Modern Man*, 87.

36. Wolin, *Politics and Vision*, 357.

37. Butler, *Sermons*, VII.15, 118.

38. Ibid., X.2, 151.

39. Pappenheim, *Alienation of Modern Man*, 83.

40. The obvious adversaries were La Rochefoucauld, Hobbes, and Mandeville. Their concern with Locke was ambivalent. Most of them were influenced by *An Essay Concerning Human Understanding* (1690), but they were bothered by some egoist strains: "Locke had supposed that each man seeks only his own happiness and is guided into the paths of righteousness by fear of punishment." William Curtis Swabey, "Benevolence and Virtue," *Philosophical Review* 52 (September 1943): 452. The quotation in the above subhead is from Butler, *Sermons*, pref. 12, 7.

41. Johnson, *Dictionary*.

42. *TMS*, I.i.1.1, 9.

43. Hutcheson is sometimes given as the exception, for he made benevolence the defining characteristic of virtue. However, he modified his position, perhaps under the influence of Butler's writings. See William Robert Scott, *Francis Hutcheson* (1900; reprint, New York: Augustus M. Kelley, 1966); Henning Jensen, *Motivation and the Moral Sense in Francis Hutcheson's Ethical Theory* (The Hague: Martinus Nijhoff, 1971).

44. Roberts, *Concept of Benevolence*, 108.

45. R. Corkey, "Benevolence and Justice," *Philosophical Quarterly* 9 (April 1959): 152–63.

46. Stanley Grean, *Shaftesbury's Philosophy of Religion and Ethics* (Athens: Ohio University Press, 1967).

47. Adam Smith differed, respectfully, with his teacher, Francis Hutcheson. He believed Hutcheson placed too much emphasis upon a form of benevolence that would require moral supererogation. However, Smith's concept of sympathy was very close to the general idea of benevolence held by most of the benevolists.

48. E. C. Mossner, *Bishop Butler and the Age of Reason* (New York: Macmillan, 1936).

49. A good general account is Austin Duncan-Jones, *Butler's Moral Philosophy* (Harmondsworth, England: Penguin Books, 1952).

50. Butler used the terms rather indiscriminately. For the sake of clarity, I will collapse them into the single word "propensity." See the thorough discussion in Roberts, *Concept of Benevolence*, 34–47. The above subhead is quoted from Butler, *Sermons*, pref. 13, 8.

51. For a discussion of the problems involved see J. Roland Pennock and John W. Chapman, eds., *Human Nature in Politics* (New York: New York University Press, 1977), and the bibliography therein.

52. C. D. Broad, *Five Types of Ethical Theory* (New York: Harcourt, Brace and Co., 1930), 56.

53. Butler, *Sermons*, II.4, 51.

54. Ibid., II.10, 54–55.

55. Broad takes this position, while Roberts disagrees. I lean more toward Broad's position.

56. Broad, *Five Types of Ethical Theory*, 56.

57. Butler, *Sermons*, XV.16, 242.

58. Ibid., pref. 39, 24.

59. Broad, *Five Types of Ethical Theory*, 62.

60. Butler, *Sermons*, I.6, 34–35. He recognized the vast difference between the love of a parent for a child and the superogatory love of all, but he was less interested in the distinction than in convincing his readers that, in all its forms, benevolence was as vital to the individual as was self-love.

61. Roberts, *Concept of Benevolence*, 47.

62. Butler, *Sermons*, I.5, 33.

63. Amelie Oksenberg Rorty, "Butler on Benevolence and Conscience," *Philosophy* 53 (April 1978): 179–80.

64. Butler, *Sermons*, I.6.

65. Roberts, *Concept of Benevolence*, 61.

66. At one point, he makes benevolence subservient to self-love where, contrary to previous sermons, he makes benevolence a "particular affection." I believe he meant it as "particular" only in regard to the fact that it must be evaluated by the moral actor. Butler, *Sermons*, XI.19, 181. For the argument that benevolence is derived from self-love, see Thomas H. McPherson, "The

Development of Bishop Butler's Ethics," *Philosophy* 23 (1948): pt. I, 316–30; 24 (1949): pt. II, 3–22.

67. Butler, *Sermons*, I.7, 37.
68. Ibid., I.15, 45.
69. Roberts, *Concept of Benevolence*, 32.
70. Butler, *Sermons*, II.8, 54.
71. Ibid., II.14, 57.
72. Broad, *Five Types of Ethical Theory*, 80.
73. Butler, *Sermons*, pref. 14, 11.
74. Ibid., XI.2, 166.
75. Ibid., I.6, 35–36.
76. Neil W. Chamberlain, *The Limits of Corporate Responsibility* (New York: Basic Books, 1973), 92.
77. Butler, *Sermons*, XV.16, 242.
78. John Kekes, "Civility and Society," *History of Philosophy Quarterly* 1 (October 1984): 429–43.
79. Ibid., 429.
80. Ibid., 430.
81. E. G. West, "Adam Smith and Alienation," in *Essays on Adam Smith*, ed. A. S. Skinner and T. Wilson (Oxford: Clarendon Press, 1975), 541.
82. Butler, *Sermons*, XII.8, 189.

CHAPTER FOUR

The Paradox of Profit

Norman E. Bowie

ONE of the more interesting philosophical paradoxes is the so-called hedonic paradox. Hedonists believe that happiness is the only good and that everything should be done with the aim of achieving personal happiness. The hedonic paradox contends that the more you seek happiness the less likely you are to find it. Consider the following situation. You awake at 7:00 A.M. and as a good hedonist you resolve to undertake each of the day's activities in order to achieve happiness. The achievement of happiness is your conscious goal in everything you do. I submit that if you adopt that strategy your day will be most miserable—probably long before noon. If you want to be happy you must pursue and successfully meet other goals. Happiness accompanies the successful achievement of those goals. To be truly happy, you must focus on consciously achieving your goals. In that way the hedonic paradox can be avoided.

I maintain that a similar paradox operates in business. Many business persons believe that profit is the only goal of business and that everything should be done with the aim of obtaining profit. I contend that the more a business consciously seeks to obtain profits, the less likely they are to achieve them. Let us call this paradox the profit-seeking paradox. What I suggest in

Norman E. Bowie is the director of the Center for the Study of Values and a professor of philosophy at the University of Delaware.

this essay is that this paradox can be avoided only if there is a rethinking of the motives for making a business decision, the purpose of business, and the values that traditional business managers hold.

SERVICE RATHER THAN PROFIT

Perhaps the place to begin is with motivation. According to the traditional view, business persons are motivated to do well—well for themselves and well for the company. By the invisible hand this self-interested behavior of individuals and individual firms is coordinated by market forces to produce the good for all. Doing good is achieved by doing well.

As several business persons said in *Ethics and Profits,*

> The American free enterprise system is not perfect, yet it has produced more benefits than any other system in history. We are the healthiest, wealthiest, best educated, most generous nation in the history of the world.
>
> The objectives of business and the achievement of social goals are the same. Without business, there is no money, no resources, no environmental protection.
>
> We believe our goals are compatible with the best interests in society.[1]

Indeed, if business were motivated to do good it would be involved in an altruistic paradox. The more business sought to do good, the more harm it would do. This paradox arises if you believe that each individual is the best judge of his or her own needs and that attempts by institutions to "do good for people" rather than letting persons help themselves is actually harmful.

But the public does not accept the business person's analysis that in seeking profit business does good. They do not agree that the material success of business persons and business executives is necessarily advantageous to the public at large. That is because the public perceives the business person as someone who would do anything for a "buck"—if not for his own buck then for the stockholder's. Poll after poll has shown that the public has little respect for business executives.[2] If business persons want respect they will have to convince the public that they are professionals rather than mere profit maximizers.

Traditionally the motive for professional conduct is the service motive; the professional skills are service skills, specifically skills that benefit humankind. Doctors, lawyers, teachers, and the clergy—the standard paradigms of professionals— exercise a special skill for the benefit of human beings. The Harvard Business School has as its motto, "To Make Business a Profession." However, I don't believe the Harvard Business School realizes just how radical that slogan is.

Business persons who view themselves as professionals are motivated to do good and in doing good the firm will do well. If a manager emphasizes the production and distribution of *quality* products that customers need and if she is *honest* and *fair* with suppliers and lenders, and most importantly if she provides meaningful work for employees, then both the manager and the firm will be profitable. If the profit-seeking paradox is to be avoided, the business person must see herself as a professional and the service motive must dominate. Business can only really do well if it seeks to do good.

We now confront two competing paradoxes. Traditionally the business person believes that business does good by doing well (seeking profit) and that if business were to consciously seek to do good, it would neither do good nor do well. Business would be enmeshed in the altruistic paradox. On the other hand, I contend, as do other critics of the traditional view, that if business is to do well, it must consciously seek to do good. Otherwise business would be enmeshed in the profit-seeking paradox. Who is right?

Let us begin by addressing that question indirectly. The theory known as ethical egoism contends that each person should act in his own perceived best interest. On a traditional, but I believe mistaken, interpretation, Adam Smith would support ethical egoism on the ground that the invisible hand would coordinate egoistic behavior so that the good of all was achieved. On the other hand, Hobbes believed that life in an egoistic world would be a war of all against all in which life was nasty, brutish, and short. There is no invisible hand to bring about utilitarian results. Instead, citizens would rationally elect to place their hands in the power of an absolute ruler (the Leviathan or state) so that the state of nature could be avoided. Who is right, Hobbes or Smith? Traditionally we have believed that Smith was right and the empirical evidence seemed to support that view. Lately however, Hobbes is having something of a renaissance.

Similarly, the traditional wisdom and the empirical evidence seemed to support the view that business should consciously seek to do well rather than to do good. Lately, however, the "business should consciously seek to do good" view is being taken more seriously. In the scholarly literature, Hayes and Abernathy's classic *Harvard Business Review* piece, "Managing Our Way to Economic Decline," pointed out how our excessive concern with short-term profit was hurting our competitive position internationally.[3] In the popular literature, Peters and Waterman's *In Search of Excellence*[4] emphasized that the profitable companies directed their concern to their employees and their customers first and were profitable as a result. In essence, *In Search of Excellence* said that a company does well by doing good. Since the publication of these well-known works, a groundswell of supporting books and articles with supporting evidence has arisen. A significant number of scholars and practitioners from a diversity of disciplines and firms accepts the paradox. The more a corporation seeks to make a profit, the less likely it is to do so. Let us say that at this point the empirical evidence is inconclusive.

I do have difficulty with the two assumptions of those who argue that if corporations seek to do good they will run afoul of the altruistic paradox, namely that people are the best judge of their own interests and that in trying to do good you necessarily do harm. Certainly there is some truth behind those assumptions. People are often the best judge of their own interests. But not always. Society has correctly not honored the judgment of drug addicts. Moreover, persons who challenge the "do good by doing well" philosophy aren't necessarily asking business to "do good for people." Rather, business is being asked to create the conditions for persons to do one of the things they most want to do, specifically to have a challenging job that allows self-development and is useful to society. If business performed that function, I do not believe it would fall victim to the altruistic paradox.

Finally, I should like to address one ethical objection to the "do good in order to do well" theme. Some ethical purists would object to the "do good in order to do well" philosophy on the grounds that the only reason a business is motivated to do good is the belief that it will do well. This, the critics contend, makes moral behavior merely instrumental. Morality is simply a means for making a profit. The business person does not believe there is anything intrinsically valuable in doing good. What would (should) a company do if it can do well by not doing good or even by doing harm?

These ethical purists seem to forget that Plato actually believed that each individual reaped the benefits of ethical behavior. The virtuous man was the happy man; the tyrant was unhappy. For Plato, virtue clearly paid. While few philosophers would go as far as Plato, many (most?) agree that morality is good for society as a whole. In that sense, as Kurt Baier among others has pointed out, a society has a morality because it is rational to do so; and by rational Baier means in the interest of society's members.[5] Similarly, morality has been seen as one possible answer to prisoner dilemma situations.[6] And recently, Robert Axelrod in his book, *The Evolution of Cooperation*,[7] has shown that the limited "tit for tat" morality has a higher payoff than taking advantage of the altruistic behavior of others.

If morality was not of benefit to society, society would not have it. Indeed, many would argue that morality is required if there is to be a society at all. I think Kant's ethical theory can be pushed in that direction. Acknowledging that fact does not diminish the value of morality.

Of course, showing that morality is in the interest of society is one thing; to show that morality is always in the interest of each member of society is quite another. It seems obvious that on occasion doing the ethical thing is not in the interest of an individual (nor in the interest of an individual corporation). In such cases the individual or corporation ought to do what is morally correct even though they won't do well by doing so. On this point the ethical purists and I are in agreement. Where the ethical purist and I might disagree is on the attitude we should take toward those cases where doing good is not compatible with doing well. In the corporate context I would argue that we should manipulate institutional structures so that we decrease the likelihood of such occasions arising. For example, in a well-run company with adequate grievance procedures and the absence of an employment-at-will contract, whistle blowing would become unnecessary. An employee could be confident that her concerns would get a fair hearing and that she would not lose her job for raising her concerns. In such cases potential whistle blowers would not face the dilemma of doing good at the expense of doing well.

The ethical purist, on the other hand, might want to instill heroic attitudes in individuals—to give them the courage to sacrifice self-interest for morality. In the absence of such courage, persons will be tempted to protect their own interests to the detriment of larger interests. People should be prepared for the hard reality that doing good can mean not doing well. My approach, the purist would argue, tries to cover over the hard demands of reality.

I frankly believe the purists have a point. However, my own view of the world and human nature leads me to think that individuals will face the hard moral choices often enough and that the likelihood of success in meeting them is enhanced when the number of times these choices must be faced is diminished.

I do not want to leave any doubt that I do believe doing good sometimes requires a sacrifice and that the sacrifice ought to be made. However, I am not concerned with such occasions here. Rather, I am concerned with the far greater number of cases where doing good really would lead to doing well. As a society I don't think people recognize the genuine value of moral behavior. Business leaders particularly need to be convinced that the profit-making paradox can only be avoided if business leaders see themselves as professional providers of a service. However, to adopt the service motive is to change one's view of the function of business.

MEANINGFUL WORK

In this section I argue that one of the main purposes of business is to provide meaningful work for employees. To get to this conclusion, we need to go through a two-step dialectic. First, the view that the sole function of business is profit making must be rejected; and second, various widely discussed alternatives to the profit-making function of business must be seen as incomplete. This prepares the way for my conclusion that the main function of business is to provide meaningful work.

The Friedmanite view that the purpose of a corporation is to maximize profits has already come under severe attack. The classical view ignores the negative externalities of the practices of the classical firm and it totally ignores effects on the distribution of income. Air and water pollution, noise pollution, and unemployment are but a few of the problems that have caused citizens to doubt that firms seeking to increase stockholder wealth actually do produce the greatest good for the greatest number.

Similarly, the classical profit-seeking firm unjustly treats labor as any other factor of production, that is, capital, machines, and land. When it pays to substitute machines for people, the profit-seeking firm should simply do it and that is the end of the matter. If the firm can hold down wages by threatening to move to another region or another country it should do so. In fact, if it pays to move a plant from one part of the country to another, the firm should do so whatever the reason. If the going wage in an industry is four dollars an hour and if it is extremely difficult for workers to live on $160 a week, that is not the concern of the employer. In fact, he should seek to lower wages if he can. Even if an economic system with profit-making firms maximizes total income, that does not establish the justice of such a system. Hence, critics argue that the higher average wealth comes at the expense of the poor. And in any case, treating employees on a par with capital, land, and machines violates a fundamental moral maxim, that is, people cannot be treated like objects but are uniquely worthy of respect.

Moreover, even if Friedman, in his analysis in *Capitalism and Freedom,* is right in claiming that profit-making firms support political liberties, Friedman ignores the fact that the employee has few liberties within the corporation. As one commentator notes, the corporation is the black hole in the Bill of Rights.[8] The Constitution simply does not apply. Moreover, the employment-at-will doctrine still predominates. In the absence of a contract to the contrary, an employee can be fired for any reason, be it a good reason, immoral reason, or indeed no reason at all. Since most people are far more involved with their job than they are with public affairs, it is not unreasonable to believe that many employees would trade some political freedom for more freedom on the job or would trade political liberties for increased job security. The classical view has a rather poor record protecting the liberties many people most want.

Of course, defenders of the classical view argue that the stockholders have rights employees do not have because stockholders are the owners of the corporation. However, the property rights argument won't do. First, property rights are not absolute. No individual can do what he wants with his property and neither can a firm. Second, from the moral point of view all property ownership is not equal. Consider the following dissimilarity between homeowners and stockowners. A homeowner who works on her home and perhaps improves it beyond what the improvements could return in resale is not judged to be irrational. A stockholder who treats his stock in that way is considered to be irrational. Which type of property ownership is most in need of restrictions? By the way, the manager and the employer usually have the most reason to treat the company as a homeowner treats her home. If the company does poorly, the costs fall more heavily on the managers and employees. They can lose their entire livelihood. Far less often does the collapse of a company mean that the stockholders lose their livelihood. Besides, analyses since the 1930s and 1940s have shown that most stockholders do not identify with the corporation in which they own stock. At this point in our history, the "big players" are the pension fund managers, and hence much of the outstanding stock is not even directly chosen by the individuals who own it. Therefore, if restrictions on personal property are legitimate for homeowners, they are even more legitimate for stockholders.

Third, if the stakeholder theory of the firm is correct,[9] there is no moral justification for maximizing the interests of the stockholders at the expense of the other stakeholders. Indeed, if other stakeholders such as labor are at a greater risk if the firm fails, morality would support giving their interests greater weight.

In place of the profit maximization view, a number of alternative theories of the function of the corporation have arisen such as:

- Seeking profits so long as it does not cause avoidable harm or unduly infringe on human rights[10]
- Seeking to do social good (correct social problems) as well as seek profit[11]
- Seeking to produce life-sustaining and -enhancing goods and services[12]
- Seeking to maximize the interests of the various corporate stakeholders rather than simply the interests of the stockholder[13]

Each of these alternative definitions has much to be said for it. All recognize that there is more to business than making a profit. Yet I am convinced that each of the alternative views to a greater or lesser degree omits or gives insufficient emphasis to something essential—namely that the *main* purpose of the corporation is to provide meaningful work.

For example, the "seek profit while avoiding harm" view simply argues that corporations should follow a moral minimum required of all individuals and institutions. It puts constraints on the competitive profit-seeking game. There is a concept of unnecessary roughness in football. Similarly, there are concepts of unnecessary roughness in profit seeking. To recognize this fact is important, but under this view the essential function of business remains profit. Management is simply reminded of the rule against avoidable harm. As such, I think such firms and their managers remain vulnerable to the profit-making paradox.

The second alternative that urges corporations to do good by correcting social problems is vulnerable to the altruistic paradox, to all of Friedman's well-known criticisms,[14] and to charges that the obligation to do social good is too open-ended.

The third and fourth alternatives require more extended discussion. Both avoid the paradox of profit making. For example, just as individuals can avoid the hedonic paradox if they pursue goals other than happiness, individual corporations can avoid the profit-seeking paradox if they pursue goals other than profit, and each specifies a goal for business other than, or in addition to, profit.

One of the criticisms of the third alternative is that it focuses on human beings as consumers rather than as producers. One of the common complaints against ethicists who criticize distributive justice under capitalism is that these ethicists ignore production at the expense of distribution. Goods can't be distributed unless they are produced. There is much merit in this criticism, but ironically the business community has forgotten its own insight. The focus is on selling to consumers; far greater attention is directed to increasing sales to consumers than it is to increasing the productivity of the employees.

Moreover, as the social commentator David Bell has pointed out, this attempt to increase consumption creates paradoxes that threaten capitalism itself.[15] Specifically, the set of values business encourages in consumers is inconsistent with the values business wants to instill in its workers. The attitudes that make Americans good consumers are not the attitudes that make Americans good workers. Business wants workers who are loyal to the company, who will delay gratification, and who will exhibit the attributes associated with the work ethic. But business urges consumers to buy and enjoy now and to pay later on credit. Thus we have, in Bell's memorable phrase, "the cultural contradictions of capitalism."

Although *In Search of Excellence* argued that excellent companies focused on their employees, the point was diluted both by the anecdotal nature of that work and by the emphasis on being close to the customer. This dilution represents a danger of the fourth alternative. Should the interests of all the stakeholders be considered equal? I would argue that there are both economic reasons and ethical reasons why they should *not* all be considered equal.

Paradoxically, the focus of American business on consumer sales has hurt profits. The "productivity crisis" is a feature story in the popular business press. Recently a number of economists have addressed this problem and have argued that business must spend more time, money, and energy on employees. In an important recent book, *The Next American Frontier*, Robert Reich argues that the United States can only maintain its economic preeminence if we make a total commitment to investment in human capital.

> Unlike high-volume production, where most of a firm's value is represented by physical assets, the principal stores of value in flexible-system enterprises are human assets. Specialized machines and unskilled workers cannot adapt easily to new situations. Flexible machines and teams of skilled workers can. Only people can recognize and solve novel problems; machines can merely repeat solutions already programmed within them. The future prosperity of America and every other industrialized country will depend on their citizens' ability to recognize and solve new problems, for the simple reason that processes which make routine the solution to older problems are coming to be the special province of developing nations. Industries of the future will not depend on physical "hardware," which can be duplicated anywhere, but on the human "software," which can retain a technological edge.[16]

Philosophers would argue that an emphasis on the individual employee is just what ethics requires. For example, Kant, in the tradition of Aristotle, recognizes that only human beings are capable of being motivated by moral rules. It is human beings that place values on other things; these other things have conditional value because they only acquire this value as the result of

human action. Human beings, on the other hand, have unconditioned value, that is, value apart from any special circumstances
that confer value. Since all human beings and only human
beings have this unconditional value, it is always inappropriate
to use another human being merely as a means to some end—as
if they had instrumental value only. Hence, Kant argues, one
should always treat a human being or a person with unconditional value as an end and never treat a human being merely as a
means toward your own ends. Each person looks at himself or
herself as possessing unconditioned value. If one is to avoid
inconsistency, one must view all other human beings as possess-
ors of unconditioned value as well.

Kant's principle of respect for persons can be applied directly
to business practice. A Kantian would take strong exception to
the view that employees are to be treated like mere equipment in
the production process. Human labor should never be treated
like machinery, industrial plants, and capital, solely in accordance with economic laws for profit maximization. Any economic system that fails to recognize this distinction between
human beings and other nonhuman factors of production is
morally deficient.

It is one thing to argue that persons ought to be respected; it is
quite another to specify how that is to be done in the employment context. A full discussion of this issue would take us into
psychology—an area where I am at best an amateur—as well as
into ethics. The psychological generalizations that follow may be
controversial. However, they are common in the popular literature and are consistent with the "respect for persons" principle.
I will take it is a given that people do not feel fulfilled unless
they are gainfully employed in jobs that they find meaningful
and important. If robots could do all our work, utopia would not
have arrived. People would be unhappy and frustrated. People
need to work.

However, not just any work will do. The work must first be
seen as useful—as making a contribution to society. Second, it
must challenge the worker. One of the problems with the assem-

bly line is that it is hard to see how putting six bolts in a car door is useful work. It is also boring and fails to challenge the worker. Our foreign competitors discovered these truths before we did. Volvo never really had an assembly-line technique and the Japanese innovations are now widely discussed and often imitated.

Moreover, the employee must be able to exercise judgment and creativity. A job where the employee simply follows orders and where all the employee's actions result from orders has no autonomy. This denial of autonomy shows lack of respect. In the corporate context, autonomy can be honored through team-work when each employee has some say in goal formation and implementation.

In summary, I take it as a psychological truth that all human beings need to be engaged in rewarding work where rewarding work is defined as work that is useful, challenging, and respect-ful of individual autonomy. Business does good when it provides jobs of these types. Moreover, that function of business is more important than the production of goods and services function. It seems obvious that a person can be deprived of nearly any product or even most of the products American industry pro-duces without suffering severe psychological harm. But if a person is denied meaningful work, the psychological harm is very great. That is why I argue that it is morally more important for business to focus on the employee rather than on the con-sumer or the other stakeholders.

Suppose business sought to do good in the sense that it focused on developing those skills and attitudes that made people happier, healthier, and more cooperative human beings. Aren't those just the skills needed to make workers more produc-tive? By doing good the corporation would also be doing well.

But isn't that just manipulative? Isn't the reason for doing good to do well? The companies behave morally because there is a payoff. We need to rethink our discussion in the first section of this essay to address this complicated question.

There are essentially three ways to seek happiness. First, one can set out consciously to do so. However, to seek happiness in that way leads directly to the hedonic paradox. Such behavior is self-defeating. Second, one can seek to achieve successful intermediate goals realizing "in the back of one's mind" that in so doing one will be happy. And third, one can seek to successfully achieve personal goals and in the process one will discover happiness. This latter means to happiness clearly avoids the hedonic paradox.

What about having happiness in the back of one's mind? Is that sufficient for avoiding the hedonic paradox? Psychologically, I think we have a borderline case. Whether or not the paradox is avoided depends on how far "in the back of one's mind" the ultimate goal of happiness is.

Similar comments can be made about management's attention to employees. If the management is creating conditions for happy and healthy employees in order to make a profit, they are simply using employees as a means to their own end. They are not motivated by the respect and dignity of personhood. Hence, the motive of such managers is not moral even if the results are good. However, most employees recognize such motives and upon recognizing them undermine management's efforts. Many a quality circle has collapsed for just that reason. The result is that immoral motives that are supposed to yield good results frequently fail to do so.

On the other hand, if the firm consciously focuses on the individual self-realization of the employees, the employees are likely to recognize this and to respond appropriately. Will such moral motivation on the part of management yield good results? Within the firm, the answer, I believe, is certainly in the affirmative. Given a stable external environment, the firm will do best by focusing on the employee. Of course, changes in the external environment affect profit too. There is no guarantee that moral motives will yield good results.

Perhaps the best strategy is for management to focus on employee self-realization while keeping profits in the back of its mind. In that way management can respond to trends in the environment. But such an approach can be dangerous. If profits aren't sufficiently in the back of management's mind, the employees will develop the same kind of cynicism found when profit is the conscious goal of "moral" behavior.

Before leaping to the conclusion that this last strategy is the only practical one, keep in mind the following distinction:

1. Management A says to its workers, "You will never be fired without cause, but if the economy turns sour, some of you will have to be let go" (moral behavior with profits in the back of the mind).
2. Management B says to its workers, "You will never be fired without cause nor will you be fired in the event of an economic downturn. If the company should go under because of circumstances beyond our control, we will all go under together" (moral behavior with profits as a happy result).

Wouldn't the employees in company B be less cynical and more productive, and hence wouldn't the profit-seeking paradox be less likely to occur? I would invest my money in the stock of company B.

In this section I have rejected the classical view that the main purpose of the corporation is to maximize stockholder wealth. Moreover, I have argued that even the well-known alternatives to the classical view do not place sufficient emphasis on what I take to be the most important function of business—providing meaningful work. The greatest contribution of business to human well-being is to provide jobs rather than goods and services for consumers. That is why firing a person without cause is such a moral wrong. That is why layoffs due to economic downturns are such personal tragedies. If Weitzman's arguments in *The Share Economy* are correct, his proposal is morally superior to current wage and layoff practices.[17]

However, if the notion that the chief function of the corporation is to provide meaningful work is to be implemented, the attitudes and values of American business must change.

New Business Values

If the primary motive of managers ought to be service and the primary purpose of business ought to be providing meaningful work for employees, what are the implications for traditional business values and business practice?

First, we have to deemphasize competition. The football and war metaphors have to be replaced. Elsewhere I have suggested the family metaphor as an appropriate device for seeing how a corporation ought to function.[18] We are not losing ground just because we are not competitive enough. We are losing ground because we are not cooperative enough. Cooperation must be emphasized over competition because cooperation is necessary to provide the cohesiveness necessary for the practice of morality. It is harder to be a free rider if you see your associates as colleagues or teammates rather than as competitors. Much is now being written in decision theory on ways to avoid zero sum games and prisoner dilemma situations. This research needs to be made accessible to managers and then applied to the business context.

One change in corporate practice might be the introduction of a notion of group merit to replace or supplement individual merit. When an economic downturn occurs, everyone could be put on a reduced work week rather than placing the entire burden on the few who are laid off. A profit-sharing system should supplement or even replace the traditional wage structure. One of the most developed suggestions is Martin Weitzman's. Worker compensation is tied to a formula that makes it vary inversely with the firm's level of employment. Although these specific suggestions may have flaws, they capture the flavor of the more cooperative collective approach.

More important than specific recommendations of the sort suggested above is a change in perspective on how the corporation is viewed. Rather than emphasizing the goals of the individual CEO, we must speak of corporate goals and organizational decisions. If we have better corporations we will have better individual corporate persons. Professor Kenneth Andrews's notion of a corporate strategy is extremely valuable in providing a focus for the ideas I have in mind.[19]

Second, we must give up our excessive commitment to individualism. In a market economy it is very difficult to overcome free-rider problems. A rational individual, in situations that require cooperation, knows that he does best when everyone else cooperates and he does not; he then free-rides on the cooperative activity of others. But if everyone reasons this way, then the cooperative activity will not occur or will occur at a level below optimum. Since morality is essentially a cooperative activity, it easily falls victim to free-rider problems. This argument has been brilliantly made in Fred Hirsch's *Social Limits to Growth* and clearly stated in Reich's *The Next American Frontier*.

> The challenge of adapting to the era of human capital exemplifies the paradox of civic virtue. To the extent that people cooperate—willingly sharing their knowledge, skills, and resources with one another—each person is rendered better off than he would be without such cooperation. The collective power of everyone's talents and resources is greater than the mere sum of the individual talents and resources involved. But each person is aware that he can be even better off if everyone *but* himself acts with an eye to the common good, so that he can benefit from the result without bearing any part of the mutual burden. If each person follows this logic and rationally opts for personal gain at the expense of everyone else, there will be no cooperation. Everyone will be worse off. What is rational for the individual is tragically irrational for the society as a whole.[20]

Morality is particularly vulnerable when the pressure is on corporations to produce short-term gains. As I indicated earlier, one of the fatal flaws in the profit-seeking motive is the excessive emphasis on short-term profit. The solution to that problem is a collective rather than an individual one. What do I mean by that? I mean the problem rests in a deficiency of the competitive system; it does not rest primarily with deficiencies in individual character.

Nonetheless, truth, trust, acceptance, and restraint—"canons of everyday face to face civility"—recognized by the classicist Theodore Levitt, is required for the conduct of business; yet the very practice of business undermines it. This is not mere academic theorizing. Observers in the field are commenting on the decline of morality and on its disastrous effects.

> Perhaps most troubling is that the atmosphere of insecurity and impermanence which characterizes all levels of American business has bred a selfish attitude among directors, managers, and employees, an egoistic mentality which is seriously undermining American enterprise. Within a productive system that increasingly depends on cooperation, good faith, and team spirit, the dominant ethic is coming to be cynical indifference and opportunism. . . . We are witnessing an extraordinary increase in self-dealing within American enterprise.[21]

As Hirsch argued, "The point is that conventional, mutual standards of honesty and trust are public goods that are necessary inputs for much of economic output."[22] However, since they are public goods, their value cannot be fully captured in the market. If business is to conduct its activities in the public good, attention should not be directed to individuals. The emphasis on individualism is part of the problem.

> American society is now rife with other "beggar-thy-neighbor" tactics, many of which are rational from the standpoint of the individual actor but are tragically irrational for society as a whole: the asset rearranging undertaken through conglomerate merger, manipulation of balance sheets, and schemes of tax avoidance; the exorbitant salaries and bonuses provided to executives in America's largest companies; the rising incidence of employee theft and insider dealings; the political demands for tariffs, quotas, and bailouts to protect companies against foreign competitors; and the refusal by many middle-income taxpayers to foot any longer the bill for social services. The vicious circle has closed: As the economy continues to decline, Americans grow more cynical about collective endeavor. Their consequential retreat into egoism merely accelerates the decline since collaboration is the only way to reverse it.[23]

Rather, the emphasis must be on collective action; and that emphasis would require changes in business practice and corporate structure. As Reich said, "It is becoming clear that America's economic future depends less on lonely geniuses and backyard inventors than on versatile organizations."

Third, we should abandon the hierarchical view of management. Sharp criticism of the view that the manager is a boss and that employees should follow orders is now commonplace. Management teams, quality-of-life circles, are all the rage. But that kind of criticism is hardly new. It came in during the 1930s. The abandonment of the hierarchical view requires more than giving up all that is implied by the word "boss." It requires reducing the separation between those who plan work and those who execute it. As Reich has argued, to adapt to the new era of international competition we need to flatten management, eliminate hierarchy, stop producing by rules, ensure that those who plan and those who execute work together. The concept of the organization chart must be given up for the concept of the team.

There are strong moral and psychological reasons for abandoning a management tradition where a boss gives orders. If employees are to be convinced to develop institutional loyalty and to put the interest of the group ahead of their own self-interest, they must feel part of a team. Inability to participate in the setting of goals certainly doesn't contribute to a team concept. In this case, psychology is buttressed by morality. In the absence of an opportunity to help set group goals, there is no moral reason for a person to sacrifice his or her self-interest for the interest of the group. Many autocrats talk the language of team loyalty, but the employees know that in such cases team loyalty is nothing more than loyalty to an autocratic boss. My arguments for team loyalty and firm loyalty must not be misunderstood. I am *not* calling for blind loyalty. I am calling for loyalty to a total cooperative enterprise. If the culture of the firm is autocratic rather than cooperative, loyalty to the firm can neither be expected nor morally demanded.

Fourth, we must bridge what Robert Reich calls "the cleavage between the business and civic cultures." Business people should see activity in the political process as a legitimate activity and even as activity required by morality. Citizens in a democracy should be active, not passive; living in a democracy brings civil responsibilities as well as benefits. For reasons already given, the notion of civic responsibilities is severely weakened in our culture. However, a limited sense of civic responsibility is strongly held by some corporate leaders. For example, business leaders usually chair the United Way and the boards of local artistic and educational institutions. Some companies actually allow employees to work for extended periods for charitable organizations. However, if business is to fulfill its aim of greater investment in employees and to emphasize full employment, government will have to be seen as a partner rather than the enemy.

But what about the charge of many conservatives, for example Milton Friedman and Theodore Levitt, that if government and business cooperate there is a danger that power will be abused? Some fear that a monolith will be created. Others pointedly remind us that corporate officials are not democratically elected. Still others argue that corporate involvement in the political process will only be self-serving.

Some thought has been given to this problem, particularly by public affairs professionals. Indeed, the profession has adopted a "Statement of Ethical Guidelines" that speaks directly to the concern of abuse of corporate power. Statement C speaks directly to our issue.

C. The *Public Affairs Professional* understand[s] the interrelation of business interests with the larger public interests, and therefore:

1. Endeavors to ensure that responsible and diverse external interests and views concerning the needs of society are considered within the corporate decision-making process.
2. Bears the responsibility for management review of public policies which may bring corporate interests into conflict with other interest[s].
3. Acknowledges dual obligations—to advocate the interests of his or her employer, and to preserve the openness and integrity of the democratic process.
4. Presents to his or her employer an accurate assessment of

the political and social realities that may affect corporate operations.[24]

Of course, it is one thing to adopt a set of guidelines and quite another to live by them—particularly when the guidelines are as general as these. However, the tone of the document represents the spirit of partnership I think necessary if business is to fulfill its function of providing full employment in meaningful jobs.

Fifth, we need to rethink the skills required for good management. Education of managers should move away from quantitative analysis to the traditional liberal arts. As Reich has charged:

> Professional education in America is putting progressively more emphasis on the manipulation of symbols to the exclusion of other sorts of skills—how to collaborate with others, to work in teams, to speak foreign languages, to solve concrete problems—which are more relevant to the new competitive environment.[25]

Such calls for a greater emphasis on liberal arts education do not come solely from academics. A symposium held in conjunction with Harvard University's 350th anniversary celebration made a call for a liberal arts component in preparation for business careers. The call came from the Corporate Council on the Liberal Arts, an organization established in 1984 representing twelve major companies. Michael Useem gave as one reason for the call the fact that "so many managers are now expected to play a role in the firm's social and political programs, the liberal arts have acquired a new importance for the long range development of a corporation's human resources."[26]

To emphasize the liberal arts is to send a signal as to what skills and attitudes the business community thinks are important. A knowledge of our history, some knowledge of other cultures, but most importantly some insight into what it means to lead a fully human life—these are the hallmarks of the liberal arts education and too often they have been missing from the education of business managers. Business can only carry out its function of providing meaningful work if it understands the ideals and aspirations of human life.

Conclusion

I have argued that, in order to avoid the profit-making para-dox, American business must turn its attention to capital invest-ment in individual employees—indeed, that business should see its essential function as providing meaningful work. By so doing, business will be doing good consistent with the demands of morality. Moreover, business will become more competitive as a result and, hence, in doing good, business will also do well. However, if business persons are to succeed in this task they will need to change some of their traditional attitudes and values.

Notes

1. Leonard Silk and David Vogel, *Ethics and Profits* (New York: Simon and Schuster, 1976), 131.

2. For just one example, see "Corporate Crime: The Untold Story," *U.S. News & World Report*, 6 September 1982, pp. 25–29.

3. Robert Hayes and William Abernathy, "Managing Our Way to Economic Decline," *Harvard Business Review* 58 (July-August 1980): 67–77.

4. Thomas J. Peters and Robert H. Waterman, Jr., *In Search of Excellence* (New York: Warner Books, 1984).

5. Kurt Baier, *The Moral Point of View* (New York: Random House, 1967).

6. David Gauthier, *Morals by Agreement* (Oxford: Clarendon Press, 1986).

7. Robert Axelrod, *The Evolution of Cooperation* (New York: Basic Books, 1984).

8. David W. Ewing, *Freedom inside the Corporation* (New York: E. P. Dutton, 1977), chap. 1.

9. R. Edward Freeman, *Strategic Management: A Stakeholder Approach* (Boston: Pitman, 1984).

10. For example, see John G. Simon, Charles W. Powers, and Jon P. Gunnemann, *The Ethical Investor: Universities and Corporate Responsibility* (New Haven: Yale University Press, 1972).

11. For example see Keith Davis, "Five Propositions for Social Responsibility," *Business Horizons* 18 (June 1975): 19–24.

12. Paul Camenisch, "Business Ethics or Getting to the Heart of the Matter," *Business & Professional Ethics Journal* 1 (Fall 1981): 59–69.

13. Freeman, *Strategic Management*.

14. Milton Friedman, *Capitalism and Freedom* (Chicago: University of Chicago Press, 1962).

15. Daniel Bell, *The Cultural Contradictions of Capitalism* (New York: Basic Books, 1976).

16. Robert B. Reich, *The Next American Frontier* (New York: Times Books, 1983), 235–36.

17. Martin L. Weitzman, *The Share Economy* (Cambridge: Harvard University Press, 1984).

18. Norman E. Bowie, "Should Collective Bargaining and Labor Relations Be Less Adversarial?" *Journal of Business Ethics* 4 (1985): 283–91.

19. Kenneth R. Andrews, *The Concept of Corporate Strategy*, 3d ed. (Homewood, Ill.: Irwin, 1987).

20. Reich, *Next American Frontier*, 280.

21. Ibid., 166.

22. Fred Hirsch, *Social Limits to Growth* (Cambridge: Harvard University Press, 1976), 141.

23. Reich, *Next American Frontier*, 239.

24. Charles S. Mack, "Ethics and Business Public Affairs," *Public Affairs Review* (Washington, D.C.: Public Affairs Council, 1980), 1:28.

25. Reich, *Next American Frontier*, 160.

26. *The Chronicle of Higher Education*, 10 September 1986, p. 42.

CHAPTER FIVE

Ethics and Responsibility

Kenneth D. Walters

As academic fields go, business ethics is still in its infancy, or perhaps toddlerhood. It can take at least several decades—sometimes a century—for a field of knowledge to really establish itself. It is true that during the past twenty years some of the most prestigious business schools have added courses in ethics—including Harvard, Stanford, Wharton, and the University of California at Berkeley. In such select company the legitimacy of the field might appear to be beyond question.

The legitimacy and future directions of the field, however, are by no means clear. Faculty debates on business ethics have been quick to criticize this new field, charging that it, among other shortcomings: has no theoretical base; does not constitute a hard social science; is not being given the benefit of vigorous research (nor does it utilize advanced mathematical techniques); and has been typically offering courses that are either designed to make, or have the effect of making, students and business people feel guilty about business careers.

These criticisms are generally invalid, irrelevant, or even unfair. Yet I believe there are valid questions which can be asked of any emerging field of study: How and why did business

Kenneth D. Walters is the dean of the School of Business, California Polytechnic State University. Dean Walters expresses thanks to the RGK Foundation for its support in this project.

ethics assume its present form? What have been the goals of the pioneering scholars in the field, and how were those goals achieved? How can the field of business ethics build on past successes and chart an intellectual course for the future? This paper seeks to answer these questions.

Intellectually, the field is evolving by following the same basic process that other academic fields have followed—a process that can best be described in three words: problems precede theory. Progress in social science seems to require that before academicians can develop theories and generalized explanations of phenomena they must realize that there are problems that deserve attention and analysis. David Riesman notes that the field of sociology was established because the existing fields of political science and economics were ignoring a number of important problems. Riesman's lectures on *Constraint and Variety in American Education* point out that sociologists

> until recently . . . could not touch the economy which belonged to the economists, and could not touch government and military affairs which belonged to the political scientists, but had to find their clientele among criminals, children, old people, immigrants, factory workers, small town folk, and other relatively powerless groups whom no one else had laid claim to.[1]

Riesman's theory that new fields arise to study the leftovers certainly explains the rise of business and society and of business ethics as academic fields, as Earl Cheit has noted.[2] Scholars who teach in business schools have been known to encounter colleagues who shy away from subjects they do not fancy or topics that may not always be amenable to analysis using mathematical and statistical techniques. If a problem is considered to be somewhat intractable, some scholars may be unwilling to risk a charge of nonstatistical or unscientific treatment. The business ethics field has experienced its dramatic growth and popularity in recent years precisely *because* it has been willing to tackle many real problems that established business disciplines were indisposed to approach.

What problems and issues have been the intellectual drivers of the business ethics field? Business ethics courses and textbooks typically have been concerned with such problems as environmental pollution, multinational marketing (such as infant formula advertising), product safety (especially consumer products such as autos and food), foreign investment policies (especially in South Africa), bribery (especially in foreign countries), false advertising or misrepresentation, mistreatment of employees (unjust dismissals), financial deception, and critiques and defenses of capitalism.[3]

One can find, of course, no shortage of cases and course materials to illustrate embarrassing or unethical behavior in each of these categories. I recently reread portions of two famous early casebooks in the field, Robert Heilbroner's *In the Name of Profit: Profiles in Corporate Irresponsibility*,[4] and Prakash Sethi's *Up against the Corporate Wall*.[5] What impressed me was the negligent or purposeful wrongdoing depicted in the cases—some people in the companies selected had done some things that were quite embarrassing, and these embarrassments had become media events. The books' message was simple: managers were seemingly quite oblivious to ethical concerns and even seemed to be poorly schooled in public relations.

Although current courses have expanded beyond the issues of fifteen years ago, there is more than a strong family resemblance between those courses and what is usually studied and taught in business ethics courses today. True, new issues have not failed to arise to keep the subject matter current and lively. Some of the main issues on today's reading lists were only gestating twenty years ago—the women's movement, child care, sexual harassment, whistle-blowing employees, public policy concerns of boards, plant relocation, employee reduction strategies, and the ethics of bankruptcy. We can be assured that the textbooks and casebooks being written today will include ample materials on golden parachutes, poison pills, greenmail, leveraged buyouts, and insider trading.

One is almost tempted to say that the field of business ethics has profited by the constant infusion of new issues. Perhaps business ethics scholars are indebted most to Ralph Nader, who saw to it in the 1960s and 1970s that big business ("the giant

corporations," as he put it) came under major new moral as-
saults every year or two in new reports issued by his task forces.
As long as interest groups found new things to criticize, scholars
seemed assured of a continuing flow of problems to study and
teach.

Current courses and reading lists tend to be better than some
of the courses and casebooks of fifteen years ago in one important sense: they offer more than just a litany of complaints
against the ethical lapses of companies. Current courses cover
strategies and procedures to sensitize management to ethical
values, ways to make ethically defensible decisions, the analyt-
ics of tradeoffs, and methods to implement and explain ethical
policies throughout the company. Additionally, there is a growing emphasis on preventative strategies in many of the materials.[6] In fact, cases on morally exemplary policies have joined
cases depicting moral backwardness, thereby giving a needed
comparative dimension to policy analysis.

Business ethics is not lacking in theory either. Many current
texts and casebooks do an impressive job of examining the
issues in the context of theoretical philosophy.[7] When philosophy is coupled with other disciplines (law, medicine, or science)
the result has happily been the enrichment of both philosophy
and the discipline involved. The philosophy of law, the philosophy of science, and medical ethics are today recognized not only
as legitimate fields of scholarship but as critical areas of intellectual pursuit in these professions.

The coupling of philosophy with business is proving to be as
intellectually challenging as the application of philosophy to law
and medicine. Morality has always been a major issue raised
about business affairs—in the Bible, in Oriental philosophy, in
the Eastern religions, and in Greek philosophy. As business
becomes a worldwide phenomenon with the relentless spread of
technology and industrialization, the morality of business practices cannot escape being a major intellectual issue in all societies. It is thus not only a natural but an inevitable development.

My argument to this point is that the field of business ethics is
a legitimate area of academic study precisely because it focuses

on a set of current "real world" problems that require appropriate intellectual tools to resolve or manage. The problems keep appearing—revelations by the press, lawsuits filed, new and proposed regulations, and political issues voiced and debated. Public moral passions can quite easily be exercised against perceived or real abuses in the marketplace—especially if a "big" business (corporation) is involved. Most business schools are trying to sensitize managers to the ethical implications of business decisions and practices.

If someone in a major company makes a major ethical blunder, it is hard to keep the company's name off the front page of the *New York Times*. Part of the manager's job is to protect against such risks.

But my real concern is: Is that all there is to business ethics? Does this concept of business ethics serve business students well? In particular, is it sufficiently comprehensive? My thesis is that business ethics, as conceived and taught today, may be overly limited in scope and purpose. Indeed, the field may be overlooking or ignoring a scandalously large number of "business actors" and "unethical activities" that deserve to move to a position of greater importance in research and teaching.

Let us examine carefully the words "business" and "ethics" and ask what might in fact be their real scope and meaning. When most people speak of business, they are using a shorthand way of describing all business companies, the largest companies, or the entire business sector of a society. In a small town, "business" may refer to something like the collective membership of the Rotarians, Kiwanians, and Lions. But speaking precisely, business is not a person, an organization, a manager or managers, the *Fortune* 500, or all companies. Business is an activity.[8] To speak of the ethics or responsibility of a large aggregation such as "the business sector" or "business" is confusing since ethical responsibilities can only be assigned to specific individuals who are capable of moral analysis. The *Fortune* 500 companies are not moral beings; they are aggregations of financial wealth, intangible and physical resources, and human beings who own and are employed by those enterprises. The people who own the *Fortune*

500 and work for them in fact do have moral responsibilities in their roles as owners, managers, and employees. It is common practice to attribute those decisions to the "company," "the management"—or indeed to "business"—but this usage can completely neglect the individual responsibilities of the millions of people involved every day in "business." William Letwin analogizes that after World War I many said that "Germany" had committed atrocities and should pay a price for those acts (in the form of reparations).[9] But were German babies born after the war guilty of atrocities? Certainly not; thus the wrongdoer was not "Germany"—although even specific guilty German individuals found it convenient to attribute their actions to "Germany" rather than take personal responsibility for their acts.

One must approach the study of business ethics by noting that the topic must include the ethical responsibilities of all people who are engaged in business activities—not only top management or owners.[10] We all are responsible for ethical behavior in our roles of buyer, producer, worker, board member, lender, borrower, manager, subordinate, tenant, owner, and employee. Most people play more than one of these roles every day in the world's business activities. Nor should one overlook each person's role in politics and government where the rules of the business game are established. Voters and citizens have ethical responsibilities—we are not merely "interest groups" who maximize self-interest in our voter and citizen roles.

What about the term *ethics?* Ethics refers to the study of the good and bad, the theory and system of moral values defining duties or responsibilities governing human conduct. Blackstone, the great English jurist, believed that law was the most nearly perfect embodiment of ethics. Examples of *legal* duties are endless and include the duty of a tenant to pay rent, the duty to support one's dependents, and the duty not to leave pets unattended in closed vehicles. Failure to perform legal responsibilities typically results in sanctions or punishment. A second class of duties are *ethical* responsibilities, which may result in praise or blame but not necessarily sanctions or punishment. I have an ethical duty to help someone who is drowning and whom

I can save. Ethics tells us to be polite to our neighbors and helpful to family and friends. Ethical and legal responsibility can coincide—as in the case of one's duty not to commit the crime of larceny by taking the private property of others.

It is important to note that moral and legal responsibility overlap but are not identical. It is impossible to turn all moral responsibilities into legal duties—even though some totalitarian societies have attempted to push matters in this direction. As Lasswell and Kaplan wrote:

> A system of maximal regimentation is called totalitarianism; the scope of the power is all-inclusive—"everything for the state, nothing against the state, nothing outside the state." All practices are coercively controlled; in the familiar phrase, everything that isn't forbidden, is obligatory.[11]

Consider a hypothetical society where everything considered moral becomes mandatory. It would be ultimately absurd, for example, for a society such as Puritan Massachusetts to try to legislate all the biblical virtues of modesty, diligence, patience, courage, kindness, and charity. Not only is it impossible for laws to mandate these admirable traits successfully, but moral voluntarism would have a difficult time existing since all virtue would be obligatory.

Do people engaged in business activities have only legal responsibilities? The question would be hardly worth asking were it not so commonly asserted today that a business person's only ethical duty is to obey the law. Since we have already seen that the law is not the totality of ethical obligations in any society, clearly a person engaged in a business transaction cannot leave ethics aside. To argue that business is constrained only by the law and not by ethics is to argue that people involved in business cease to be moral beings when they are involved in business transactions. Such a view, which leads to a pejorative statement of "That's business," is untenable. We have far too many examples of unethical, immoral, or inhumane acts explained away by, "That's business." Human beings cannot carry on the ordinary affairs of life in a moral vacuum; they have duties—some of which are legal, others of which are ethical, and some, though not all, of which are both.

A significant number of roles, relationships, and responsibilities must be examined if we are to truly understand the ethics of business. Discussions of business ethics have tended to ignore a number of important relationships. For example, one of the most popular subjects in current business ethics courses and research is the ethical responsibilities of managers or "employers" toward employees. The specific issues include whistle-blowing, sexual harassment, employee reduction policies, plant relocations, unlawful discharges, and numerous others. These issues are nearly always prominently covered in courses in business ethics and social responsibilities of business. Another major topic is the relationship of large corporations and the consumer. These relationships nearly always emphasize the way the companies mistreat the consumer through violations of product safety and the like. The ethics of employer-employee and seller-consumer relationships are not unilateral, however.

When discussing the ethics of managing employees a few years ago, an MBA student raised the question: What about the ethical responsibilities of employees toward the company? The ensuing discussion elicited strong sentiments from several students who had worked alongside employees who had felt no ethical obligations whatsoever toward their employers. Not only did employees have ethical responsibilities to the employer; the students added other ethical obligations of employees: to the company's customers, to fellow employees, to other companies doing business with the employer, and to individuals from other companies with whom one comes in contact at work. Other students pointed out that these are not only bona fide ethical issues (involving strong beliefs about right and wrong) but issues which are highly pertinent to the problems of managing human resources efficiently.

Ethically responsible employees are essential to efficient, productive, humane, and happy organizations. Can employees be taught ethical responsibilities? The answer emerging from Japanese managerial theory and experience appears to be that they can. It is paradoxical that American society—the society which springs from the Judeo-Christian heritage—is now being painfully forced to relearn the lessons of personal ethical responsibility from the Japanese.

While Japanese management is the subject of some jokes these days, those who go to Japan soon learn to appreciate how Japanese concepts of business ethics operate in actual practice. Those who observe Japanese ways of doing business state quite unequivocally that the Japanese employee's attitude toward his boss and toward the company he works for ("his company") and the company's customers are considered to be serious *ethical* responsibilities. Such obligations are a centerpiece of Japanese ethics and culture.

Mark Pastin's book, *The Hard Problems of Management*,[12] contrasts two cases. In the first case, a group of Japanese employees assemble a car door which is defective—a window flashing is improperly installed. Worker Miko puts the locks in the door, while worker Hako installs the window flashing. On seeing the defective flashing, Miko will readily say: "I have made a bad door." In the other case, an otherwise excellent and conscientious American professor who knows some of his colleagues teach poorly determines to do nothing about it in that he is not responsible for the poor teaching by others in his department.

The contrasting cases raise the obvious question: Who is the more ethical employee? Miko has a concept of her job that includes what her fellow workers do and for what they are producing together. She feels *responsible* for what Hako does— much like all parents feel responsible for their child's behavior. But the American professor does not feel responsible for the "job" of his colleague—even though it reflects on the performance of his department.

Pastin's critical insight is this: Miko's sense of personal responsibility can only be explained in terms of ethics, not in terms of financial incentives. She is not causally responsible for the defective door, nor legally responsible. But she assumes ethical responsibility for the door because she is part of the work group who made it. In Pastin's words, "Responsibility means the ability to act independently of reward systems."[13] *"Genuine responsibility begins where mere response to reward systems ends."*[14]

A relevant (and perhaps embarrassing) question to ask is: Which concept of responsibility do we teach in American business schools?

Japanese management theorists do not overlook the importance of financial incentives to motivate employees. But the Japanese recognize that efficient management depends on instilling a sense of ethics and personal responsibility into the attitudes of workers. Japanese managers managing American workers have quickly perceived that the attitudes of many American workers are deficient and pose a barrier to productivity; they are irresponsible. Their attitudes, their intentions, their *ethics* have to change in order for the company they work for to be more productive. In place of the limited concept of *legal responsibility* that American workers tend to hide behind, the Japanese managers have strived to urge the workers to substitute the concept of ethical responsibility for the product being produced. A professor at Tokai University, Hajime Karatsu, explains:

> In the U.S., work is broken down into individual functions, with each employee responsible for certain tasks. A worker is required to do his or her own job competently, but isn't expected to bother about other aspects of the operation. This neat division of labor seems efficient, except that factories and assembly lines don't function on one job.
>
> No longer is it enough to do your own job properly; each worker is responsible for the whole product. Unless everyone pitches in to get the belt moving again, not a single car is turned out. One person's carelessness can slow down production.[15]

It is quite reasonable to ask why the topic "ethical responsibilities of employees" does not appear to be an issue generally covered in business ethics courses. Although all American business students do not become managers, almost all become employees. To understand the responsibility an employee owes to other employees, to the owners, and to customers would seem to be highly important knowledge. If American employees indeed appear to be less aware of their ethical responsibilities today than in the past, how did this occur? If no one is teaching these responsibilities—not parents, certainly not television, not humanities courses, nor even business schools or business ethics courses—then who will do it? Employers may have to learn to teach employees business ethics or continue to suffer the consequences of ethically deficient employees. Ethical education doesn't just happen, as Jonathan King states so well:

> If virtue is found where virtue is honored, so, too, ethical education. To a considerable extent, ethical dialogue must be institutionalized in business decision processes: in the classroom, in business schools, and in the business world.[16]

King notes that just as the intellectual fiber of a nation is weakened by pervasive functional illiteracy, so too is the moral fiber weakened by ethical illiteracy. Both are necessary components of a productive and civilized society. What good is a person who can speak five languages if he or she can't tell the truth in any of them?

I have spent a good deal of time discussing the ethical obligations of employees because I believe that topic to be one that is overlooked in discussions of business ethics. But I cite that as just one example of issues that deserve greater analysis and attention in research and teaching. Consider also the ethical obligations of the buyers of products—the buyer's relationship to the seller. How many products are negligently used or abused, only to be returned to the seller for a refund or replacement? Such cases involve not only buyer-seller ethics, but the responsibilities of a buyer to other buyers as well.

Cross-cultural examples are again quite helpful. I have a student whose family owns cherry orchards. They ship cherries to Japan, where there is so much demand that cashiers cannot handle the tremendous volume. Consequently, shoppers are asked to put their money in a basket by the cherry display. The honor system works beautifully. Judging from the story, buyer ethics are more highly developed in Japan than one is likely to find in a random U.S. grocery store. The ethic of employee loyalty and buyer honesty may be important competitive edges held by the Japanese.

In a society in which shoplifting has reached staggering proportions, surely some attention might be devoted to buyer ethics in business ethics courses. Who will bother to teach buyer ethics in American universities? With nearly one-third of all college students today declaring themselves to be business majors, perhaps the business schools would be as good a place to begin as any. The 275,000 students who graduate each year with bachelor's degrees in business are unlikely to have learned about the ethics of being a consumer (or an employee) in their general education courses, marketing courses, or even their business ethics courses.

One may fairly ask the question at this point: Since business ethics involves multiple activities and relationships, all of which can have an ethical dimension, which relationships are more important, which are less important, and where do ethical responsibilities end? Surely we are not responsible to everyone for everything. This problem was brilliantly analyzed by Adam Smith in his book *The Theory of Moral Sentiments*,[17] published in 1759. Smith told a hypothetical story of a European who hears about a natural disaster in which China is swallowed up in a catastrophic earthquake. The European is indeed saddened by hearing of the tragedy. Although the sheer loss of life is enough to momentarily depress him, the tragedy is not of lasting consequence to him. Smith continues the story by hypothesizing that the next day the same European loses his little finger. This loss—inconsequential in comparison with the millions of Chinese deaths—distresses the European so profoundly that he does not sleep that night.

Smith's point, which we may call the proximity principle, is that we are naturally inclined to be more sympathetic toward issues and events close to our own lives. Similarly, ethical duties to others depend on our proximity to them. One has a duty to assist people in need, but it is reasonable to first give assistance to family and dependents, then to friends and neighbors, and only then to people we do not know. In business, each person is in close proximity to those with whom one works, with bosses, customers, subordinates, and others with whom we transact business daily. Following Smith's proximity principle, these would become the critical relationships to study and understand using the tools of ethics. Yet, these concerns are receiving little attention in our business ethics courses. Perhaps they pale next to the glamorous shenanigans of Boone Pickens and Ivan Boesky, and the scandals depicted in the popular business press. To be sure, Boesky's transactions are *safer* to analyze in class—precisely because they are so far removed from the lives of most undergraduates and MBAs. Felix Rohatyn's characterization of investment bankers as "a bunch of samurai who will do anything for money"[18] may or may not be true, but it does little to help educate our students in how they can live more ethical business lives. It is comfortable and easy to question the Ford Motor Company engineers who designed cheap gas tanks; it is far harder to discuss with students why cheating is so rampant and what should be done to raise the level of honesty in academic life.

A general rule can be stated: the more exotic (or far removed) and idiosyncratic the business ethics case, the more likely it is to be included in a textbook and the less likely that students will find themselves in such a setting in their own careers. Upon applying the proximity principle to the normal fare in business ethics classes, one might conclude that the topics are more media-driven than they are driven by student everyday needs or industry's need for ethical, honest, and conscientious employees.

To summarize, too much emphasis in business classes is being placed on what "business" (big companies) does to "society" (millions of "victims"), while insufficient attention is being given to how individuals can more ethically interact with each other in their daily business affairs. Our choice of villains and victims reveals a great deal. For every Love Canal there must be a million people who throw beverage containers in our streets and landscapes and another million who breathe carcinogens in our faces. For every deceptive ad campaign hatched on Madison Avenue there are a million shoplifters and taxpayers who cheat on their income taxes. For every exploding Pinto gasoline tank there are countless drunk drivers who kill and maim at random. And for every manager who sexually harasses employees there may be a score of employees who call in sick when they are not.

Then why is so much of our moral energy in business ethics focused so intently on the big companies and on someone we call "management"? Perhaps it is just more popular to talk about the problem being "them" instead of "me" and "us." But if solutions to our problems of the lack of ethical sensitivity in American life lie in the renewal of a sense of responsibility in individuals, then the issues of personal business ethics must become centerpieces of our curricula. If we do not know how to teach personal business ethics, then that alone should become a major research priority.

The issue can be raised another way. We who teach business ethics do not even *pretend* that our courses are value-free. We know better than to make such claims; in fact, we actually *design* our courses to examine values. This is correct and begins to address the vast academic deficiency which William Scott and Terence Mitchell describe so well in their recent article "Markets and Morals in Management Education."[19]

The question is: What is the underlying "message" of the business ethics course? What values, skills, and attitudes are we aiming to instill? Here is a multiple-choice question for professors of business ethics: When a student finishes a course in business ethics, which one of the following is most likely to be the message he or she got from the course?

Message 1: Capitalism stinks. There has got to be a better system than this. Greed and avarice are creating sheer chaos. We should nationalize business and run things for the public good instead of for profit.

Message 2: Business stinks. It deserves to be regulated and forced to behave. In the meantime, I want no part of it. I'd better go to law school or find work in a respectable career.

Message 3: Business people are an unethical bunch. I will *never* do those terrible things we studied about in this class. My generation will set things right when we get high enough in the organization to run things ethically.

Message 4: Business is business, ethics is ethics, and never the twain shall meet. I'm thoroughly confused.

Message 5: I am personally responsible for my own behavior. As a future manager, a big part of my job will be showing people how to be responsible for the quality of the jobs they are doing.

Peter Drucker, in his book *Managing for Results*, may not have been referring to business ethics when he wrote that "the pertinent strategic question is not how to do things right, but how to find the right things to do and to concentrate resources and efforts on them." Warren Bennis makes the point even more succinctly when he states that "doing things right" is not as important as "doing the right things." As a field of study, business ethics must define what "the right things" are. If one critical need is for more personal responsibility from people engaged in business activities, there is no shortage of innovative ways to see that this can be achieved in business education.

Notes

1. David Riesman, *Constraint and Variety in American Education* (Garden City, N.Y.: Doubleday, Anchor Books, 1958), 91.

2. Earl F. Cheit, "What Is the Field of Business and Society and Where Is It Going?" in *Rationality, Legitimacy, Responsibility: Search for New Directions in Business and Society*, ed. Edwin M. Epstein and Dow Votaw (Santa Monica, Calif.: Goodyear, 1974), 183–202.

3. James W. Dean and Richard Schwindt, comps., *Business, Government & Society*, vol. 11, Business Administration Reading Lists and Course Outlines (Durham, N.C.: Eno River Press, 1985).

4. Robert Heilbroner, et al., *In the Name of Profit: Profiles in Corporate Irresponsibility* (New York: Doubleday, 1972).

5. S. Prakash Sethi, *Up against the Corporate Wall* (Englewood Cliffs, N.J.: Prentice-Hall, 1971).

6. Dean and Schwindt, *Business, Government & Society.*

7. See, e.g., Thomas Donaldson and Patricia H. Werhane, *Ethical Issues in Business: A Philosophical Approach* (Englewood Cliffs, N.J.: Prentice-Hall, 1979).

8. This idea is beautifully developed in William Letwin, "Social Responsibility of Business in an Insurance State," in Epstein and Votaw, *Rationality, Legitimacy, Responsibility*, 131–55.

9. Ibid., 132.

10. Ibid., 133.

11. Harold D. Lasswell and Abraham Kaplan, *Power and Society* (New Haven: Yale University Press, 1950), 222.

12. Mark Pastin, *The Hard Problems of Management* (San Francisco: Jossey-Bass, 1986). Pastin's book, a highly creative series of essays on business ethics, states: "The Japanese are onto something, and it concerns responsibility. Responsibility solves the Rubics Cube of Japanese management," 157.

13. Ibid., 160.

14. Ibid., 158.

15. "America Needs Japan-Style Managers Now More Than Ever," *Asian Wall Street Journal Weekly*, 12 January 1987, p. 7.

16. Jonathan King, "The Fundamental Goals in Teaching Business Eth-

ics," Oregon State University School of Business, working paper. See also Jonathan King, "Teaching Business Ethics," *Exchange* 18 (1983): 25–32.

17. Adam Smith, *The Theory of Moral Sentiments* (New York: Augustus M. Kelley, 1966), 192–93.

18. Myron Magnet, "The Decline and Fall of Business Ethics," *Fortune*, 8 December 1986, p. 66.

19. William G. Scott and Terence R. Mitchell, "Markets and Morals in Management Education," *Selections: The Magazine of the Graduate Management Admission Council* 3 (Autumn 1986): 3–8.

CHAPTER SIX

The Motivating Power of Ethics
in Times of Corporate Confusion

Margaret J. Wheatley

FOR the past several years I have worked for or consulted to a number of crazy organizations. To label these organizations crazy is not to differentiate them substantially from the vast majority of organizations that exist. I doubt that few would challenge the statement that to work in today's world is to witness constant degrees of irrational behavior, at both the micro and macro levels. Certainly it is not rationality that explains the power plays, political infighting, mergers, divestitures, takeovers, reorganizations, and other characteristics of contemporary organizations.

Profound changes are occurring in today's corporations. These large organizations, once seen as stable and secure bastions of activity, are being swept by currents of change that in many cases threaten their future existence. They have become volatile, unstable environments; none can guarantee lifelong employment or even deliver on the promise of a steady career trajectory upward through the organization. As a direct consequence of this instability, we are keeping a deathwatch on

---

Margaret J. Wheatley, formerly professor of management at Cambridge College, is executive vice-president of Ibis Consulting Group, Incorporated, Cambridge, Massachusetts.

corporate loyalty—those shared commitments and values that create a context for productive work. Although corporate loyalty has been an integral part of American life since the rise of the corporation in the 1920s, a recent Harris poll reported that 65 percent of mid-level managers feel their employees are less loyal to their companies than ten years ago. [1]

This erosion of loyalty dramatically alters the work environment. No longer is there as clear a context for one's actions. Instead of feeling part of some larger whole and acting accordingly, employees are forced back on themselves as referents for their behavior. Understandably, this loss of context has led to very different employee-employer relations. People have become fixated on their personal interests. One career advisor noted that the only allegiance people now exhibit is to their own careers. Another called it the emergence of "Me, Inc."[2] Increasing numbers of people are feeling betrayed, apathetic, depressed, alienated.[3] Other individuals seem to be running amok with opportunism. People talk about how they beat the system or made a killing, language that reflects the violence and striving of individuals isolated in systems that they perceive as often acting to destroy them as to support them. It is no wonder that we are confronted with a mushrooming concern about ethics in organizations.

None of these phenomena are surprising; in fact, they are entirely predictable according to our basic intuitions about people, or from the more theoretical perspective of motivational theory. But in every crazy organization I've worked in, I've observed something that has surprised me, a phenomenon that has perplexed me for some time. In these chaotic organizations, where decisions are made only to be unmade, where even the semblance of rationality has disappeared, there are always a few people who continue to work at high levels, who continue to do quality work. Why are these people behaving so strangely? Why are they continuing to do excellent professional work for organizations that really don't deserve it?

Like all exceptions, this one is worth a closer look. In fact, the dramatic upheavals in organizational stability may create many "exceptions" to behaviors we would predict from current theory. Most investigations of organizational behavior occurred in settings of growth and expansion. Now that we are faced with environments of destabilization and reconfiguration, our theories about organizations are somewhat suspect. At the very least, we need to test our assumptions in the light of empirical observations of life in declining organizations.[4]

As I've observed people behaving in ways that current motivation theory cannot explain adequately, I've begun to observe motivators whose existence seems to have been masked by times of organizational prosperity. I offer my observations and conclusions in the hopes of contributing to a more inclusive theory of what motivates people to work.

My hypothesis is this: People who work in chaotic organizational situations where there is no longer a sense of being connected to some greater whole can continue to work productively if they actively engage in constructing meaning for themselves and those they manage. In the absence of an organizational context that makes sense, they connect with some other context, some meaning that inspires them to keep working well.

To search for meaning in our lives is to search for an answer to "Why?" If our search for answers leads us to look beyond ourselves, we enter the realm of ethical inquiry. We become aware of some greater system of which we are a part. We become concerned with the impact of our behavior on others. This greater system can be defined in many ways. It can be connecting with the ethics of our profession, or the obligations of leadership, or principles of right and wrong. Whatever form it takes, the effect of such inquiry is transcendent; it forces us to view ourselves as part of something beyond ourselves.

My observation is that when people engage in this search, they become energized. The very act of meaning making, of assuming responsibility for making choices about one's behavior, is motivating. Ethical inquiry, then, is a strong motivator.

In linking ethics and motivation together, I am not only

141

challenging weaknesses in current motivation theory but also departing from populist notions about the role ethics should play in our work lives. So much of the current groundswell of interest in ethics stems from a need to find new ways of controlling people. From a managerial perspective, the search for ways to instill values in people is a means of creating boundaries, or like a bit in the mouth of a horse, a means for controlling otherwise willful inclinations. In fact, I believe one reason why ethics is a managerial fad is that managers have come to view it in terms of their traditional function, control.

Yet what I've observed is that ethics serves not to restrain, but to motivate, that a strong ethical base inspires people to behave in productive ways. What I'm suggesting turns the current managerial interest in ethics on its head. We need to explore the role of ethics in organizations because it is ethics that provides sources of motivation when organizations no longer can. Ethics can motivate people to transcend organizational circumstances and continue to be productive contributors.

Our current perceptions of motivation have precluded us from appreciating the important role that ethical inquiry plays in motivating people. As I will discuss in detail, motivation research has focused so intently on the individual's internal constructs that it has largely ignored the energy to be found when links are made between the individual and some greater value.

To take this one step further, it may be that our current perceptions of human motivation contribute to the ethical problems we encounter. Research and practice have focused on the primacy of individual growth. In the days of business expansion, this was a beguiling concept, and one that empirically seemed to make a great deal of sense. We now have a culture that supports the notion of self-actualization, but without the resources to provide for rapid and frequent growth for large numbers of individuals. With people focused on personal development, the spectre of scarce resources can easily lead to desperate acquisitions for self-gain. What we have been saying to ourselves about self-actualization, and how we have structured expectations that employment is primarily a means for actualizing ourselves, may be contributing to the ethical problems now facing us.

Our current understanding of what motivates behavior in organizations is firmly rooted in a psychological approach. For the past fifty years, attention has been focused almost exclusively on what needs or drives cause an individual to respond to certain activities and not to others. Early efforts at understanding motivation focused on defining the inherent drives in human beings, but in the 1940s this work was eclipsed by need theorists who strove to define our basic needs. Needs are seen as motivators because an unsatisfied need is thought to create a state of tension that releases energy and provides direction. This purposeful energy guides individuals toward a goal that will fulfill the unsatisfied need.[5] As Douglas MacGregor stated it: "Man is a wanting animal—as soon as one of his needs is satisfied, another appears in its place. This process is unending. It continues from birth to death. Man continuously puts forth effort—works, if you please—to satisfy his needs."[6] Two different courses of inquiry into needs were pursued. The first track was occupied by researchers who were not trying to scope out the entire needs landscape but, rather, were trying to define one or two additional primary human motives that seemed especially important. Examples of such motives include affiliation, equity, competence, and achievement.[7] Each of these specific motives, in addition to other primary needs, is thought to cause us to be attracted to certain situations.

Other researchers took a different course and attempted to define a comprehensive system for classifying all human needs. The value of such a system is that it would allow us to predict which outcomes are attractive in which sets of circumstances. This approach has proven very popular because of its easy applicability to managerial problems, and its perceived predictive power. Abraham Maslow's work on a hierarchy of needs has been paramount in this field. Many researchers have expanded, simplified, or otherwise built on his hierarchical formulation, but it is his approach that has been popularized by many management writers, beginning with MacGregor's *The Human*

Side of Enterprise. By now, Maslow has been so thoroughly integrated into popular culture that almost everyone at least has heard the phrase "self-actualization."

Maslow's premise was that our needs exist in hierarchical order of prepotency, such that the lower order or more basic needs are inherently more important than the higher or less basic needs. Before any higher-level needs become important, a person must have satisfied the preceding level of need.[8] Once a need is satisfied, it no longer is a motivator. The strength of any need is determined by its position in the hierarchy and by the degree to which it and all lower needs have been satisfied. Maslow states that our behavior is governed by a constantly changing set of "important" needs.[9]

Other theorists have supported the notion of a need hierarchy but have contributed some significant differences. Clay Alderfer reduced needs to three levels: existence, relatedness, and growth.[10] He agrees with Maslow's premise that the satisfaction of a need influences its importance and the importance of higher-level needs. However, he argues that any need can be influenced by the satisfaction or frustration of needs above and below it. Interaction between need levels extends in both directions. He also believes that all needs can be activated simultaneously, which Maslow's theory of prepotency denies.

In summing up the variety of work done on needs classification systems, Lawler concluded that there are six areas of needs for which strong empirical evidence exists. These are:

- A number of existence needs—primarily hunger, thirst, sex, and oxygen
- A security need
- A social need
- A need for esteem and reputation
- An autonomy or freedom need
- A need for competence and self-actualization

Lawler also concluded that there is little evidence for suggesting that more than a two-step hierarchy exists, with existence and security needs at the lowest level and all higher-order needs at the next level. However, people do not seem to be simultaneously motivated by needs from the two different levels.[11]

Lawler summarized the popularity of the hierarchical need concept:

> The concept, if valid, provides a powerful tool for predicting how the importance of various outcomes will change in response to certain actions by organizations. It also can provide some important clues concerning what is likely to be important to employees. It suggests, for example, that as people get promoted in organizations and their lower-level needs become satisfied, they will become concerned with self-actualization and growth. *It also suggests that if a person's job security is threatened, he will abandon all else in order to protect it* (emphasis added).[12]

Self-actualization is the capstone to Maslow's original need hierarchy, a concept interpreted similarly by several important researchers over the past fifty years.[13] It is also the need most central to this inquiry into ethics and motivation. Self-actualization refers to our need for growth and development. In Maslow's words, "What a man *can* be, he *must* be. This need we may call self-actualization . . . the tendency to become actualized in what he is potentially . . . the desire to become more and more what one is, to become everything one is capable of becoming."[14]

Although not all people are self-actualizing, Maslow argued that the concept is important in explaining behavior in organizations, particularly at the managerial level. There has been an impressive amount of research to support this, and most of us have become aware of how our needs for growth and challenge are independent of any extrinsic rewards. For self-actualizing people, Maslow constructed a reverse motivational premise. He said that whereas other needs motivate by their absence and cease to motivate once fulfilled, self-actualizing needs increase as they are satisfied. The more opportunities for growth we experience, the more we seek out additional ones.[15]

In the years since Maslow, motivation theory has grown more sophisticated and complex, moving beyond individual needs to examine how organizational circumstances affect behavior. Yet even with the addition of organization factors to the motivation equation, the concept of self-actualization underpins these as well.[16] For example, a key variable in Rosabeth Moss Kanter's work on the structural determinants of behavior in organizations is "opportunity," the real and perceived situations that allow employees to experience growth, development, and recognition.[17]

The concept of the need for self-actualization has become so ingrained in our culture that it pervades not only management theory concerned with job design issues, but for some the categories by which they gauge themselves. I remember as a management graduate student filling out a questionnaire to rank myself on a self-actualization scale. I was relieved to learn that on almost all dimensions, I had "made it." To have ranked less on the scale would have been a blow to my self-image.

But in the years since I enthusiastically embraced self-actualization, I have encountered behaviors in chaotic organizations that have not been predicted by these motivational theories. I have seen self-actualizing people, whose job security was threatened and whose futures were uncertain, respond with noble efforts, respond with professional activities that did nothing to foster their own personal growth. Their behaviors were undertaken for reasons not anticipated by motivational theory. Their concerns were not with actualizing themselves, but with responding to the needs of their people for a sense of meaning. Where they succeeded, they were able to carry on productively with their work.

The first manager who called my attention to this phenomenon was a woman in her early thirties who had worked for the same corporation since completing college. She had risen rapidly and was on the company's high potential list. She seemed well adapted to life in a large corporation; she had achieved notable results and had the reputation of being well connected with more senior managers. In discussions with her, she radiated what seemed an appropriate mix of astuteness, self-confidence, and experienced cynicism for life in a large corporation.

Within the space of a few months, however, dramatic upheavals occurred in the company. Two large divisions were merged into one. In the desire to create a unified product line, the company suddenly had two of every function and department. One doesn't need to know much about corporate life to envision the fierce political battles that ensued as managers from twin departments competed for the right to retain leadership of their function and, in many cases, to maintain their jobs. As key managers were moved out, those below, including this mid-level woman manager, found years of alliances suddenly destroyed. She and others were left defenseless as they approached their own battles with competing departments. She was thrown into conflict with a twin department that was much less sophisticated than her own and that had a far less lustrous track record. For three months her time was spent engaged in a political fight for survival, even though in less chaotic circumstances her organization would have easily eclipsed its rival.

Her department was completely demoralized. Their fine work of the past seemed to have little bearing on the decisions being made at higher levels. No reasonable justification existed for the turmoil they found themselves in, nor the threat to their existence that prevailed. Their futures depended simply on who won the political wars several levels above them. As I observed this situation over a period of months, it was truly an organization that had abandoned any facade of rational behavior. Employees could find no meaning in corporate actions beyond raw power plays. In such an environment, most employees checked out either psychically or physically. There appeared no reason to do otherwise.

But it was in this setting that I saw this one manager, and a few others, display behaviors that at first seemed incredible and then led me to question my understanding of human motivation. I saw her engage in a personal and deliberate effort to create meaning for her people when their organization no longer provided that meaning.

She did this in several ways. Her first approach was to be honest and forthright with her staff about the craziness around them. She did not try to protect them from difficult information, nor did she attempt to mask the situation or make it seem different than what it was. She communicated frequently to them through a variety of means, including a newsletter (her organization totaled nearly two hundred people), conference calls, and frequent personal visits around the different facilities. She gave them the information she had and listened to their concerns and fears. She was frank to admit what she didn't know or what ideas she was thinking of but hadn't yet decided on. Her communications were designed to give people an accurate picture of current realities, and she trusted them to deal with that information in a thoughtful and adult manner.

Second, she supported her staff as they went through their own sufferings resulting from loss and change. She provided forums and workshops where people could vent their feelings, share their grief, and support one another. In structured workshops she encouraged both humor and sadness as ways to deal with their situation.

With these types of supports, she prepared the way to lead her people to what we came to call "the abyss." She confronted them with the fact that the organization they had all relied on to provide them with meaning for their work no longer could provide that meaning. In many ways the organization was acting as if it no longer cared (although this was viewed as temporary). She told them that they would have to make choices about their professional behavior based not on the expectations of the corporation, but from a different source, which they would have to provide. Where there was to be value in the work they were to do, they would have to define that value among themselves. Their entire function might be dissolved within a few weeks, yet she asked them to continue to work at high professional standards if that was important to them intrinsically.

During and after this period, she commented often on how transformational an experience it had been. She described feeling more centered and more clear than at any time in her professional life. She was warmed by the response and respect she received from her employees. And her department rolled along, meeting its responsibilities and even putting energy into developing a few new services, all while its fate hung in the balance.

This is only one story, but the theme of it has become familiar to me as I've wandered through these crazy organizational settings. A staff member in the organization just described commented: "If the corporation won't give me a direction, then all I can do ethically is establish what I think is right—for me, my people, our customers, and the company—and proceed." Another manager said: "The business is unmanageable. I've stopped trying to manage it. The only thing of value is the people. They have to come out of it with some goodness—and I have to find ways to foster it."[18]

There are several interpretations one can give to statements and behaviors such as these. One thing they have signalled to me is that some managers realize that one of their primary responsibilities to their people is to help them find meaning in their work. This effort to construct meaning for their activities provides strong motivation to act, and this becomes especially evident in situations where other incentives to act have disappeared.

With this assessment, I was led to the work of Viktor Frankl and logotherapy. Logotherapy (derived from *logos*, the Greek word for both "meaning" and "spirit") is based on the belief that man is not interested primarily in any psychic conditions of his own but rather is oriented toward the world, toward the world of potential meanings and values which are waiting to be fulfilled and actualized by him.[19] Based on a "will to meaning," logotherapy stands in sharp contrast to the motivational perspectives of need theory. In need theory, it is the drive to reduce tension caused by an unsatisfied need that motivates behavior. Things, tasks, people can be seen as instrumentalities for restoring peace to the individual's psychological system. As Maslow stated: "The environment is no more than the means to the person's self-actualizing ends."[20]

Logotherapy deals with our transcendence beyond individual needs, to an encounter with the world. The world has its own objective reality; we are players in that reality, but it exists independent of us. This objective world, Frankl states, makes demands on us.

> We need to stop asking about the meaning of life, and, instead, to think of ourselves as those who are being questioned by life. . . . Life ultimately means taking the responsibility to find the right answers to its problems and to fulfill the tasks which it constantly sets for each individual.[21]

In this objective view of reality, our identities are not something we invent, but something we discover through our encounters with things beyond the self. The world is not an instrument for our gratification, but the locus for meaning we must discover. "Meaning is more than mere self-expression, or a projection of the self *into the world*. The meaning that each of us must fulfill is something beyond ourselves, it is never just ourselves."[22]

As its central concept, logotherapy defines a "will to meaning," an innate desire to give as much meaning as possible to one's life, to enact one's values. Meaning making is distinct from needs. If it were a need, we would seek to satisfy it just to be rid of it. Meaning is something we are concerned with for itself; and it is, says Frankl, the highest value. Meaning is something that summons us, that goes before us and keeps drawing us towards it.

> Meaning must not coincide with being; meaning must be ahead of being. Meaning sets the pace for being. Existence falters unless it is lived in terms of transcendence toward something beyond itself.[23]

Frankl asserted that there is a tension we experience between being and meaning, a tension that is inherent in being human and, therefore, ineradicable. In fact, this tension is indispensable to mental well-being. More important by far than self-actualization, from a motivational perspective, is this tension we experience to find a personal meaning in life, to have a point of reference outside our personal existence. The feeling of real fulfillment comes not by more strenuous efforts at self-actualization, but by more meaningful contact with the objective, external world.[24]

Although will-to-meaning is an independent construct from need theory, self-actualization does play a role. It occurs spontaneously as a result of our successful encounters with meaning. Like happiness, Frankl argues, self-actualization is a by-product of living correctly; neither goal can be pursued for itself. The more one pursues them directly, the more one will be disappointed, for they are not end states; they exist only as consequences of the achievement of more fundamental primary goals.[25]

Frankl's work adds an important dimension to motivation that has been overlooked in the management literature. Will-to-meaning exists independent of any needs hierarchy and independent of the motive for self-actualization. It is activated when a person consciously encounters the objective world and is challenged to make choices about how he or she will respond to that world. The motivating energy comes from the tension between the world and the individual, from the choices that are waiting to be made, and from the sense that the rightness of those choices can be verified outside of the individual. Will-to-meaning is a powerful motivator. Even in the most dire circumstances, as Frankl's own experience at Auschwitz demonstrated, people can find the energy to go on if they have determined a meaning for their trials.

I believe all of this makes sense to us at a deeply intuitive level. But it has not had an impact on the models of motivation currently in use. The need for meaning making is, however, creeping into the management literature. In a study that examined the behavior of employees in organizations undergoing severe cutbacks, it was noted that employees responded better to their own personal distress if management had made clear *why* all of this was occurring. By creating a context of meaning, employees were able to deal more effectively with high levels of stressful change.[26]

It bears emphasizing again how radically different Frankl's theory is from the work of other motivational theorists. In almost all the others the focus has been on the individual. The environment is considered for the potential impact it has on the individual's needs. It is a theoretic perspective that, unintentionally or not, leads to an instrumental view of life. By contrast, Frankl focuses on encounters between the individual and the outside world. This objectification of reality is dramatically different from the filter by which self-actualization theory interprets the world.

It is not new to complain about self-actualization as a corroding concept. Daniel Yankelovich, as he explored the attitudes of the new workforce in the late 1970s, excoriated the prevailing tendency to focus only on self-actualization.[27] And the recent spate of publicity given to upwardly mobile young professionals who are leaving profitable careers to work for little pay on such issues as poverty and peace led one psychiatrist to comment that conflicts over values have become the prevailing psychological problems therapists are treating. We are beginning to see, he said, an alternative vision of adulthood, where we realize that life has to be fulfilling and meaningful in the here and now, that we can't postpone meaning in pursuit of other rewards.[28]

I believe we must take a serious and long look at current approaches to motivation, and begin to factor in other dimensions known to give people the capacity to act. Such work is important not just from a theoretical perspective. As America's large organizations continue to go through their numerous gyrations to be equipped to meet the demands of our world, we will be faced with several crises that center on employee motivation. How will we continue to motivate people to be productive in the midst of constant change? How will we motivate people in settings where political battles rage? How will we motivate people when the organization can make no guarantees for future employment? How will we motivate people as they increasingly explore sources of satisfaction other than work?

The answers to these questions will involve a number of complex factors. But it seems clear that we will be directed to look at the interactions of people with themselves, with one another, with their profession, and with their lives rather than focusing only on the individual-organization dimension. In many cases it will mean doing what I've done here, bringing theory that already exists in other disciplines into the management literature.[29]

I hope that the current faddish interest in ethics leads us deeper into the realm I've begun to explore—namely, that the encounter with ethical issues can give people power. Rather than being a safeguard, ethics can contribute enabling energy to the organization system. If we can move beyond our control needs, we will perceive that people who are prepared to engage actively with the meaning of their lives at work will not only be the most trustworthy, but also will be the most highly motivated performers.

Frankl said that his philosophy ultimately involved education toward responsibility.[30] With this in mind, I'd like to propose some directions for the education of managers that would help move us toward preparing them to engage in work from a different motivational basis.

First, we need to create subtle changes in the language we use to describe careers. Our language needs to move away from the constant talk about individual growth, satisfaction, and development and into the realm where we describe careers in terms of the opportunities that will be present for making choices and assuming responsibility. In and of themselves, such language changes would do little; but as part of a reorientation process, more effective and accurate language can play an important, if subtle, role.

Second, we need to think of ways to encourage people to experience the world on its own terms, not as an instrument for their own needs. The best way I know to do this is to create experiences that develop a systems way of thinking, where the interconnectedness of seemingly discrete parts becomes apparent. Another way of expressing this would be to encourage a sense of community or a holistic approach to thinking. Whatever terms one uses, the concept requires a sophisticated approach to solving problems. It argues for management training that expands the borders of whatever problem is being studied, for training that forces people to encounter the complex web of relationships that underpins every situation. Nothing is so humbling as a good systems analysis. It quickly develops a sense of awe for the small but powerful place each of us occupies in the system. It is the best way I know to awaken consciousness toward responsibility and humility.

And finally, educators need to find ways to support and encourage each individual's sense of his or her own uniqueness. I've witnessed that we counsel promising students in terms of where to use their particular skills to foster career success. This is different than talking to students about the constellation of their talents and the unique opportunity they represent to the rest of us to cause things to progress. Again, it is a subtle difference in the messages we send that over time can lead to important changes in self-consciousness.

The task for educators is not to be beguiled into approaching our ethical morass by focusing on questions of right and wrong. This is important; but beneath this surface lies the need to educate people to a higher sense of themselves, to the responsibility to encounter life and make meaning from those encounters. My experience suggests that people respond strongly and positively to this. Frankl once described his approach as a "summoning philosophy." To the extent that we can make real to ourselves that we are being summoned by life, that responsibleness lies at the heart of management, we will have found a wellspring of energy that will enable us to work productively through times of organizational confusion.

Notes

1. "The End of Corporate Loyalty," *Business Week*, 4 August 1986, p. 42.

2. Ibid.

3. In examining endemic stress experienced by employees under conditions of continued losses, chronic shortages, and inadequate role opportunities, Fried found that people tend to give up and manifest depression, apathy, alienation, and denial. Behaviorally, people tend to withdraw and decrease their productivity. M. Fried, "Endemic Stress: The Psychology of Resignation and the Politics of Scarcity," *American Journal of Orthopsychiatry* 52 (1982): 5.

Kanter and Stein described the emotions felt by those watching things fall apart as "erratic behavior, suspicion and mistrust, self-protective disinterest in the organization, and departure from the routine practices. The 'rules' cease to have the same compelling meaning under conditions of extreme uncertainty." Rosabeth Moss Kanter and Barry A. Stein, "Organizational Deathwatch," in *Life in Organizations*, ed. Rosabeth Moss Kanter and Barry A. Stein (New York: Basic Books, 1979), 377.

4. Katherine C. Esty, "Job Distress in Contracting Organizations: When Smaller is Not Beautiful" (Ph.D. diss., Boston University, 1984), 3–4.

5. W. Warner Burke, *Organization Development: Principles and Practices* (Boston: Little, Brown, 1982), 24.

6. Douglas McGregor, *The Human Side of Enterprise* (New York: McGraw-Hill, 1960), 36.

7. For a more detailed journey through the literature of motivation theory, see Edward E. Lawler III's excellent summary "Drives, Needs and Outcomes," in *Managing Organizations: Readings and Cases*, ed. David A. Nadler, Michael L. Tushman, and Nina J. Hatvany (Boston: Little, Brown, 1982), 79–100.

8. Maslow's five need categories are:
- Physiological needs, including the need for food, water, air, etc.
- Safety needs, or the need for security, stability, and the absence from pain, threat, or illness.

- Belongingness and love needs, which include a need for affection, belongingness, love, etc.
- Esteem needs, including both a need for personal feelings of achievement or self-esteem and also a need for recognition or respect from others.
- The need for self-actualization, a feeling of self-fulfillment or the realization of one's potential.

Abraham Maslow, *Motivation and Personality*, 2d ed. (New York: Harper and Row, 1970).

9. Lawler, "Drives, Needs, and Outcomes," 89.

10. Clayton P. Alderfer, *Existence, Relatedness and Growth* (New York: Free Press, 1972).

11. Lawler, "Drives, Needs, and Outcomes," 94–95.

12. Ibid., 92.

13. Lawler lists nine of the most prominent, including Erich Fromm, Karen Horney, David Riesman, Carl Rogers, Rollo May, and Gordon Allport. "Drives, Needs, and Outcomes," 88.

14. Abraham H. Maslow, "A Theory of Human Motivation," in *Management Classics*, 2d ed., ed. Michael T. Matteson and John M. Ivancevich (Santa Monica, Calif.: Goodyear, 1981), 244.

15. Maslow, *Motivation and Personality*, 211.

16. The one exception to this trend is the work on expectancy theory by Victor H. Vroom, *Work and Motivation* (New York: John Wiley and Sons, 1964). Expectancy theory focuses not on needs, but on outward behaviors, so it avoids the self-actualization question altogether. The theory posits that three factors influence our motivation: the belief that if I do "X," it will lead to "Y"; the assessment that "Y" is of value to me as a reward for effort; and the belief that I can actually do "X," that is, perform to the required levels. Expressed formulaically, the amount of motivation = E x V (Expectancy times the valence of the reward). Where any of the three factors is zero, there is no motivation to perform the act. See David A. Nadler and Edward E. Lawler III, "Motivation—a Diagnostic Approach," in *Managing Organizations*, 102–3.

17. Rosabeth Moss Kanter, *Men and Women of the Corporation* (New York: Basic Books, 1977), chap. 6.

18. Author's notes during conversations, July-November 1986.

19. Viktor E. Frankl, *Psychotherapy and Existentialism: Selected Papers on Logotherapy* (New York: Washington Square Press, 1967), 40.

20. Maslow, *Motivation and Personality*, 117, quoted in Frankl, *Selected Papers*, 45.

21. Viktor E. Frankl, *Man's Search for Meaning* (Boston: Beacon Press, 1962), 122.

22. Ibid., 10. This sense of an objective meaning to each life pervades Frankl's work. He conveys a strong belief that we are all unique. "No one is replaceable nor is his life repeatable. This twofold uniqueness adds to man's responsibleness." Frankl, *Selected Papers*, 8–9.

23. Ibid., 12.

24. Robert C. Leslie, *Jesus and Logotherapy* (Nashville: Abingdon Press, 1965), 72.

25. Frankl, *Selected Papers*, 44.

26. Esty, "Job Distress," 3–4.

27. Daniel Yankelovich, "New Rules in American Life: Searching for Self-Fulfillment in a World Turned Upside Down," *Psychology Today* 15 (April 1981): 35–91 (an in-depth review of his book by the same title [New York: Random House, 1981]).

28. Televised interview, Channel 5, Portland, Oregon, 15 January 1987. Frankl termed such psychological disturbances "noogenic neuroses," rooted in the unrewarded longing and groping of man for that hierarchically highest value—an ultimate meaning to his life. Frankl, *Selected Essays*, 43.

29. Among the literature that needs to be incorporated is that of Adult Development research. Although in my informal observations, I noted no difference in managerial behavior predicted by age, I've been intrigued by Vaillant's work on what constitutes good mental health in adults. Based on a thirty-year longitudinal study of male achievers, Vaillant noted that the critical defenses that enabled people to engage in life fully were stoicism and altruism. Where his subjects used these defenses, they could effectively adapt to the stresses of life. "It is not stress that kills us. It is effective adaptation to stress that permits us to live." See George E. Vaillant, *Adaptation to Life* (Boston: Little, Brown, 1977).

30. Victor Frankl, *The Doctor and the Soul: From Psychotherapy to Logotherapy* (New York: Alfred A. Knopf, 1972), xviii.

For those who still tend to view the recalcitrant, erring, corrupt corporation as some sort of institutional entity, unmanaged by the human touch, the events of the last three decades, the period encompassed here, should be sufficient to remove the last vestiges of such innocence. Corporations are managed by men; and men, never forget, manage corporations to suit themselves. . . . And, as we have seen in 15 case histories, the basic cause of the business disaster is greed, human greed, simple and unadulterated.

—Isadore Barmash

For the things which are important in the analysis of democracy are those which bind the hands of good men. We then learn that something more than virtue is necessary in the realm of circumstance and power.

—Philip Selznick

I never met a corporation that has a conscience.

—George Meany

CHAPTER SEVEN

Organizational Ethics: Paradox and Paradigm

J. Bonner Ritchie

E XTRAPOLATING from the quotations on the facing page one could argue that organizational ethics are only the ethics of the individuals who make up an organization. One could further argue that not only don't organizations have a conscience, they can't. These arguments have face validity, and I would hold them to be basically true. Values, goals, and actions do belong to people. And, while we attack, criticize, sue, and often hold organizations responsible for immoral actions, it is clearly *people* who state the values and goals and act on behalf of organizations. But, while these notions lay a necessary foundation for discussing organizational ethics, they are not enough. We need to look at more than individual ethics *in* organizations. We need to develop a *new* framework for thinking about the ethical role of individuals in an organizational setting.

As Barmash states on the facing page,[1] it seems clear that individuals without ethics can play havoc with an organization—an observation that many people would agree with and

J. Bonner Ritchie is chairman of the Organizational Behavior Department, School of Management, Brigham Young University. Professor Ritchie acknowledges the thoughtful assistance of Robert A. Page, Jr., University of California, Irvine, in the preparation of this essay.

would probably define as the essence of organizational ethics. However, the Selznick reference suggests that in the complex process of aggregating individual behavior in organizational roles, something more than individual ethics may be required.[2] He implies that even people "with virtue" need constraints as they attempt to administer a productive *and* moral organization. It is this subtle dynamic of people acting in organizations, with either their own personal motives *or* the best interest of the organization as the driving force, that constitutes my area of inquiry. In order to pursue this issue, we need to explore several different levels of abstraction. I would propose that this area of inquiry be identified as organizational philosophy.

Organizational philosophy is not just the study of the philosophy of organizations. It is the application of the tools of philosophy to the analysis of organizational phenomena. More specifically, it is the burden which rests upon each of us to ask the difficult questions, to push assumptions, to question criteria, to verify facts, to ascertain logic, and to determine whether a decision, behavior, or outcome is useful and good. By design or default we are continually making such judgments; my assumption is that with better organizational philosophy we could develop better analysis.

In this philosophical analysis it is the challenge of each organizational member or observer to satisfy the questions of organizational ontology, epistemology, logic, and ethics. While testing assumptions regarding the nature or purpose of the organization, ways of knowing about the organization, or the limits of our organizational knowledge, we are always encountering the structural relationships of people in the organization. Organizations are sets of relationships with rules, expectations, and consequences beyond the domain of individual ethics. Understanding people in groups/organizations is different than understanding people alone. As Lewis Thomas argues in *The Lives of a Cell*, the problem is not the inherent corruption of people, but rather "what we've always known and never had enough time to worry about, that we haven't yet learned how to stay human when assembled in masses."[3] One of the reasons we have not learned that lesson, I would suggest, is that we have not yet refined the concept of organizational ethics to account for the complex organizational factors which must be added to individual ethics. Abraham Zaleznik has said that "conscience is a fragile thing. It needs support from institutions, and that support is weakening."[4]

The fact that answers to the organizational philosophy questions will not be universally accepted suggests an even greater significance to the inquiry. Organizational effectiveness depends on the careful statement, and resolution, of different positions, and the constructive problem solving and planning— which depends on an accurate application of others' positions. This is all impossible without thoughtful ethical analysis.

It should be noted at this point that this discussion is not primarily about business ethics or social responsibility. There are obviously interrelationships and overlaps, but business ethics involves an analysis of the proper conduct of business. And, social responsibility involves the role of the organization in concerns of the larger community. While "truth in advertising" or support of the local ballet company are important topics for business ethics and social responsibility, they do not directly constitute the field of organizational ethics. I would argue that a careful standard of organizational ethics would likely lead to honest advertising, but the focus of this inquiry is at a different level. The issue is organizations in general, not just in their business activities, and we are considering those internal processes which may or may not be ethical, independent of social responsiveness.

To illustrate, I would consider the following items to be illustrative of the domain of organizational ethics:

- Management executive decisions which may result in employees performing work which may be dangerous or immoral
- Whether employees have adequate information regarding the effect of their work on themselves and others
- Decision processes and criteria (by management, employees, unions, etc.) which determine standards, rewards, and punishment for different work situations

- Whether leaders order subordinates to perform irrelevant tasks in order to validate leader power or to test subordinate loyalty
- Use of organizationally privileged information to disadvantage someone or to pressure someone for personal gain
- Lying with respect to quality control because of competitive pressure to get a product on the market
- Faking test results in order to meet project target dates
- Intended or unintended job or promotion selection criteria which result in discrimination against a minority group
- Promise of a future reward when organizational resources are not available
- "Excellent" leaders telling members what their goals "should" be because the leader has decided it

In summary, organizational ethics are inseparable from organizational relationships—up, down, and lateral. They involve the definition of a process of decision making, structure, motivation, rewards, and behavior which is consistent with criteria for quality and ethical organizational relationships.

I should mention at this point that I do not propose to solve the problem of how to create an ethical organization, but I do want to raise some concerns and to participate in the dialogue. If we can develop better questions, communicate more sincerely, and pursue with passion a more ethical organizational framework, we will be on the right path.

A CONCEPT OF ORGANIZATION

In order to place a discussion of organizational ethics in context, a brief statement regarding a theoretical framework of organization is needed. As Karl Weick suggests, I prefer to think of organization as a verb rather than as a noun.[5] This means we consider a variety of simultaneous activities under way as contrasted to a static structure. These activities may involve such things as raising children, producing a product, many ways of reducing equivocality, playing games, building

162

social networks, exercising political power, teaching students, or changing the world. All are activities which will serve many second- or third-level purposes in addition to the primary organization function.

In his landmark work redefining organization theory, Weick suggests that there are more significant reasons for becoming part of an organization than just attempting to achieve a specified organizational goal. And, while there are many useful and appropriate ways to define organizations, for this discussion I suggest the following limited and somewhat unusual perspective: Organizations are the stage upon which we act out our identity—the place we decide who and what we are. Within organizations we find and develop the resources for life's organizational drama.

Peter Drucker suggests that "the only way to find what you want is to create a job. Nobody worth his salt has ever moved into an existing job." A job is the means for you to find out who you are. Drucker argues that "one doesn't marry a job. A job is your opportunity to find out—that's all it is. You owe no loyalty to your employer other than not betraying secrets. Be ruthless about finding out whether you belong."[6]

There may be some troublesome ethical implications in Drucker's prescription, especially when you push it to the extreme of endorsing the use of an organization only for your selfish interests. In the current world of "organizational culture," "excellence," "shared values," and "organizational family," some would feel that Drucker's employee would be neither happy nor productive. But, his position does highlight the important aspect of organizations as the place where we discover who we are. That does not mean we need to exploit other members of the organization or be indifferent to the organization's mission in order to use it as a means to learn about ourselves.

Shakespeare asked in *Measure for Measure,* "Would you know a man?" and answered, "Give him power." If Shakespeare is correct, it is only in organizations, where we can exercise and understand power, that we can come to know ourselves and others. The process by which we discover those roles or activities in life that provide meaning is by functioning in organizational positions. As we search for meaning and purpose we may try out many different parts or even stages. Comedy may serve some better and tragedy others. Some may even find that they gain greater satisfaction building props than performing in front of a large audience.

But regardless of the specific activity, a variety of people are depending on us and evaluating our contribution. Often there are several such evaluators who put our names on a chart signifying some level of achievement; or who promote, grade, or terminate us based on some performance standard; or who use us as a role model for their behavior. While all of this may seem prosaic, it is imbued with underlying contradictions and tensions. We are not just doing a job, we are putting our, and others', intrinsic worth on the line. It is human beings' lives we are dealing with, not just an amalgamation of faceless people. It is this idiosyncratic process of exploration, learning and growing (or failing) which makes organizational science so difficult and organizational ethics so crucial.

With all of the performance anxiety, peer pressure, manipulating reward systems, and ambiguity of a fast-changing world, no wonder people often become destructive (of self or others) on the organization stage. This is especially true in today's setting where so many special interest groups are struggling to redefine their identity in a world of newfound individual rights. As we observe people in racial, religious, age, gender, educational, and occupational categories fighting for their dignity and rights, we see the great opportunity—and potential for terrible destructiveness—opened up to an unethical leader who can more easily exploit those with less power.

Organizations are the bridge we see taking us across the chasm between our dreams and reality. We observe where we are (reality) and where we would like to be (dreams) and then define our organizational involvement as the means to close the gap. In a world of increasingly higher aspirations, complex technology, intense worldwide competition, and great uncertainty, there is so much at stake that our ethical systems are under more and more strain.

PARADOXES

Questions of organizational ethics present several paradoxes which must be managed. One has to do with simple realities of organizational life. Things such as bounded rationality, limited information, imperfect communication systems, functional specialization, multiple and conflicting goals and rewards, informal group norms, and environmental pressures—all put ethical choices in a matrix of conflicting assumptions and criteria. All of these conditions mean that people in a variety of positions make decisions that affect others without those making the decisions, or those being impacted, having a chance to evaluate the effect of the decision on them. We simply do not have enough information to account completely for the effects of our decisions. And, when we are on the receiving end, we often do not even realize the decision is being made, or what inputs are being considered in the process. A leader, for example, may be acting with the best ethical intentions and yet employ a procedure or make a decision or promulgate policy that results in perceived immoral effects by an individual or group inside or outside the organization. It is this *unintended* effect that results in an ethical leadership dilemma, or paradox. In addition, of course, there is the more obvious unethical impact of those with *immoral* motives. I suspect that the analysis (although probably not the solution) would be much easier if only immoral motives resulted in immoral effects.

Another paradox is found in Reinhold Niebuhr's struggle to find a resolution between individual and organizational needs. Niebuhr concluded that there is an "irreconcilable conflict between the needs of society and the imperatives of a sensitive conscience."[7] He argued that individuals have a better chance of being moral or ethical when they can define their own interest plus the interest of another individual and develop rules of conduct which satisfy conditions for a benevolent interpersonal relationship. He states that people "are endowed by nature with a measure of sympathy and consideration for their kind, the breadth of which may be extended by an astute social pedagogy."[8] However, this potential for the individual to learn and manifest ethical behavior toward others is not contained in the social organization.

Niebuhr goes on to say that "these achievements are more difficult, if not impossible, for human societies and social groups. In every human group there is less reason to guide and to check impulse, less capacity for self-transcendence, less ability to comprehend the needs of others."[9] It seems that even if an ethical leader wants to make the organization sensitive and benevolent, an ethical contradiction may result. The dilemma occurs when the leader makes decisions demanding similar sacrifices from other organizational members that the leader is willing to make and that others *may* make if they had the free choice. But, does the leader have the right to be unselfish with other individuals' interests? Or to tell them what their moral obligation should be? After all, their own analysis might lead to a different conclusion. It may be easier to teach ethical behavior in a classroom because students can hold in reserve what they learn and then, when it is time for action, consider one ethical value system versus another. By contrast, organizational leadership is more likely *committing* the resources and forcing the values of other people rather than inviting them to consider his or her approach.

A third paradox can be found in Laczniak's argument that ethical conflicts are inherent in organizational decision making.[10] Referencing several other studies, he stated that at some point in their careers 75 percent of responding managers felt a conflict between profit considerations and ethical conduct.[11] Other studies extend this dilemma to conclude that most managers consider not just a given choice itself to be an ethical dilemma, but pressures in making the choices are themselves unethical.[12] In another study 65 percent of the managers surveyed at times felt pressure to compromise personal ethical standards.[13]

Part of the problem stems not only from the growing lack of consensus in society, but a lack of consensus within the organizations regarding the nature of ethical standards. There is also evidence that consensus regarding what constitutes ethical behavior in decision-making situations diminishes as the level of analysis becomes more specific and as you move to lower levels in the organization.[14] Even if general rules can be defined and agreed upon, the agreement has a high probability of breaking down in specific circumstances, especially those handled by low-level participants in the organization.

My own experience has validated this dilemma. In one organization where I was conducting training programs, I used the questionnaire from which some of the above conclusions were developed and found that, of about fifty middle managers queried, each at one time in his career felt his boss had asked him to do something that he considered immoral, illegal, or unethical. The more interesting aspect of this finding was that about two-thirds of the group did not feel that the boss had intended or was aware of the negative impact. While lack of information, time pressure, and honest differences of opinion were often mentioned as causes of the problem, a more important concern was that the boss was not sensitive to the functional or ethical perspective of the subordinate. Those surveyed felt that in many cases a different leadership style would reduce the problem. In those cases where the boss was aware of and sensitive to a subordinate's position and made a difficult decision the subordinate disagreed with, the resentment and perception of unethical behavior was almost eliminated.

A fourth paradox is addressed in Arlie Russell Hochschild's book, *The Managed Heart*. She questions the ethics of managing feelings or emotions—of requiring employees to act as if they feel a certain prescribed way. This "emotional labor" is defined as that which "requires one to induce or suppress feeling in order to sustain the outward countenance that produces the proper state of mind in others."[15] With the increase in the service sector in our labor force, more and more people are hired to project an attitude of safe, happy, confident, caring, loving feelings toward customers or clients. What happens to individuals when they do not really feel the way they are ordered to and the resulting duplicity affects their mental state or offends their sense of ethics? For example, is it ethical to require a clerk to pretend endorsement of a product when it is not sincere? Or is it just a job (a question that will be discussed later)? In the organizational setting we are buying time and labor; but can, or *should*, we buy feelings?

For example, one of the challenges of being an effective food server is always being pleasant, always smiling whether or not one is feeling good physically or emotionally. But being pleasant regardless of how one actually feels might be postulated to be an ethically acceptable *requirement*, considering that the amount of tips as well as the image of the establishment are affected by the degree of pleasantness of the servers. That is, it might be ethically argued that, say, food servers who don't feel they should have to smile if they don't feel like smiling can be invited to seek work as a server in some other, perhaps less popular, establishment that may attract lower-tipping customers.

I find it ironic that we often describe as our greatest leaders those who are most manipulative. The logic is simple: the greatest leaders are the ones who mobilize resources, who change perceptions, and who reputedly of their own accord accomplish great results. We are overwhelmed by the "ethics of consequence." The utilitarian criterion of the "greatest good for the greatest number" becomes the rationale for a positive evaluation even though the means may have included deception, promising rewards which couldn't be and were not delivered, or pitting innocent people against each other in order to use competitive drive as a motivating force.

Lest I imply that I have an alternative theory of leadership, I admit that the term "manipulation" is often cast in a negative, ethically undesirable connotation. As a matter of fact, "nonmanipulative leadership" can be a contradiction in terms. Consequently, there have been many attempts over the years to idealize the nonmanipulative organizational culture or leadership style. Litwin and Stringer claim that we have been avoiding the real issue; that is, we should not look to democratic participation as a way to eliminate manipulation.[16] We may thereby *reduce* exploitive behavior or make leadership more consistent with a particular ethical system, but we do not eliminate the reality of management control functions, of the burden of making decisions with limited information, or of firing people. The very title of William Dyer's book *The Sensitive Manipulator*[17] implies an interesting perspective on this issue. It seems, therefore, that our quest should not be to eliminate manipulation but to manage it within a given value system.

In John Gardner's book *Grendel*, he retells the Beowulf legend from the perspective of the monster. In the discussion of the rights of the people versus the rights of the government, there is a debate about the legitimate use of power and when revolutionary violence is justified. One old man's justification for such violence was very simple. He said, "All systems are evil. All governments are evil. Not just a trifle evil. *Monstrously* evil."[18] While this position is not universally shared, those who do accept it would defend violent overthrow. So, while we cannot eliminate power, it must be managed and restrained.

It is in this context that the immorality of leaders/organizations can be seen as an opportunity for one to invoke the "consent of the governed" or "checks and balances" as an optimistic means of control rather than the pessimistic means of resignation or revolution. Revolution may be a situational strategy but not a universal response to the imperfection of organizations. This idea is reflected in another of Niebuhr's maxims: "Man's capacity for justice makes democracy possible; but, man's inclination to injustice makes democracy necessary."[19]

Some years ago I did a review of studies of leadership and participation.[20] Since the degree and quality of subordinate participation and the leadership style employed in the interaction are key ethical dimensions in organizational behavior, the conclusions of that inquiry ought to be relevant. The literature made clear that certain conditions must exist for participation to be effective; in fact, when those conditions did not hold, the attempted participation seemed to backfire and both morale and productivity suffered. The criteria for effective participation were found to be as follows:

1. Individuals need relevant skills and information to be effectively involved in the participative decision-making process.
2. Individuals must be convinced that their involvement will really affect the outcome of the decision.
3. Individuals must perceive that their contributions will be rewarded.
4. The primary unit of participation should be the supervisor-subordinate team.
5. Individuals must perceive the involvement and decisions as legitimate (moral/ethical/legal).
6. There must be a reciprocal climate of trust, honesty, and confidence between supervisors and subordinates.

In each of the above contingent variables it is interesting to note that there is a strong ethical dimension. In fact, the overriding criterion for overall effective participation is the ethical quality of the superior-subordinate relationship. While points five and six are explicit statements of that variable, each of the other contingent criteria rest on that important foundation of leadership—reciprocity. That is, there must be the understanding that subordinates will receive the information and training they need to do their jobs. Subordinates must perceive that others in the organization will honestly listen to them and reward their inputs and not just go through the motions. In other words, people will not see the organization or its leaders as ethical if they feel they are only being used as a variable in a production function.

Given the above conditions, it is no surprise that so many attempts at participation are ineffective. When people feel they are being deceived and that behavior is not consistent with real intent, they resent the abuse and often undercut their supervisors' objectives. A sensitive, informed boss would not make that mistake. These violations are more than bad management. They insult, demean, and abuse the members of the organization the leader is supposed to respect and productively employ.

As a reinforcing concept, James MacGregor Burns's definition of "transforming leadership" describes the great potential of a powerful leader who embodies the implicit ethical imperative, which is such a crucial, but often neglected, dimension in discussions of leadership. He states that transforming leadership occurs

> when one or more persons *engage* with others in such a way that leaders and followers raise one another to higher levels of motivation and morality. Their purposes, which might have started out separate but related, as in the case of transactional leadership, become fused. Power bases are linked not as counterweights but as mutual support for common purpose. Various names are used for such leadership . . . : elevating, mobilizing, inspiring, exalting, exhorting, evangelizing. The relationship can be moralistic, of course. But, transforming leadership ultimately becomes *moral* in that it raises the level of human conduct and ethical aspiration of both the leader and led, and thus has a transforming effect on both.[21]

It is no small task to balance the many conflicting forces and achieve this transforming effect.

In recent years there has been an attempt to change the perception of leadership from a functional task focus to a transforming personal focus. Leadership is often contrasted to the role of management. I regard management as taking care of things—money, inventory, equipment, production processes—while I define a leader as one who develops people. Things are managed; people are led. Thus the high ethical concern surrounding leadership. There are still the difficult questions, however. Who decides in what way people are led or changed? By what process are people informed—or warned—about where they may be led or what the costs may be? These questions imply that any potential leader should carefully and continually consider the high ethical ingredient in all his or her leadership actions.

Paradigms

In the attempt to find an ethical resolution between honestly held but conflicting criteria for organizational roles, leaders often invoke a variety of metaphors to help decide a future course of action or to rationalize a past one. These metaphors or paradigms are often very useful and give us a way of abstracting to a higher level of analysis. However, they can also be a trap— we may think we are in a Superbowl, keeping careful score and trying to win at all costs, while others may be expecting a loving family support system. This difference of perception and metaphorical approach, while not unethical on its face, becomes very unethical when the metaphor employed causes dependent individuals to feel betrayed or abused and they emerge from the encounter with a lower sense of self-esteem or a reduced organizational commitment.

The basic question of the appropriate role we want to play builds on the overarching metaphor of the stage. As Shakespeare suggested in *As You Like It*, "All the world's a stage, and all the men and women merely players. They have their exits and their entrances, and one man in his time plays many parts." Regardless of the type of organization (business, family, university, church, government, athletic, musical), we continually must decide what role we are going to play and how we will play it. Other individuals may have a strong influence on our decision, but *we* decide, and in that role decision we explicitly or implicitly define our ethical criteria.

There are many interesting questions we can ask about our role definition and performance. Who writes the script? Who creates the set? Who directs? Who is the drama critic? What happens when you think you are in one play and you are really in another one (or, at least, everyone expects a different play)?

In considering possible paradigms we might employ in our thinking about organizations and our involvement in them, it is crucial to consider the implications of each. Several examples follow.

Laissez-faire

In this paradigm we have the classical economic assumption of the power of the free market. The invisible hand will aggregate individual motives and actions into a larger public good. Some would argue that it is, in fact, the mechanism which will turn private vice into public virtue. Advocates of a laissez-faire model do not deny individual or organizational abuse but feel that social Darwinism is preferable to welfare capitalism and that there are ways to handle the abuse other than government control. Their position is often stated in an attack on social responsibility. As Milton Friedman's famous argument goes, the only socially responsible behavior of a manager is to increase profits, as long as there is no deception or fraud.[22] K. R. Andrews interprets this position in terms of a manager whose socially responsible decisions reduce profits of a firm, in effect imposing a tax on shareholders and acting without authority as a legislative body.[23]

As Andrews states, unethical behavior may be too profitable to assume that the market will discipline corporations fast enough to correct the problems. He concludes:

> Given the slow rate at which verbalized good intentions are being converted into action, many critics of the large corporation suspect that for every chief executive announcing pious objectives there are a hundred closet rascals quietly conducting business in the old ways and taking immoral comfort in Friedman's moral support.[24]

Finally, observes Harold Williams, chief executive of the Getty Foundation: "The concept of 'let the market govern' relieves one of one's sense of responsibility."[25] The laissez-faire paradigm finds support in a great amount of nostalgia about the good old days. The cowboy who rode the open plains alone and was fully self-sufficient, for instance, impresses us with his independence and resourcefulness. But, the usefulness of such a metaphor today is limited: unlike the open plains, the business market is not infinite; and unlike the cowboy's necessary

ability to do anything and everything, people must have special-
ized skills to survive in today's workplace.

Games

Competitive games are fun and compelling paradigms. For
example, Robert Keidel states, "If ever a sport epitomized
modern business, it is football. The game is a metaphor for the
factory, for the office and for much of our thinking about
business management. . . . The language of football is used
regularly by virtually every executive in America."[26]

Sitting in on a corporate executive committee meeting recently, I heard a CEO state that "we need fewer tight ends and
more wide receivers in this outfit." The metaphor was unmis-
takable, at least for those who know football. And, of course,
therein lies one of the problems. Everyone does *not* know
football. What about those who do not share a macho competitive sports frame of reference? Is it strategically or ethically
defensible to use symbols that employees—who need to
understand—do not understand?

Another down side of sports analogies is the risk that they will
create a win-at-all-costs mentality, which sees everything in
terms of the scoreboard. A score of 3–2 makes it very clear who
won the ball game, but organizational effectiveness is not so
precisely measured. The gamesman[27] is a macho individual who
loves the challenge of the confrontation, is the ultimate strate-
gist, and has very basic self-serving individual rules in addition
to the "rules of the game."

In a critique of a game paradigm applied to business, A. Z.
Carr looked at management as a poker game. In both business
and poker, success requires good strategy and skill as well as
the ability to manage uncertainty and chance. One must have an
intimate knowledge of the rules, insight into the other players,
and the ability to maintain and manipulate appearances. At
some point, however, both the strategy and ethics of poker
diverge from those of management. Deception and bluffing may
be appropriate in a card game, but can they be justified in a

corporate setting where, for example, you have two division managers going after one vice-president position? The extreme application of this metaphor to the business world is described in the words of one executive:

> So long as a businessman complies with the laws of the land and avoids telling malicious lies, he's ethical. If the law as written gives a man a wide-open chance to make a killing, he'd be a fool not to take advantage of it. If he doesn't someone else will. There's no obligation on him to stop and consider who is going to get hurt. If the law says he can do it that's all the justification he needs. There's nothing unethical about that. It's just plain business sense.[28]

One of the more troublesome uses of the game paradigm surfaces when the stakes are high. In such circumstances, an executive's ability to engage in questionable activities with finesse and style is often admired. Beating the system, not getting caught, and dominating the other players are valued within this metaphor; but such values become troublesome, if not dangerous, criteria in everyday organizational life. And, of course, at times the subtle behavior may give way to more overt action. "A Smith and Wesson beats four aces" is a cowboy and gamesman prescription for justifying extreme, Watergate-type behavior when "the presidency is on the line."

Another use of the game logic is found in competitive performance ratings. The motivating force of a chart listing top sales people must be juxtaposed to the destructiveness of unjustified comparisons. Different situational realities may lead some individuals to lie or engage in illegal sales tactics in order to look good in the comparison. Or, they may have a nervous breakdown when pushed too far with unfair or unreasonable criteria.

Interestingly enough, even some sports apologists see limits or reversals to the paradigm. As Keidel quotes Paul Zimmerman of *Sports Illustrated,* he states that today we see a style of football management often labeled "corporate football."

> It's a game of situation substitutions: You move your pieces on the board, we move ours. Cerebral football played on synthetic

grass. Ironically, as football has grown ever more "corporate," the game has become less relevant as a model for business corporations to follow. It has become less human and less fun.[29]

When James F. Bere, chairman of Borg-Warner, commenting on the destructive effect of the insider trading scandal, stated that "we know in our minds that the playing field wasn't level,"[30] he was invoking a useful game metaphor. The officials must enforce the rules fairly, and the game must be fair; but, ofttimes it shouldn't even be a game.

Administrative Policy

In this paradigm, administrative edit and policy manuals are the means for controlling behavior. Bureaucratic structure sets up a decision-making system where those who have responsibility and expertise tell everyone else what to do. This approach often works well where a rational division of labor creates high efficiency. However, this paradigm often makes unrealistic assumptions about employee motivation and behavior. People don't always do things just because they are told to. In fact, rebellion against bureaucratic orders is legendary.

This paradigm has a simple and compelling logic for many people. Ethical behavior simply means obedience to company policy and procedure. Through responsible top management, well-designed internal policies, and a careful control system, people have something to fall back on in addition to their own judgment. The organization may also have someone assigned to monitor compliance or to help individuals who need instruction or reinforcement. There is always a person or a rule to support one's behavior.

One of the problems with this model is that executives or employees may feel that by simply having the policy, or by simple technical compliance, they absolve themselves of any further analysis or choice. Often fundamental changes in policies are needed to create an ethical climate.

Central to the policy paradigm is the organizational code of ethics. Such codes can be a means of forcing management to identify areas of concern and to put in writing where they stand. While this may be helpful to all members of the organization, it can also be a very self-serving device to barely avoid running afoul of the law—a means of achieving higher profits without an expensive lawsuit. A code also usually addresses a limited range of issues and may allow individuals to claim ignorance when their behavior is not specifically precluded by the code.

On the other hand, there is some evidence that a code of ethics does make a positive contribution to organizational practice.[31] Sometimes members of an organization simply do not know many of the ethical dilemmas they may encounter and how to think about them. A review of a code of ethics can be very helpful in generating advance consideration of problems and in developing personal principles. Cherrington and Cherrington, for example, found that conditions which contribute to honesty in retail stores are (1) top management having a well-defined standard of honesty, (2) a very explicit code of ethics, and (3) leadership which has not been guilty of dishonest decisions.

In an area such as sexual harassment, a policy may take on additional meaning. AT&T, for example, is seen as having a sexual harassment policy that is truly effective.[32] The impact is not just on those who may do the harassing, but on those who are harassed. The precise statement of steps to follow when victimized gives individuals confidence that they have recourse beyond complaints to immediate supervision. However, a general comment in the employee handbook is not enough; the organization must spell out the specifics. Another example of a well-regarded specific policy is Bank of America's policy on AIDS, which accounts for both business and ethical issues in defining the appropriate administrative behavior for supervisors with subordinates who have AIDS.

In a final critical comment suggesting that codes of ethics may be codes of convenience, Cressey and Moore state:

> In our judgment, in fact, 106 of the 119 codes are either paternalistic or authoritarian in tone, telling employees in effect that ethical expertise is correlated positively with salary and status. This assumption is particularly ironic in view of the

fact . . . that managers, especially lower-level ones, find pressure from above to be a significant factor in the compromising of personal ethics and also in view of the fact that top-level executives were frequently implicated in, if not the initiators of, much of the ethically questionable behavior those codes were intended to correct.[33]

Culture

Moving beyond "organizational culture" as the buzz-word of the decade, we have a level of meaning that is very different from the other paradigms. With strongly shared systems of beliefs and values the organization may take on a distinctive and powerful public or private identity. In a world that many people feel has increasingly disintegrating ethical standards, the organization has the opportunity to unite its work force around a strong set of ethical values. As Peters and Waterman note, organizational members "desperately need meaning in . . . [their] lives and will sacrifice a great deal to institutions that will provide meaning."[34] Of course, this potential strength is also a potential weakness. We are back to the ethical dilemma of leadership. The strong identity which can produce noble behavior can also solidify individuals behind an immoral cause or push them to abdicate individual responsibility.

Regardless of the danger, the culture paradigm gets to the heart of the organization as a symbol of meaning. In *Leadership in Administration,* Philip Selznick notes that distinctive organizational values result in "discernable and repetitive modes of responding to internal and external pressures."[35] This force in the socialization process can determine, with or without written rules and formal policy, the way people interact, the process and criteria for decision making, and the essence of the informal social structure of the organization. In elaborating on this point Selznick states the following:

> In what is perhaps its most significant meaning, "to institutionalize" is to *infuse with* value beyond the technical requirements of the task at hand. The prizing of social machinery

beyond its technical role is largely a reflection of the unique way in which it fulfills personal or group needs. Whenever individuals become attached to an organization or a way of doing things as persons rather than as technicians, the result is a prizing of the device for its own sake. From the standpoint of the committed person the organization is changed from an expendable tool into a valued source of personal satisfaction.[36]

We see, then, that the same process that provides meaning allows individuals to default by finding support in conforming with the "company way." Organizations which have such strong cultures may also regard their policies and practices as *inherently* moral. And, remaining true to this culture becomes the criterion for ethical behavior. An application of this idea is found in the following statement of Bowen McCoy, president of Morgan Stanley Realty:

> Business ethics, then, has to do with the authenticity and integrity of the enterprise. To be ethical is to follow the business as well as the cultural goals of the corporation, its owners, its employees, and its customers. Those who cannot serve the corporate vision are not authentic business people and, therefore, are not ethical in the business sense.[37]

An additional negative possibility of the strong culture model comes with the rapidly changing environment. As conditions change there may well be a need for new strategies which conflict with the old culture. An advance in technology or a rapid increase in the size of the organization can create a situation where a culture, developed in a small firm with simple technology, is unable to adjust. In such a situation, members often feel betrayed and unsure of their values and direction.

Overall, I suggest that paradigms are not objectively good or bad; they are more or less useful or appropriate within a specific context. They have their strengths or weaknesses in helping us to think more clearly and to act more ethically.

I find it interesting to note two broader paradigms which I like that are increasingly used in describing and leading organizations. One is the educational paradigm where "life is a learning experience." The capacity to learn from all experiences is a rare skill. And while some would argue that it may suppress action in favor of reflection, it offers a useful framework for many of our organizational encounters.

A second paradigm I like comes from the world of music. In the Zubin Mehta training films *Bolero* and *Commitment and Fulfillment as a Way of Life*, we find the values and metaphors of music applied to organizational life. Things such as harmony, balance, rhythm, conductors, score, inspiration, and passion reflect the less competitive, less destructive world of the symphony or the jazz group. I have found that these metaphors serve many organizations well when it comes to describing ethical relationships. In fact, in one organization I have worked with, organizational change was particularly effected by encouraging a transition from cowboy to music metaphors.

CONCLUSIONS

Ethics as a Topic for Instruction

In an attack on the current interest in business ethics, Peter Drucker states that we are witnessing "another fad" and "only the latest round in the hoary American blood sport of business baiting."[38] While I agree with much of his argument, I am very troubled by his conclusions. He is concerned that attempts to teach ethics could result in simply more elegant arguments that managers could use to rationalize irresponsible behavior. He feels that by focusing on the consequences of the action, managers would learn to justify practices whose means were troublesome but seemed to create benefits for a number of individuals. I strongly share that concern but wonder why he rejects the increased interest as inferior because of assumed weaknesses in one of the means. Clearly the utilitarian logic of "greatest good for greatest number" could be used to defend payment of a bribe to secure a contract in order to maintain employment for thousands of individuals. But I think we can do better than teach people to rationalize.

As this essay argues, and as Williams discusses in his rejoin-

der to Drucker, moral judgment requires much more than evaluation of the consequences of the action.[39] While many individuals may reject the attempt to improve understanding of ethics
because they do not like one particular school of thought, I think
they either miss the entire point or are consciously developing a
subterfuge. Organizational ethics requires a careful consideration of many different ethical perspectives (which, of course, is
itself an ethical prescription) prior to passing judgment or acting.

Managing the Paradoxes

It is said that "dancers always dance with pain, and usually
with injury." I would argue that those who hold positions of
responsibility in organizations similarly manage with pain and
usually with injury. The burden of resolving a variety of paradoxical demands and choosing defensible strategies will always
be painful if one is really sensitive to the ethical considerations
in organizational life.

Organizational ethics cannot be controlled only by leaders.
Such issues must be managed by both leaders and members—
people of all levels must be involved in disciplining the system.
We need not just rules and policies (although we do need those),
but a way of thinking about organizations, leadership, and
membership which respects and supports ethical relationships.
It is understood that strategic demands or emergencies may
require decisive and perhaps exploitive action at times. However, a larger climate of ethical decisions and behavior would
create enough slack that such occasional action would have less
harmful effect. But, the real test is what people feel the decision
makers really understand and value, and how they act with
respect to the organization and the individual.

The Increasing Complexity

For an increasing number of people there is an ethical dimension to organizational activities which serves as an end itself.
For them, efficient performance is neither a necessary nor

sufficient justification for unethical behavior. They assume that people ought to behave with decency and respect toward others in the organization, and they are unwilling to accept or consider means or ends which are inconsistent with their values.

In a world with so many vulnerable subgroups and so many people trying to find "their role" on the organizational stage, ethical dilemmas are likely to continue to increase. As we struggle for the institutional equity an ethical system demands for racial groups, religious minorities, women, senior citizens, youth, people at different socioeconomic levels, and other emerging subsets of the population, we have to realize that definitions, commitment, and ability will be severely challenged. As we have seen in the Middle East, when a group feels it has been treated unethically, rational discourse is not a quick panacea. It will be a great test of our potential to see if we can develop ethical systems soon enough to prevent a destructive fight.

My hope is that we can be sophisticated enough to apply the appropriate paradigm when it fits and to reject it when it doesn't. I also hope we can be simple enough to stand by an ethical principle even when it is unpopular or costly to do so.

As I said in the beginning, I perceive the purpose of this essay to be one of increasing the dialogue, asking questions, and suggesting topics for reflection. I hope the dialogue will continue. Our effectiveness and our humanity may both depend on it.

Notes

1. Isadore Barmash, ed., *Great Business Disasters*, rev. ed. (New York: Ballantine Books, 1972), 292.

2. Philip Selznick, *TVA and the Grass Roots* (New York: Harper, Torchbooks, 1966), 266.

3. Lewis Thomas, *The Lives of a Cell* (New York: Bantam Books, 1974), 129.

4. Myron Magnet, "The Decline and Fall of Business Ethics," *Fortune*, 8 December 1986, p. 65.

5. Karl E. Weick, *The Social Psychology of Organizing* (Reading, Mass.: Addison-Wesley, 1979), 18.

6. Mary Harrington Hall, "A Conversation with Peter F. Drucker: Or the Psychology of Managing Management," in *Organization and People: Readings, Cases, and Exercises in Organizational Behavior*, ed. J. B. Ritchie and Paul Thompson, 3d ed. (St. Paul: West, 1984), 27.

7. Reinhold Niebuhr, *Moral Man and Immoral Society* (1932; reprint, New York: Charles Scribner's Sons, 1960), 257.

8. Ibid., xi.

9. Ibid.

10. Gene Laczniak, "Business Ethics: A Manager's Primer," *Business* [Georgia State University School of Business] (January-March 1983): 23–29.

11. Raymond C. Baumhart, "How Ethical Are Businessmen?" *Harvard Business Review* 39 (July-August 1961): 16.

12. Steven N. Brenner and Earl A. Molander, "Is the Ethics of Business Changing?" *Harvard Business Review* 55 (January-February 1977): 57–71.

13. Archie B. Carroll, "A Survey of Managerial Ethics: Is Business Morality Watergate Morality?" *Business and Society Review* 13 (Spring 1975): 58–60.

14. Laczniak, "Business Ethics," 27.

15. Arlie Russell Hochschild, *The Managed Heart* (Berkeley: University of California Press, 1983), 7.

16. George H. Litwin and Robert A. Stringer, *Motivation and Organizational Climate* (Boston: Harvard University, Graduate School of Business Administration, 1968).

17. William G. Dyer, *The Sensitive Manipulator* (Provo, Utah: Brigham Young University Press, 1972).

18. John Gardner, *Grendel* (New York: Ballantine Books, 1971), 104.

19. Reinhold Niebuhr, *The Children of Light and The Children of Darkness* (New York: Charles Scribner's Sons, 1944), p. xi.

20. J. Bonner Ritchie, "Supervision," in *Organizational Behavior*, ed. George Strauss et al. (Madison, Wis.: Industrial Relations Research Association, 1974), chap. 3, 51–76.

21. James MacGregor Burns, *Leadership* (New York: Harper and Row, 1978), 20.

22. Milton Friedman, *Capitalism and Freedom* (Chicago: University of Chicago Press, 1962).

23. Kenneth R. Andrews, "Can the Best Corporations be Made Moral?" *Harvard Business Review* 51 (May-June 1973): 57–64.

24. Ibid., 687.

25. Magnet, "Decline and Fall of Business Ethics," 68.

26. Robert W. Keidel, "Professor Bear," *M.B.A.: The Magazine for Business Professionals* 1 (January 1987): 44.

27. M. Maccoby, *The Gamesman* (New York: Bantam Books, 1976).

28. Albert Z. Carr, "Is Business Bluffing Ethical?" *Harvard Business Review* 46 (January-February 1968): 146.

29. Keidel, "Professor Bear," 49.

30. Ford S. Worthy, "Wall Street's Spreading Scandal," *Fortune*, 22 December 1986, p. 28.

31. See William G. Dyer and W. Gibb Dyer, Jr., "How Organizations Lost Their Integrity," *Exchange* (Brigham Young University School of Management), Fall 1982, 26-31; D. R. Cressey and C. A. Moore, "Managerial Values and Corporate Codes of Ethics," *California Management Review* 25 (Summer 1983): 53–77; O. F. Williams, "Business Ethics: A Trojan Horse?" *California Management Review* 24 (Summer 1982): 14–24; and David J. Cherrington and J. Owen Cherrington, "The Climate of Honesty in Retail Stores," in *Employee Theft: Research, Theory, and Applications*, ed. William Terris (Park Ridge, Ill.: London House Press, 1985), 3–16.

32. Anne McGrath, "The Touchy Issue of Sexual Harassment," *Savvy*, April 1987, 18–19.

33. Cressey and Moore, "Managerial Values," 63.

34. Thomas J. Peters and Robert H. Waterman, *In Search of Excellence* (New York: Warner Books, 1982), 56.

35. Philip Selznick, *Leadership in Administration* (New York: Harper and Row, 1957), 16.

36. Ibid., 17.

37. Bowen H. McCoy, "The Parable of the Sadhu," *Harvard Business Review* 61 (September-October 1983): 107.

38. Peter Drucker, "Ethical Chic," *Forbes*, 14 September 1981, p. 160.

39. Williams, "Business Ethics."

CHAPTER EIGHT

Reason of State as Political Morality: A Benign View

John A. Rohr

THE purpose of this essay is to examine the meaning of "political morality," that is, a morality that is appropriate for statesmen. My concern is limited to the federal government of the United States. Concretely, therefore, I am writing about a morality to guide members of Congress and their staffs, federal judges and their clerks, and relatively high-ranking officials in the executive branch of government and in independent federal agencies.

Needless to say, such an essay is a venture in political realism. It is therefore appropriate that I should turn at the outset to the foremost American political realist of our century, Reinhold Niebuhr. In the introduction to his classic treatise on realism, *Moral Man and Immoral Society*, Niebuhr insists that "a sharp distinction must be drawn between the moral and social behavior of individuals and of social groups, national, racial, and economic."[1] The book goes on to argue most persuasively that we ignore this distinction at our peril. By the end of the book the reader must be impressed with the powerful case

John A. Rohr is a professor of public administration at the Center for Public Administration and Policy, Virginia Polytechnic Institute.

Niebuhr makes to show why it is unwise, unfair, and even dangerous to apply to governments the sorts of moral analyses we apply to matters of individual conscience. Niebuhr's readers will remember this point years later because the pithy title of the book—*Moral Man and Immoral Society*—captures the argument so nicely.

The careful reader, however, might be a bit perplexed by a puzzling concession Niebuhr makes on the very first page of his introduction. Referring to the distinction between individual and collective morality, he notes that "the title 'Moral Man and Immoral Society' suggests the intended distinction too unqualifiedly, but it is nevertheless a fair indication of the argument to which the following pages are devoted."[2]

The reason the title exaggerates the distinction between individual and collective morality is that Niebuhr does not maintain that society itself is simply immoral. Instead, his point is that collective morality is *inferior* to personal morality. He does not say there is no collective morality at all. Throughout his book, however, he tells us precious little about this inferior morality that is nevertheless *morality* in some sense, despite its inferiority. When he does talk about it, the discussion is usually framed in descriptive rather than analytic terms. We come to know this inferior morality not in its principles and foundation, but in the way it is expressed in human affairs—as, for example, when man indulges his acquisitive or warlike passions. The thrust of Niebuhr's argument is to urge the folly of applying lofty personal standards to such messy and complicated affairs because such efforts lead either to fanaticism or to cynicism.[3] He has little to say about the inferior moral principles that govern such affairs.

Moral Man and Immoral Society was first published in 1932. It was reprinted in 1960 with the addition of a one-page preface. Looking back over the decades, Niebuhr restates the thesis of the book: "The central thesis was, and is, that the Liberal Movement both religious and secular seemed to be unconscious of the basic difference between the morality of individuals and the *morality of collectives,* whether races, classes, or nations."[4] Thus in 1960, as in 1932, it was quite clear to Niebuhr that there is a collective morality. In this essay, I examine one aspect of collective morality, the collective morality of the state. What does it mean in practice to talk about a political morality that is quite different from personal morality and yet in some sense can be called "morality?"

Such questions did not begin with Niebuhr. The elaborate and extensive literature on "reason of state" in the sixteenth and seventeenth centuries represents an effort to save some semblance of morality in public affairs on the part of thoughtful men who could not dismiss out of hand the brilliant, but shocking, insights of Machiavelli.[5] The expression "reason of state" did not originate with Machiavelli. Indeed, he never used the term. It first appeared in the writings of authors who set out to refute Machiavelli on his own grounds. For the most part, they were religious men who objected strenuously to Machiavelli's cynical advice to the prince to subordinate religion (along with everything else) to political ends. Their interests went beyond religion, however. They saw the need to answer Machiavelli's hardheaded realism if traditional morality was to influence statecraft. Instead of denying Machiavelli's argument that the prince must be cunning and deceptive, the reason-of-state authors developed an elaborate casuistry to justify questionable actions *within* the framework of traditional morality. A favorite topic was to show how the prince might deceive others without actually lying. Thus Pedro Ribadeneyra, a prominent sixteenth-century Jesuit, condemned Machiavelli roundly but developed a sophisticated argument to assure the prince that certain forms of equivocation were not really lies. "So likewise is it no lie . . . to say certain true words in one sense, although he who says them should believe that he who hears them, because they are equivocal, will be able to take them in another way."[6] Giovanni Botero's *Ragion di Stato* provides abundant examples of similar types of moral reasoning addressed to statesmen.[7]

This sort of casuistry has been severely criticized over the centuries as shallow and contemptible. What the self-righteous critics forget, however, is that Machiavelli's work demanded some kind of answer. Machiavelli was being read by real princes.

The early reason-of-state authors were trying to formulate a political morality that took Machiavelli seriously but was still in some sense a genuine, though inferior, morality that would guide statesmen in managing their weighty affairs. Machiavelli's work required counterarguments as well as condemnation.

In France, the doctrine of reason of state was closely linked with both Jean Bodin's famous work on the legal concept of sovereignty and the remnants of the medieval tradition that celebrated the sacral character of the king. The offspring of this fertile union of legal principle and religious tradition was the doctrine of the divine right of kings. That is, the king is chosen by God to rule the people and temporarily embodies in his person the plenitude of sovereignty that passes to his successor upon his death. Reason of state in the service of a king chosen by God was a two-edged sword. On the one hand, it provided a rationale for the arrogance that accompanies any form of absolutism and eventually contributed to the overthrow of the *ancien régime*. On the other hand, however, the religious underpinnings of rule by divine right urged caution and restraint on the king in the exercise of his powers. Although as sovereign he was above the positive law, court preachers never wearied of reminding the king that he was *God's* representative among men and should conduct himself accordingly. Thus the practical application of reason of state in political affairs was tempered by the softening effects of religious traditions that recognized both a natural law and a divine revelation that even kings chosen by God could not violate. Cardinal Richelieu was perhaps the consummate practitioner of the morality of reason of state. He was wily and shrewd, but not unscrupulous. His famous *Political Testament* clearly indicates a distinction between two kinds of morality—one for public affairs and the other for one's personal life.[8]

The quest for precedents for Niebuhr's political morality need not end with the era of royal absolutism. One can go back even further and find hints of a distinctively political morality in such an unlikely source as St. Thomas Aquinas.

Aquinas's moral teaching rested on his magisterial exposition of the natural law tradition. Although he held that certain activities were morally demanded and others morally prohibited by man's nature, he was quite circumspect in applying his doctrine to concrete human behavior. His moral teaching was characterized by careful attention to the way in which the complexity of circumstances confounds the best of principles. Nowhere is this clearer than in his elegant treatment of the virtue of prudence, where *gnome* ("the wit to judge the exceptional") is treated as one of the virtues he describes as an "ally" of the virtue of prudence *(de virtutibus adjunctis prudentiae)*. *Gnome* is a virtue in its own right because "sometimes it happens that something has to be done which is not covered by the ordinary rules of conduct." That such a situation can arise is itself an important concession from an adherent to the natural law tradition—far more important than a similar concession from a contemporary philosopher who is likely to reject teleology and, along with it, the finely structured moral universe of St. Thomas Aquinas. For St. Thomas, prudence is the virtue that inclines man to apply general principles correctly to specific situations. If, however, a situation arises that does not fall under a general rule, prudence will be of no avail. Enter *gnome*, which is variously translated as "the wit to judge the exceptional" or "the ability to judge rightly over the extraordinary things of life." Quite significantly, the only example Aquinas gives of *gnome* is taken from political life—we need not "return a deposit entrusted to us by a would-be attacker of our country."[9] The ordinary rule of justice is that deposits should be returned upon demand, but political events create a situation that overrides that principle. If Aquinas had been a modern utilitarian or a modern "situationist," his discussion of *gnome* would be unremarkable. But he is neither of these. He is the most authoritative exponent of the natural law tradition and for that reason does not take lightly exceptions to general moral rules. In political matters, however, he does make an exception and maintains that the exception itself is grounded in a virtue: the virtue of prudence.

I do not suggest that Aquinas was a political realist as that term is attributed to Niebuhr today. Nor do I suggest that he anticipated the *raison d'état* authors of the sixteenth and seventeenth centuries. My purpose in mentioning Aquinas is simply to establish the point that even in the morally conservative natural law tradition there is willingness to recognize at least two levels of morality for political affairs.

In the opening sentence of this essay I stated that my purpose was to examine the meaning of "political morality." Thus far I have not *proved* that such a morality exists nor do I intend to do so. I simply call upon the authority of Aquinas, Niebuhr, and the reason-of-state tradition to *assert* the existence of such a morality. If my assertion is wrong, I shall find comfort in such distinguished company. My purpose in writing is to see what this political morality might mean in practice for American statesmen.

Before getting into the practical details of what such a morality might look like in practice, however, there are other preliminary matters that must be clarified or at least acknowledged if they cannot be clarified.

Political morality is necessarily problematic because moral principles are usually announced in universal terms, but politics is necessarily particularistic. The moralist asks if it is wrong to lie. He does not ask if it is wrong for Englishmen or Russians to lie. Political life is necessarily led within the confines of a regime that is based on certain specific principles—or at least on certain specific events or myths that enjoy some sort of normative influence. Thus, politics contrasts sharply with science, religion, and the arts. These forms of human activity transcend national boundaries. A symphony that was pleasing only to Italians would be a strange symphony. This is why scientists, artists, and religious men and women make life so difficult for statesmen. They cannot be counted on to yield to the blandishments of patriotic rhetoric. They have seriously grounded reasons for standing in judgment on the ways of statecraft. This is even more true of philosophers, as we know from Plato's account of the death of Socrates and even more importantly from the argument of the *Republic*.[10]

Before we examine the meaning of political morality, we must somehow establish the justice of the particular regime we are discussing—in our case the United States. Obviously, a full discussion of such a topic would take us too far afield to pursue the stated purpose of this essay. Once again, I shall settle the problem by fiat and simply assert that the United States is a fundamentally just regime. If it is not, then it is futile to discuss how one can be a moral statesman in such a regime. The proper postures toward fundamentally unjust regimes are emigration, subversion, or revolution—but not public service.[11]

I use the term "reason of state" in the title of this essay. I do so with some misgivings because political scientists tell us that we Americans have a weak idea of "state."[12] I think this is a sound observation and I was tempted to use the term "reason of society" to capture more precisely the moral dimensions of American statecraft. I decided against this neologism, however, because I want to highlight my attempt to write in a reason-of-state tradition, even though that tradition does not accommodate nicely the American political heritage. Americans cannot be expected to look kindly on a doctrine that spent its finest hours defending the divine right of kings.[13]

Reason of state has been burdened with some terrifying meanings in recent political science literature. For example, it has been defined as "the doctrine that whatever is required to insure the survival of the state must be done by the individuals responsible for it, no matter how repugnant such an act may be to them in their private capacity as decent and moral men."[14] That definition is too broad; "whatever is required" includes far too much. Such a definition goes beyond the "problem of dirty hands" because it says statesmen *must* do nasty deeds when state survival is at stake.[15] I am not prepared to go that far. The more realistic question is not what must be done but what may be done.

Even the question of what sorts of foul deeds may (as opposed to must) be done to insure the survival of the state is somewhat peripheral to what I have in mind. There have been times when

American statesmen have had to worry about the survival of the regime itself. The Civil War is the most obvious example and may be the only one before the arrival of the nuclear age. I am not really interested in such dramatic issues as the survival of the regime, important as such questions are when they arise. My focus is more pedestrian. I am interested in the statesman's *attitude* toward governing that permeates his approach to questions that are of moral significance but fall short of such ultimate questions as the survival of the regime.

If this is reason of state at all, it is a rather benign version of that doctrine—a point I have tried to capture in the title of this essay. I am not really interested in the question of when the courtier may dissemble in the service of his prince. I am interested in whether an American statesman might be morally justified in using the stability of the existing political order as the basic motive for his decision in two types of situations: (1) when serious moral considerations can be found on both sides of a two-sided issue, and (2) when he is inclined to engage in activities that are morally suspect but not absolutely prohibited.[16] I examine the substantive issues of sanctions against South Africa and of affirmative action to illustrate the first situation. For the second situation I examine the morality of a public official attempting to influence religious beliefs about abortion in order to discourage certain tendencies in the abortion debate that threaten political stability.

My discussion of all three topics is instrumental. That is, I mention South Africa, affirmative action, and abortion only to give concrete examples of political issues freighted with moral values that will enable me to explain my benign view of reason of state. My discussion of these substantive areas is highly selective and the canon of selection is based on what will clarify my argument rather than anything I might have to say on the merits of each of these issues. Finally, I must acknowledge that some readers will find the outcome of the argument distasteful and perhaps even shocking. I would remind such readers that the morality I am trying to explain is *ex hypothesi* different from and inferior to personal morality.

SOUTH AFRICA

To consider the meaning of political morality in the case of South Africa, let us put ourselves in the position of a congressman on 29 September 1986. The House of Representatives is about to vote on the motion to override President Reagan's veto of an earlier congressional action imposing sanctions on South Africa. The moral arguments on both sides have been straightforward. Those favoring sanctions maintain that American trade with South Africa gives aid and comfort to the supporters of apartheid. If the United States reduces or eliminates its trade with South Africa, the Botha government will begin to change its ways. Those opposing sanctions maintain that poor blacks in South Africa will be hurt far more severely than the leaders of their government. Sanctions will encourage these leaders to "hunker down" in a siege mentality. They have the military force to "hang tough" for decades. By imposing sanctions, the United States will lose what little influence it has through application of the "Sullivan principles."

Let us assume our congressman has followed all these arguments carefully and finds himself undecided. He honestly does not know which argument is more persuasive. This is an important assumption. (If he were certain that a vote for sanctions would have disastrous results for South African blacks and only reinforce the apartheid regime, his moral duty would be quite clear.) Let us further assume that he is from a district that shows little interest in the whole issue. The indifference of constituents makes it relatively easy for him to "vote his conscience" on the motion to override.

If he were to think in terms of a political morality, he might decide in favor of sanctions in order to give black congressmen and the black leadership throughout the United States a sense of accomplishing a serious foreign policy victory. As a matter of fact, this was how many black leaders interpreted "their" victory over President Reagan when Congress did override the veto. Congressman Mickey Leland, a prominent member of the Congressional Black Caucus, described the override as "probably the greatest victory we've ever experienced." Similar sentiments were echoed by other black congressmen such as William Gray and John Conyers.

The congressman in our example (he is white) would make this decision on hardheaded reasons of state and not on sentimental or condescending grounds. He would see a serious public interest at stake in having the black leadership realize that its effectiveness is not limited to inner city/ghetto/urban poverty issues. There is a public interest involved in encouraging a new generation of black leaders to raise their sights beyond the traditional issues that have understandably preoccupied civil rights groups in the past. Such a consideration is particularly attractive in an era of budget cutting when pleas for new social programs are likely to fall on deaf ears. It is important for ambitious black leaders to see themselves as persons solidly integrated into the American political system. To see themselves this way, they must win a few of "the big ones." Sanctioning South Africa is one of the big ones.

If our congressman had been paying more than ordinary attention to the moral arguments that enveloped the sanctions debate, he would recall the conservative complaint that the United States was being inconsistent in the way it pursues moral goals in foreign policy. Conservatives wonder why we go out of our way to increase trade with such repressive regimes as the People's Republic of China and the Soviet Union, while we come down so hard on South Africa. Our congressman would recognize this argument as the kissing cousin of the liberal complaint that we grant political asylum to refugees from the Soviet Union and other Communist countries, but we will not extend the same gracious treatment to refugees from El Salvador and Haiti. Although consistency is an important element in moral reasoning, our congressman would realize that the call for evenhandedness in foreign policy is suspect. First of all, no nation has an obligation to right all wrongs. It is morally defensible to be selective in the wrongs we choose to right. Certainly one criterion for selection would be that we try to right wrongs where there is a reasonable chance that we might be successful.

There is very little we can do to change the ways of the Soviet Union or the People's Republic of China. Like ourselves, they change as their interests indicate. This may not be the case with South Africa. At present there is a "reasonable chance" (though surely no more than a reasonable chance) that we might be able to encourage salutary changes in that ill-starred nation.

There is another reason for singling out an apartheid regime as the object of our sense of moral indignation. It is our own unhappy history of racism, a history we are trying to put behind us. Some might argue that our own checkered past exposes our hypocrisy when we preach to those who support apartheid. Political morality is not impressed with that line of argument; it understands that hypocrisy is the tribute that vice pays to virtue. Political morality reminds us that we should be particularly sensitive to issues of racism—more sensitive than most other nations that have been spared our sorry history in this matter. In a sense we are like reformed smokers and reformed alcoholics. We may make ourselves obnoxious when we preach to the rest of the world about the evils of racism. Perhaps the rest of the world pays little attention to us, as it pays little attention to crusading ex-smokers. Nevertheless, our preaching is good *for us*, even if no one else pays us any heed. In singling out South African racism for our moral outrage, we are serving our national interests. We make it less likely that we will become backsliders in our own moral struggles against racism. We are like the athletes who once used illegal drugs and now tell our children to say "no to drugs." It is hard to tell if their preaching keeps any youngsters from using drugs, but it may keep the athletes themselves on the straight and narrow path.

There is one final consideration that might trouble our congressman. Some critics of sanctions maintain that they will impose serious hardships on our own economy. If this is true, it would certainly be a powerful argument against sanctions. Unfortunately, this argument never got a serious hearing. The argument was lost in the midst of Donald Regan's incredible blunder when, referring to anticipated reductions in the importation of diamonds from South Africa, he asked, "Are the women of

America prepared to give up all their jewelry?"[17] This remark was immediately denounced as sexist by those who took it seriously and as ludicrous by those who consider Regan an inept buffoon. What was quickly forgotten was the context in which Regan made this remark. He was briefing reporters on the administration's position on the likely effects of the proposed sanctions. He had some pointed comments about possible adverse effects on our domestic steel industry and our need for "industrial diamonds—things that we need for etching, cutting, shaping of tools and so forth."[18] In this context he uttered his ill-fated remarks about women's jewelry. If there was any merit to the broader point he was making, it was lost in the uproar over his sexist comment. If it turns out that sanctions do have an adverse effect on our own economy, the fault will lie as much with Regan for his ineptness in making his case as with the proponents of sanctions who hooted at Regan. Political morality is unforgiving. Donald Regan sinned against political morality in permitting what might have been a serious consideration to become lost in a remark that was both ludicrous and offensive.

AFFIRMATIVE ACTION

To examine affirmative action in the light of political morality, we shall put ourselves in the place of a federal district judge who must decide whether an affirmative action program for promoting minority police officers violates either the Civil Rights Act of 1964 or the equal protection clause of the Fourteenth Amendment. The plaintiffs in the case are white officers who maintain they are the victims of "reverse discrimination." Let us assume that the facts of this case are such that strong legal precedents can be found to support both the plaintiffs and the defendant municipality.[19] The purpose of this assumption is to take our judge out of the situation in which he mechanically applies absolutely clear precedents to factual situations. In a word, our judge must make a policy choice that will be driven to a considerable extent by his assessment of the moral claims raised on both sides of the issue.

The moral case for affirmative action looks to the past. It stresses the lasting effects of historical wrongs perpetrated against a racial or ethnic group. These people are disadvantaged today because of injustices visited upon their forebears decades or even centuries ago. Their slogan is, "Let's play catch up."

The counterargument looks to the present. Disgruntled whites sympathize with the plight of minority groups but complain that they are being punished for wrongs they did not commit. The equal protection clause protects *persons*, not groups. As individual persons, they are being made to expiate the guilt of others. Their slogan is, "Two wrongs don't make a right."

If our judge is favorably inclined toward the moral argument for affirmative action, he will need a principled response to the complaints of white policemen who correctly point out that their parents or grandparents suffered considerable injustice when they arrived in the United States from Italy, Poland, Ireland, or Greece. Why should the government take more seriously the injustices perpetrated against blacks, Hispanics, and Native Americans than those perpetrated against Italians, Poles, and Greeks?

There is one answer to this question that is particularly helpful for establishing a principled distinction between historic injustices against blacks and traditional immigrant groups. Quite simply, blacks were not immigrants. Their ancestors were brought here against their will. They entered the United States (or a British colony that eventually became one of the United States) with a different and inferior *legal* status from that of the traditional immigrant. The injustice against blacks was *state* injustice—formal and quite legal. The injustice against Poles, Italians, et al., though quite real, was societal, informal, and extralegal.

This does not mean that blacks necessarily suffered greater injustices than the traditional immigrants. It may well be that some slaves and their freedmen progeny lived happier lives than some immigrants and their progeny. This consideration, however, is irrelevant to my argument. I am not interested in standing Bentham on his head and constructing a calculus of suffering. In my argument it makes no difference how *much* one's ancestors suffered. What matters is the *source* of the suffering. For blacks it was the state; for traditional immigrants it was society. Affirmative action programs mandated by the state are appropriate remedies for righting the wrongs perpetrated by the state against the members of a once-enslaved race. It is appropriate that these remedies benefit only those who were the victims of state-sponsored injustice. That is why it is fair for the state to sponsor a promotion policy in a police department that prefers black officers to, say, Italian officers.

Affirmative action programs for minorities benefit groups other than black Americans. The favored groups (in addition to blacks) are Hispanics, American Indians, Alaskan Natives (Aleuts), Asians, and Pacific Islanders. Does the state/society distinction help to justify a principled difference between these groups and the traditional immigrant groups? I think it does, but the argument is not nearly as clear as it is when applied to blacks. Nevertheless, let us see where the argument will take us.

Each of the preferred groups can claim that the injustices against their ancestors were the result of state action. This is because their ancestors became "Americans" as a result of state action rather than by immigration. Take the case of Samoans, who are Pacific Islanders. Their land originally came under American jurisdiction through a tripartite protectorate agreed to by Germany, England, and the United States in 1889. Samoans are Americans for reasons of state. So are Aleuts; they entered the American community as a result of our purchase of Alaska from Russia in 1867. The injustices they have experienced as Americans can be traced to the state actions that made them Americans.

At least some Asiatics were the object of state-based discrimination because of the Chinese Exclusion Act of 1882 which severely restricted Chinese immigration. Other Asiatics suffered legal disabilities imposed by certain western states during the first half of this century. American Indians were the losers in a series of wars and military skirmishes fought against white settlers bearing arms in the name of the state. They are singled out as a group apart from the rest of Americans in the first and eighth sections of the first article of the Constitution.

Hispanic Americans present the most difficult case. It is necessary to distinguish between Puerto Rican Americans and Mexican Americans. The former are clearly Americans by state action—conquest during the Spanish-American War. The latter are more problematic. Those Mexicans residing in territories conquered by the United States during the Mexican War clearly became Americans by state action. Those who came to the United States of their own volition are like the traditional immigrants from Europe and have no stronger moral claim upon the state for compensatory treatment than the descendants of immigrants from Poland, Ireland, or Italy.

By applying the distinction between injustices perpetrated by the state and those perpetrated by society, we can offer a principled reply to non-Hispanic whites who correctly point out that their ancestors also suffered discrimination. Although the fit is not perfect, it comes close to justifying the status quo that favors blacks, Hispanics, Asians, American Indians, and Aleuts at the expense of other racial and ethnic groups. The fit is not perfect because the distinction I have drawn between state discrimination and societal discrimination is not as neat and tidy in fact as it is in principle. Also, some of the preferred groups are over-inclusive; that is, they include persons whose ancestors did not suffer any state-based wrongs—for example, Mexican immigrants who came here voluntarily. (I set aside the question of illegal immigrants. Their presence in the United States outrages political morality, regardless of the strength of their claim on higher moral grounds. The integrity of national borders is a state imperative of the highest order.)

Of all the preferred groups, however, blacks have the most serious claim. The state-based injustices visited upon the other groups were the results of ordinary state action—treaty, war, and control of immigration. This is not true of slavery. Slavery was a form of state-based injustice that was extraordinary even as it flourished. The civilized world looked on the slave trade as a moral abomination.[20] It did not so regard imperialist wars or the acquisition of an empire by treaty or by purchase. To be sure, there were always critics of imperialism, and many indeed were the domestic and foreign critics of the morality of our war with Mexico and of our war with Spain. But these were matters of opinion. Good and decent men were found on both sides of the argument. Not so with slavery. The slave trade flouted a settled consensus that such practice was simply wrong. American Negroes are the descendants of persons who were wronged by the state in a way that no other group in this country has been wronged. The state tolerated and at times encouraged the institution of slavery. By "the state" in this case, I mean both the mother country and the colonies during the colonial period and both the United States and the slave states after independence. Today, the United States is heir to all these earlier "states." If reason of state is in any sense a moral doctrine, it demands that some restitution be made.

If the argument from reason of state is pressed, it seems to me one could justify far more ambitious programs of affirmative action for blacks than we have known hitherto. Political morality is at ease when moral considerations coincide nicely with positive law. This is the case, if one wishes to argue that this nation should go much further in its affirmative action efforts for blacks. The first section of the Thirteenth Amendment prohibits slavery. The second section provides: "Congress shall have power to enforce this article by appropriate legislation." This provision is pregnant with possibilities for taking legal action to better the condition of blacks today. On several occasions, the Supreme Court of the United States has held that the constitutional prohibition against slavery reaches "the badges of slavery" as well.[21] In *Jones v. Mayer Co.* (1968),[22] the Court invoked the second clause of the Thirteenth Amendment to uphold a suit brought under the Civil Rights Act of 1866 which upheld the right of blacks to purchase property. Jones, a black man, maintained that the Alfred H. Mayer Co. had refused to sell a home to him because he was black. He brought his action under the nineteenth-century statute because the denial of purchase took place before the Open Housing Act of 1968 was in effect. The importance of the case, however, lies in the Court's sweeping language that gives Congress the authority to define what constitutes a "badge of slavery"—in this case the refusal to sell a home to a man because he is black. This argument will benefit only blacks because they alone are descended from slaves and therefore they alone can seriously claim to be burdened even today with the badge of slavery.

The Thirteenth Amendment prohibits slavery and (by judicial interpretation) the badges of slavery. Unlike the Fourteenth Amendment, the Thirteenth does not mention state action.[23] Therefore, private forms of discrimination against blacks that are tantamount to badges of slavery can (and have) been reached by federal law.[24] If there was a political will to take bold and imaginative steps to better the condition of American blacks today, constitutional arguments might well be found to justify affirmative action programs far beyond anything we have known to date. Perhaps even the constitutional prohibition against racial quotas in affirmative action programs would yield to Thirteenth Amendment considerations.

At present, of course, there is no such political will. Far-reaching affirmative action programs for blacks alone have about them an aura of political fantasy. This is due not only to the current mood of the conservative 1980s. The reason lies deeper in the American political tradition. The sort of affirmative action program I have suggested presupposes that one takes reason of state seriously. As Americans we do not take it seriously because we do not take the idea of "the state" seriously—as opposed, for example, to the way the French understand *l'état* as an abiding presence superior to *le gouvernement*.[25] To take seriously the idea of the state redressing wrongs *it* has committed in the distant past requires a political imagination that welcomes the idea of a legal personality extending over long periods of history. Such ideas smack of "corporatism" and are alien to our political traditions, even though they hold an honored place in our commercial relations.

Let us return to our federal judge whom we left pondering

these weighty matters some pages back. If, despite the frail American notion of state, he is still inclined to justify affirmative action on grounds of political morality, there is another line of argument he might pursue. This new line is not altogether appealing. It is devious and manipulative, but political morality has no pretensions about its place in the moral universe. It is a second-class citizen and is quite willing to act accordingly.

Let us join the judge as he looks at affirmative action for blacks from the point of view of what such a program can do for the state rather than what it can do for blacks. In the tenth *Federalist*, James Madison set forth his famous argument on why it is only a large republic that will successfully safeguard individual rights against the likely defects of republican government. In small republics, it is too likely that one permanent and stable faction will overwhelm another and leave nothing for the vanquished. In a large republic, however, there is such a diversity of economic interests that no one interest nor any one group of interests will combine on a *permanent* basis to overcome the rest. There will be constantly shifting alliances among men committed to diverse interests. A political system based on shifting economic alliances will provide a low but solid public life, free from a dangerous, strident politics based on such volatile grounds as religious opinion or other considerations we would call "doctrinaire" today.

Madison's proposition has passed into the canon of political science as the "Madisonian model" of contemporary pluralism. The First Amendment has successfully privatized religion so that public attention can be focused on lower but safer matters such as economic well-being. Indeed, so private is religion that we find ourselves constantly scolding preachers and prelates about the dangers of "imposing" their religious beliefs on society at large. We have learned from history how dangerous it is to ground a political system on religious belief. Indeed, who needs history? We need only look at Iran today.

In some ways, a political system based on race is no less volatile and therefore no less dangerous than a system based on religion. It is not good that the Democratic party virtually owns the black vote today. It is not good for blacks; but, more importantly, for the purposes of this argument, it is not good for the state.

Affirmative action holds out some possibility of dividing the black community along economic lines. More precisely, it holds out for blacks the possibility of reinforcing the tendency to divide along economic lines that one finds in nearly all American racial and ethnic groups. Critics of affirmative action have often noted that middle-class blacks are the most likely beneficiaries of most affirmative action policies. Admission to college, preferential promotions, and contractual "set-asides" for black businessmen are not the sorts of social programs that will accomplish anything for black people trapped in the vise of grinding poverty. Affirmative action programs can benefit only those black persons who have positioned themselves to make use of them. They give a slight edge to those who have just about "made it" on their own. Perhaps what holds them back are those vestiges of racism in our society (as opposed to our state which has thoroughly purged itself of racism). An aggressive affirmative action may just be enough to offset these unfair disadvantages.

From the point of view of the state, affirmative action has the advantage of accelerating the entrance of large numbers of blacks into the middle class both in an economic sense and, more importantly, in a social, political, and attitudinal sense. Once blacks are in the middle class, the statesman can hope that they will do what all other Americans do. They will think and feel and vote and spend in ways that further their economic interests rather than in ways that favor members of their race.

If our judge is a statesman, he will applaud this development because he fears race-based politics. He understands that the strength of his country lies in its massive middle class. His is not a bleeding heart. The suffering of the poor during the Reagan years troubles him because he is a decent man; but it troubles him far less than the threat of a gradual erosion of the middle class. He is especially alarmed at the prospect of large numbers of blacks falling from middle-class status to below the poverty line—a breeding ground for violent and revolutionary zealots. Churchmen, like the Catholic bishops, can be counted on to prick the nation's conscience with biblical injunctions on how the character of a nation is judged by the way it treats its poor. Perhaps the bishops are right, at least in terms of the criteria by which the bishops know we will all eventually be judged. The statesman, however, must remain clearheaded in such matters and adhere to the principles of political morality that prompt him to favor affirmative action because it will accelerate the arrival of great numbers of blacks into the middle-class culture that is the foundation of our liberal democratic regime. He admires from afar the exalted teaching of Jesus who tells us that whatever we do unto the *least* of his brethren we do unto him. Noble as this teaching is, it is not for the statesman to follow. Soberly, and perhaps a bit sadly, he puts the statesman's gloss on the sacred text—"Whatever you do for the most advantaged members of the least advantaged groups, you do for the state." This is the great merit of affirmative action. It helps not those who are most in need of help, but those who will know how to use it in a way that will stabilize the existing order.

ABORTION

In considering the abortion controversy in the light of political morality, we shall place ourselves in the position of an experienced and senior career civil servant in the Department of Health and Human Services. Unlike our congressman and our judge, he does not have a specific decision to make. His problem is that he must live day after day with the nasty controversies that surround the abortion issue. He is religious but not profoundly so. He realizes that his Roman Catholic background has strongly influenced his opposition to abortion. With twenty-five years of federal service to his credit, however, he has learned how to play the game by pluralist rules. At an earlier period in his life he had studied genetics. His scientific background has reinforced his religious beliefs on abortion. He thinks this may be the reason he finds himself in basic agreement with his church on the abortion issue, whereas he is in fundamental disagreement on other issues such as birth control and remarriage after divorce.

What he finds most troubling about the abortion issue is the large numbers of abortions that have taken place since the Supreme Court handed down its 1973 pro-choice decision in *Roe v. Wade*.[26] He has read reliable estimates that put the number in the range of sixteen million. He understands the pro-choice argument; it is grounded in a woman's claim to certain rights over her own body. Sometimes the argument is linked to a confident assertion that the fetus is not human. At other times the argument proceeds in disregard of the status of the fetus. In either case, however, the pro-choice position seems to have led to an inordinately large number of choices in favor of abortion. If sixteen million is an inflated figure, then what is the correct number? Fifteen million? Fourteen million? No matter what the exact number might be, it is large enough to be quite distressing for anyone with serious reservations about the morality of abortion. Despite these misgivings, our senior civil servant has never joined a pro-life group nor has he ever participated in any pro-life demonstrations. Although he supports the goals of the pro-lifers, he is embarrassed by their rhetoric and their tactics.

When he thinks in terms of political morality, his embarrassment turns to alarm. As a statesman, he is appalled at what the abortion controversy is doing to important state interests. Perhaps the most important matter is the way the abortion controversy has distorted the process by which federal judges have been selected by the Reagan administration. He is profoundly disturbed by reports that a prospective judge must be "right" on abortion before he or she will be seriously considered for an appointment. Secondly, he is concerned by the tendency of the abortion issue to encourage single-issue voting. This distorts the electoral process. Thirdly, he finds the bombing of abortion clinics quite distressing. As a statesman, he is instinctively uneasy about any form of lawlessness; but he is especially disturbed at lawlessness based on moral principle. Principled lawlessness forces the state to create prisoners of conscience;

but such actions tend to weaken the moral underpinnings of the legal system and threaten eventually to expose the system as raw power.

Our senior civil servant does not think it likely that serious pro-lifers will moderate their behavior. After all, many of them are quite serious when they say that every abortion is a murder. They believe that a human being is present at the moment of conception. If this is their position, why *should* they moderate their behavior? It is futile to appeal to their sense of patriotism by pleading with them to consider what they are doing to our political institutions. They would surely dismiss such pleas by asking why they should care about the well-being of a political order that has condoned sixteen million murders. They would find the Nazi analogy quite pertinent. It would be like asking decent and caring Germans to stop their lawless efforts to smuggle Jews into Switzerland. They would remind their critics that as far as they are concerned there is no difference between this nation's policy on abortion and a public policy that would permit the extermination of the handicapped, the insane, or any other group—racial, religious, or whatever—that happened to displease those who were able to shape the law to their wicked ends. Under such circumstances what would we think of people who did no more than "write their congressman" or march meekly in protest while the handicapped were being legally slaughtered by relatives who found their care burdensome?

With such thoughts in mind, our statesman would soon realize that the problem pro-lifers present to the state is not one that can be solved at a behavioral level. The problem is with their beliefs. Indeed, given the nature of their beliefs, it is remarkable that they have not been more obstreperous. The task of the statesman is to get the pro-lifers to reconsider their belief that every abortion is a murder. This is an extremely delicate matter. The American statesman has taken an oath to uphold the Constitution of the United States which protects one's right to believe whatever one wishes to believe. Political morality will not permit him to renege on that pledge, but there may be some actions he could take that would not violate his oath of office. He is, after all, not simply a statesman. His career does not exhaust his humanity. He is still a member of society as well as a man of the state. As a member of society, he could enter into a dialogue with pro-lifers and especially with his fellow Catholic pro-lifers to try to persuade them to reconsider their position on abortion as murder.

In the paragraphs that follow I sketch the main points of the argument our statesman might make in an effort to persuade pro-lifers to reconsider the grounds for their opposition to abortion.

He would begin by pointing out that one can certainly oppose abortion without believing that every abortion is a murder. The notion of murder implies an *intention* to kill an innocent human being. If a hunter kills another hunter he has mistaken for a deer, he has not committed murder. When he fired his gun, he intended to kill, but he did not intend to kill another human being. Likewise, an abortionist is not a murderer if he sincerely believes that the fetus he kills is not a human being. From the pro-lifer's point of view, an innocent human being is dead despite the abortionist's sincerity; but the same is true in the case of the dead hunter. Of course, there is no way of knowing just what a given abortionist believes. Some may be murderers and others may not be. The point of all this, however, is to convince the pro-lifers that even if there have been sixteen million abortions in this country, it does not necessarily follow that every one of them has involved a murder. This argument is not legalistic. The statesman is not talking about the *crime* of murder. It is obvious that the abortionist has committed no such crime under current American law. The statesman addresses murder as a *moral* offense, which is what the pro-lifers have in mind when they say abortion is murder.

Even if the pro-lifer should accept this argument, he would surely respond that it is not very helpful. The point about the subjective state of mind of the abortionist ignores the fact that, as far as a pro-lifer is concerned, every abortion results in the taking of the life of an innocent human being. This, of course, is the central issue for the entire abortion controversy. The states-man approaches it by reminding the pro-lifer that one might still oppose our current public policy on abortion even if one had some doubt about whether the fetus was a human being from the moment of conception. If I have some doubts about just when the fetus becomes human, then I would oppose abortion not because it involves killing an innocent person but because it *might* involve killing an innocent person. For example, suppose I should hear a footstep on my front porch late one evening. As a precaution I take my gun to the front door to investigate. I see a stranger on my porch and I shoot and kill him. The reason I kill him is that he might be a burglar, a kidnapper, a murderer, or whatever. It turns out, however, that he was a traveler who was lost and approached my home for directions. Clearly, I have done a terrible deed both legally and morally. I have shown a wanton and willful disregard for human life.

The same is true of anyone who supports our present policy of permissive abortions, if that person has serious doubts about the human status of the fetus. If a person is absolutely certain that the fetus is not human, then, of course, he or she by definition has no doubts and shows no disregard for human life in supporting an unfettered right to abort. If a person, however, simply does not know whether the fetus is human, he or she is in a state of doubt and therefore should not condone abortion except for the most serious of reasons. The great moral weakness of *Roe v. Wade* was that Justice Blackmun's argument ignored this point. He correctly noted that there was and always has been considerable doubt about the humanity of the fetus, but then he drew the outlandish conclusion that a woman and her physician were therefore free to decide to terminate the life of the fetus. The constitutional argument about a right to privacy and the moral argument about a woman's right over her own body cannot mask the faulty structure of the Court's argument: I am in doubt, therefore I can kill. It is as though my right to have my front porch free of uninvited strangers authorized me to kill a stranger who appeared on the porch simply because I was in doubt about why he had appeared.

The argument that the human status of the fetus is doubtful should lead to a moderate public policy conclusion that would preclude both absolute prohibitions against abortion and support for abortion on demand. If as a society we really don't know whether the fetus is human or not, then we should permit abortions for serious reasons—but only for serious reasons. An affluent, healthy, childless, married woman of twenty-eight should not be permitted to have an abortion because an ill-timed pregnancy interferes with a planned ski trip to Aspen. If, however, the pregnancy presented a serious threat to her life or to her health, she should be able to have the abortion. This would be a sound public policy for a society that was unable to resolve its doubts about the human status of the fetus.

A pro-lifer should find our statesman's line of reasoning attractive. It has the advantage of supporting a strong opposition to the present public policy on abortion, which is, for all practical purposes, a policy of abortion on demand. If it were to become public policy, it would dramatically reduce the number of legal abortions. Regardless of whether it prevails as public policy, it would give the pro-lifer a good reason for opposing abortion *without maintaining that every abortion is a murder.* One cannot cry "murder" until one is certain that the deceased is human. If there is some doubt on this point, then we are not talking about murder. We are talking about taking a life of a being that might have been human. If this is done for trivial reasons, it is morally wrong; but it's not murder.

The pro-lifer might tell our statesman that he cannot accept this argument. He might say that the argument is fine for one who honestly has some doubts about the humanity of the fetus but that he has no such doubts. For him it is absolutely certain that the fetus is human from the moment of conception.

To respond to such a pro-lifer a different line of argument is in order. Consider the usual aftermath of a bombing of an abortion clinic. Law enforcement officers and pro-choice spokespersons appear on camera to condemn the latest outrage. Interestingly, however, they are not alone. Prominent pro-lifers often join in the condemnation of violence and lawlessness. If the perpetrators are apprehended, they justify their behavior on the grounds that an attack against a piece of property is of no moral significance when one is attempting to discourage the murder of innocent babies. They realize their argument carries no legal weight, but they are willing to take the punishment for their actions against property. They usually insist that their actions were not "violent" because no persons were injured.

Let us change the scenario. Let us take the case of a leading spokeswoman for a prominent national pro-choice group. It so happens she owns three abortion clinics in the city in which she resides. She is a nurse by profession and has spoken often and proudly of her direct involvement in assisting physicians who perform abortions. One afternoon she is assassinated by a pro-life activist. The crime takes place in a state that permits capital punishment for first-degree murder. The pro-life activist turns himself in and announces that he is willing to pay for his crime even if he should be executed for it. He insists, however, that he has done nothing morally wrong even though he understands why the state must punish him. He compares the assassinated nurse to a high-ranking Nazi official who presided over a camp where Jews were being exterminated.

How would other pro-lifers react to this situation? Presumably, the overwhelming majority would be horrified and condemn the assassin outright. Our statesman might then ask one of the pro-lifers why he or she takes this position. If the answer is that he condemns all forms of violence, the statesman would have nothing further to say. That position is perfectly consistent. Suppose, however, that he came upon a pro-lifer who did not condemn all forms of violence. Suppose this person would support a war that was clearly justified or capital punishment for certain particularly heinous crimes. There would be no inconsistency here. One can be opposed to abortion and still support capital punishment because abortion involves killing one who is innocent and capital punishment involves killing one who has been proven guilty of a terrible crime. It is not at all unusual to find a pro-lifer who supports capital punishment or who is proud of having fought against Hitler in World War II.

If such a person were asked why he condemned the assassination, he would not give opposition to violence as his reason because we have already seen that under certain circumstances he approves of violence. Perhaps he would say he opposes the assassination because it is illegal. We would tell him we know this and so did the assassin. Does he think the assassination was immoral as well as illegal—that's the interesting question. Since he is a pro-lifer, he is clearly committed to a distinction between the moral and legal spheres. He is no legal positivist; if he were, he would not maintain abortion is morally wrong, since everyone knows it is legally permissible. It is obvious that our pro-lifer is quite capable of distinguishing a moral from a legal question. Perhaps he would say that even though there is a distinction between morality and legality, it is always morally wrong to break a law. Such an argument is vulnerable to the rejoinder: "What about Nazi Germany?" Would it be morally wrong to break a law in Hitler's Germany that supported anti-Semitism? Surely not. The main reason for conferring moral value on positive law is that adherence to a rule of law (positive law) helps to maintain the stability of a fundamentally just regime. Such an argument does not extend to Hitler's Germany, the prototype of the fundamentally unjust regime. The statesman can surely ask his pro-life friend if it reaches contemporary America where we condone over a million legal abortions (i.e., "murders" for the pro-lifer) every year with no end in sight. Can a pro-lifer who believes he lives in a society that tolerates a million murders a year seriously consider such a society fundamentally just? If the regime is not fundamentally just, then what *moral* reason can there be for upholding its rule of law?

It would seem that the pro-lifer would have to justify his condemnation of the assassination on the straightforward grounds that the victim did not deserve to die. Can this proposition be defended by one who maintains that abortions are murders? The assassinated nurse has made a career and perhaps a lot of money out of what the pro-lifer must consider the murder of babies. She does it every day. She advertises her lethal service in the classified section of the daily paper. Let us say she is forty years of age and gives every sign of dedicating herself to this sort of activity for the rest of her working career. From the pro-life point of view, she is a mass murderess who has killed thousands of innocent victims and has every intention of killing thousands more. It is clear that the law will not restrain her. From the pro-life point of view, how can it be morally wrong to assassinate such a woman under such a legal order?

The pro-lifer might reply that perhaps the assassinated nurse did not realize that every abortion involves the killing of an innocent human being. Pro-lifers know better, of course; but the nurse may have been a victim of invincible ignorance and, therefore, monstrous as her deeds were, she did not deserve to die. This argument is faulty. Suppose the nurse went mad one day and started to shoot the people in her clinic—the patients, the physicians, the other nurses, the secretaries—anyone who came into her line of fire. Suppose, further, that no policeman was in sight to put an end to this dreadful scene. Suppose one of the patients happened to have a gun with her, took careful aim, and killed the mad nurse before she could kill anyone else. Surely we would praise the woman whose marksmanship was so effective and, even if she had no business carrying a gun, we would applaud her decision to take decisive action. But we would also maintain that the mad nurse did not *deserve* to die. The insane never deserve any punishment—let alone death. They deserve compassion, care, and if possible, rehabilitation. Their exemption from moral responsibility, however, does not mean nothing can be done to prevent them from carrying out their mad acts, if these acts clearly and immediately threaten the lives of innocent bystanders. In such a crisis situation, the moral accountability of the mad killer is quite irrelevant. The task at hand is to protect the innocent whose lives are in peril.

This is the sort of reasoning that justified the slaying of the man who went berserk in a MacDonald's restaurant in San Diego and killed some innocent people several years ago. If he was insane, he did not deserve to die; nevertheless, under the circumstances, the person who killed him acted correctly. This line of reasoning is relevant to the abortion argument if one looks at it from the point of view of a pro-lifer who maintains that all abortions are murders the state will not prevent. Even if the abortionists do not realize they are killing innocent people day after day, the pro-lifer knows that they are and that he cannot turn to the police for help. Under such circumstances, why would it not be morally permissible to assassinate the nurse?

If the pro-lifer answered that such an action might lead to a backlash against his movement, the obvious response is that this is merely a prudential calculation. Indeed, the assassination might have just the opposite effect. It might deter abortionists from pursuing their trade. Unfortunately, we have some rather painful evidence of just how effective other forms of terrorism can be. The whole discussion of consequences, however, would be an embarrassment to the pro-lifer. He does not want to be put in the position of saying that abortionists' lives are forfeit to pro-life zealots in principle, even though prudence might dictate considerable caution in putting this principle into practice.

With this line of reasoning, our statesman would hope to convince the pro-lifer that perhaps he is not certain after all that every abortion involves the killing of an innocent human being. He has shown that such a belief leads to a conclusion that is shocking and clearly unacceptable—that is, that the assassination of an abortionist could be morally justified. No responsible pro-lifer has ever held such a position. Indeed, no irresponsible pro-lifer has ever held such a position. It is simply wrong. But if this wrong conclusion follows logically from the belief that every abortion is a murder, then there must be something wrong with that belief. This is what our statesman has been trying to do all along. His objective has been to convince the thoughtful pro-lifer that he cannot really believe that every abortion is a murder. What the pro-lifer really believes is that every abortion *might* be a murder. In switching the foundation of his belief from certitude to doubt, he assures the collapse of the elaborate superstructure of the case for assassination.

Since our statesman is a Catholic, he would probably be involved in many of these discussions with his coreligionists. To them he could make additional arguments to show that, despite their church's unequivocal opposition to abortion, this opposition does not necessarily rest on the belief that every abortion involves the killing of an innocent human being. There are several indications that this is the case.

The most important argument is that the Catholic church has never put its full teaching authority behind the proposition that every abortion involves the taking of a human life. The code of canon law excommunicates any Catholic who procures an abortion, but this means only that the church considers abortion a terrible evil; it does not necessarily mean that it equates abortion with murder.

Prominent Catholic pro-lifers, including even some bishops, have at times condemned abortion because of the evils to which it is likely to lead. For example, Bishop John Roach, a former president of the National Council of Catholic Bishops, once told a congressional committee that there are several reasons to support a pro-life amendment to the Constitution. One of his reasons for condemning a permissive abortion policy was that it might create a mentality that would easily justify other forms of killing—for example, euthanasia and infanticide.[27] This is certainly a plausible consideration, but it doesn't make any sense if it comes from one who is *certain* that all abortions involve the killing of a human being. Such a person lives in a society where a million people are killed by abortion annually. This is surely enough evil for anyone to worry about without raising concerns about where it will all lead. To discuss the evil of abortion in terms of its leading to euthanasia is like condemning Hitler's killing of the Jews because he might soon start killing the Lutherans.

Joseph Califano, a prominent Catholic layman, has written thoughtfully on the moral problems that face a public official who personally opposes abortion but whose official duties require him to take part in policies that encourage it. During the Carter administration, Califano served as secretary of the Department of Health and Human Services (HHS). In that position he had statutory responsibilities for issuing regulations on the funding of abortions. The exercise of his administrative discretion had a direct impact on the number of legal abortions performed in this country. Califano agonized over the dilemmas that confronted him. He sought expert advice from Catholic priests and theologians well versed in the complexities of church teaching on this matter. There is no doubt that Califano looked on abortion as a moral abomination.[28]

Despite his firm personal opposition, however, his memoir reveals some interesting exceptions. For example, he says that he thought "that when a woman has been the victim of rape or incest, a case can be made to permit an immediate abortion."[29] Perhaps many Catholics would agree with Califano on this point, but it is logically indefensible if one believes that the evil of abortion consists in the taking of an innocent life. Why make an exception for rape or incest? If the evil of abortion consists in the taking of the life of an innocent human being, rape and incest are irrelevant considerations. A fetus conceived by rape or through an incestuous union is no less human than a fetus conceived in the most tender and loving marital relationship. If one emphasizes Califano's stress on an *immediate* abortion, one might support his position on the grounds that if the physician does a dilitation and curettage quickly enough, the "abortion" can take place before conception. In this case, there has been no abortion in the moral sense of the term. The same conclusion would follow, however, regardless of the circumstances of the sexual union—rape, incest, or the most conventional form of union. In a word, rape or incest are irrelevant for those who consider abortion the taking of a human life.

Then why did a man as thoughtful and as intelligent as Califano make this distinction—a distinction that surely has intuitive appeal? Let us suppose he did so out of sensitivity to the feelings of the woman who has been raped. This would show that Califano is a good and decent man, but it would not say much for his reasoning powers. It is morally unjustifiable to attempt to comfort a woman who has been raped by killing another human being. If the woman's brother found the rapist and killed him, he would face a murder indictment. If it is wrong to kill the rapist who is guilty, it is surely wrong to kill the newly conceived "baby" who is innocent. This argument hangs together as long as one is certain that there is a human being

215

present from the moment of conception. But suppose one has some doubts along these lines. Suppose one thinks there *may* be a human being present from the moment of conception. Then Califano's exception for rape is quite logical. In performing an abortion in these circumstances one cannot be certain if one is taking a human life, but one can be certain that one is taking a major step toward relieving the sense of outrage and degradation that the raped woman surely feels. There is room for moral maneuvering.

Califano, of course, did not go into all this, but it may well be that his real reason for opposing abortion is that he believes abortion *may* involve the killing of an innocent human being. If this is the case, his exception for rape and incest makes perfectly good sense.

Another remarkable incident in Califano's memoir concerns a visit with Pope Paul VI during Califano's tenure as secretary of HHS. Califano's views on abortion had alarmed women's rights groups and had been the topic of extensive media coverage during his confirmation hearings. Immediately after his audience with the pope, reporters called Califano to inquire as to whether the pope had discussed abortion with him. He had not, Califano assured them. Instead the pope directed most of his comments to "the failure of the food-rich nations such as the United States to feed the world."[30] Now, there can be no doubt that Pope Paul VI was an adamant foe of abortion. But if he believed that every abortion was a murder, it is quite unlikely that he would have failed to bring the subject up in an audience with a Catholic official from a country where over a million abortions were taking place every year. His talk about third-world hunger would be a shocking dereliction of duty. Today many people criticize Pope Pius XII for doing too little to help Jews who suffered and died at the hands of the Nazis. Pope Paul's failure to discuss abortion with Califano would be a far greater evil than anything Pope Pius XII did or failed to do. This is true, of course, only if the pope believed that every abortion necessarily involves the taking of a human life. Perhaps even Pope Paul had some doubts along these lines.

Our statesman rests his case. He has gone as far as he properly can in trying to channel the public argument over abortion along lines that are less threatening to important state interests. If he could convince important pro-lifers that there may be some doubt about the humanity of the fetus, he would give them a principled basis for opposing abortion as perhaps the first of many evils in our society rather than as an evil so vast as to dwarf all others. Pro-life activities would, of course, go on unabated, as they should under First Amendment protections. Pro-lifers would continue to look forward to the day when the Supreme Court will overrule *Roe v. Wade,* as it surely will. In the meantime, however, they could in good conscience abandon single-issue voting as well as their demands that judges be selected primarily on the basis of their position on abortion. Above all else, they would have a principled basis for condemning resorts to violence on the part of their fellow pro-lifers who exceed the legitimate bounds of legal protest.

During the celebration of the bicentennial of the Constitution, our statesman might have encouraged serious pro-lifers to compare themselves to the men and women who supported adoption of the Constitution in 1787 and 1788 despite that document's compromise with the vicious institution of slavery. This comparison is appropriate, however, only if one is not certain that the fetus is human from the moment of conception. If one is certain that the fetus is human, then the evil of abortion is far worse than the evil of slavery. It is a terrible thing to buy and sell an innocent human being, but it is far worse to kill one; not one, alas, but millions. If our statesman succeeds in planting the seed of doubt in the minds of pro-lifers, he will then have given them grounds to see themselves as men and women who must learn to live with certain evils even as they work against them. This, we may confidently assume, was the mind-set of the most conscientious men and women of the founding era of the Republic as they weighed the evil of slavery against the blessings promised by the new Constitution.

The statesman's concern is similar to our congressman's position on South Africa and our judge's position on affirmative action. In each case, the governing principle is to scale down the ideological fervor of our democratic politics. On South Africa, the goal is to lift the black statesman's vision above traditional "black issues" and to experience himself as an important force in world affairs. On affirmative action, the goal is to encourage middle-class blacks to be like other Americans and to take their financial interests more seriously than their racial identity. On abortion, the goal is to persuade pro-lifers that, as serious as the issue of abortion is, the evil of abortion may be less than the evil of sixteen million murders condoned by the state.

Conclusion

The purpose of this essay has been to examine the meaning of political morality. I have done this by giving a few examples of what it might mean to think in moral terms derived from the stability of the existing order as a first principle. I have not attempted to announce any sort of grand theory; I have merely given examples. The examples themselves are somewhat tentative. Under slightly different circumstances of either fact or perception, I could have reached quite different conclusions. On the issue of affirmative action, for example, I would hope our judge would reach a very different conclusion if he took seriously the likelihood of a white backlash against minorities because of affirmative action. The same is true if he thinks affirmative action will seriously undermine Americans' belief in the importance of individual rights. This is an important article of faith in our civil religion. Serious and widespread doubts about individual rights would have a destabilizing effect on our institutions. His readiness to change from support for affirmative action to opposition does not suggest any inconsistency on his part. He is quite consistent in judging events of the day in terms of state interests. Under one set of circumstances he is for affirmative action and under another against it. This is quite consistent because the merits of affirmative action are instrumental to state interests.

The same would apply to our congressman who votes to override President Reagan's veto of the sanctions against South Africa. Presumably, he would change his mind if he were convinced that these sanctions would simply play into the hands of the African National Congress and that this organization is really as dangerous as the president thinks it is. Perhaps events would convince him that Bishop Tutu is a pawn of African Communists who, in turn, are lackeys of their Kremlin masters. A Russian satellite astride the Cape of Good Hope would augur ill for American strategic and commercial interests—and so on and so forth. If events gave credence to such a view of the world, the congressman should change his mind and reluctantly support the apartheid regime in the hope that it can hold the line against those who would turn South Africa into a Soviet satellite.

I conclude with a few more examples of the sort of thinking that is congruent with political morality. My examples are sketchy but will suffice to suggest the drift of the argument.

The easiest case is Iran. It is obvious that both President Carter and President Reagan were severely humiliated by their failure to think of the hostages in terms of reason of state. They are both good and decent men who approached the problem in terms of the well-being of American citizens who were mercilessly exploited by their contemptible captors. As a great power, the United States has both an interest and an obligation to support the orderly management of international affairs. This means that the president must play the statesman and instruct the American people on why their captured fellow citizens may be expendable. Such instruction should be supported with a rhetoric that looks on terrorism as the "moral equivalent of war." The warriors are the American journalists, clergymen, scholars, diplomats, soldiers, sailors, and businessmen who go abroad to pursue their respective callings, callings that represent the best in the American tradition. They should be encouraged to go abroad but should be advised that they are at risk when they do so. Their bravery should be celebrated. They should be advised that military efforts to free them may be undertaken even if such efforts might endanger their lives. If military efforts are unlikely to be effective, our government may decide simply to ignore the kidnappers and their demands. Americans abroad should be warned of this as well. Americans abroad should be looked upon as our own version of "freedom fighters," who voluntarily risk their lives to preserve the right of free men and free women to travel where they please. This sort of thinking would present in a more positive light our former policy of not accommodating terrorists.

The national holiday in honor of Martin Luther King is an event of profound moral importance. The teaching power of the symbol of King-as-great-American-hero cannot be overestimated. Most importantly, it is a lesson that our children will learn in a way they will never forget because King's birthday gives them a day away from school. What better way to impress children with the seriousness of Martin Luther King? Unlike affirmative action, King's birthday deprives no white man or woman of any rights or benefits. It creates no culture of poverty. It is virtually cost-free. The handful of protestors against the holiday betray themselves as shameful racists. Statesmen should support this national holiday enthusiastically.

The dreadful prospect of nuclear war creates a particularly difficult problem for political morality. Ordinarily, one thinks of reason of state in hawkish terms—a willingness to use force to defend national interests. Nuclear war, however, presents a different set of issues. War is above all else an act of state. It is intended to defend state interests or perhaps even the survival of the state. It is hard to see how nuclear war could achieve either of those goals. This is especially true in view of expert testimony suggesting that a nuclear war once begun might not be able to be controlled by the legitimate authority of the state. That is, it may escalate beyond what anyone intends. This is all quite speculative, of course, and may it ever be so. This speculation, however, raises fundamental questions about the morality of nuclear war even in terms of reason of state. A war that is likely to destroy the state and massive numbers of its people as well cannot be justified on grounds of reason of state.[31]

Perhaps these examples will suffice to fulfill my purpose of examining what political morality might look like in practice. It is not a very attractive picture that I have painted. Perhaps some readers will conclude that my political morality is no morality at all. In writing this essay, I have struggled with this conclusion myself; but I have resisted it because of Niebuhr's compelling argument against using the norms of personal morality to judge political affairs. If Niebuhr is correct, we need some kind of political morality. I have tried to offer a benign view of reason of state, American-style. If my argument is wanting, perhaps someone else will offer an alternative political morality.

Notes

1. Reinhold Niebuhr, *Moral Man and Immoral Society* (1932; reprint, New York: Charles Scribner's Sons, 1960), xi.

2. Ibid.

3. Ibid., xii.

4. Ibid., ix (emphasis added).

5. Alexander Passerin d'Entreves, *The Notion of the State* (London: Oxford University Press, 1967), chap. 5, 44–49.

6. Pedro Ribadeneyra, *Tratado de la Religion y Virtudes que deve tener el Principe Christiano, para governar y conservar sus Estados Contra lo que Nicolas Machiavelo y los Politicos desle Tiemp ensenan* (Madrid: Luis Sanchez, 1601) (*Religion and the Virtues of the Christian Prince: Against Machiavelli*, trans. George A. Moore [Washington, D.C.: Country Dollar Press, 1949], 282).

7. Giovanni Botero, *Della Ragion Di Stato Libri Dieci* (*Practical Politics*, trans. George A. Moore [Washington, D.C.: Country Dollar Press, 1949], 33–246).

8. William F. Church, *Richelieu and Reason of State* (Princeton: Princeton University Press, 1972), pt. I, 13–102, and pt. V, 481–504. Armand, Cardinal Duc de Richelieu, *Testament politique* (Amsterdam: H. Desbardes, 1688) (*The Political Testament of Cardinal Richelieu*, trans. Henry Berfram Hill [Madison: University of Wisconsin Press, 1961, 1972]). For further discussion of reason of state, see d'Entreves, chap. 5, 44–49, where a distinction is drawn between this doctrine and that of *Machtstaat*. See also Friedrich Meincke, *Die Idee der Staatsräson in der neueron Geschichte* (1925) (*Machiavellianism: The Doctrine of Raison d' État and Its Place in Modern History*, trans. Douglas Scott [New Haven: Yale University Press, 1962]).

9. Thomas Aquinas, *Summa Theologiae* II-II, question 51, art. 4; trans. Thomas Gilby, O. P. (London: Eyre and Spottiswoode, 1974), 105.

10. I refer to the problematic role of the philosopher in political life. This point is discussed in the "interpretive essay" that accompanies Allan Bloom's translation of the *Republic* (New York: Basic Books, 1968), 307–436.

11. For a brief discussion of the meaning of a "fundamentally just regime," see John A. Rohr, *Ethics for Bureaucrats: An Essay on Law and Values* (New York: Marcel Dekker, 1978), 82, n. 39.

12. Kenneth H. F. Dyson, *The State Tradition in Western Europe: A Study of an Idea and Institution* (Oxford: Martin Robertson, 1980), passim.

13. Because of John Locke's profound influence on American political thought, we can hardly expect Americans to have any patience with the doctrine of divine right of kings. Everyone has read Locke's famous second treatise on government. The first treatise, which few read today, attacks Robert Filmer's defense of divine right. See John Locke, *Two Treatises of Government*, ed. Thomas I. Cook (New York: Hafner, 1947), 5–118.

14. Arthur S. Miller, "Constitutional Reason of State," in *Encyclopedia of the American Constitution*, ed. Leonard W. Levy, Kenneth L. Karst, and Dennis J. Mahoney, 4 vols. (New York: Macmillan, 1986), 2:491.

15. Michael Walzer, "Political Action: The Problem of Dirty Hands," *Philosophy and Public Affairs* 2 (Winter 1973): 160-80.

16. If a particular action is absolutely prohibited, then it simply cannot be done regardless of consequences. This is true whether one is discussing personal or political morality. This rather obvious consideration soon collapses into the more fundamental question of what (if anything) is absolutely prohibited.

17. David Hoffman, "Regan Remark Assailed as Sexist," *Washington Post*, 18 July 1986, sec. A, 27.

18. Ibid.

19. In support of affirmative action, see *Fullilove v. Klutznick*, 448 U.S. 448 (1980) and *Steelworkers v. Weber*, 443 U.S. 193 (1979). For a more critical position on affirmative action see *Firefighters Local Union No. 1784 v. Stotts*, 104 S. Ct. 2576 (1984) and *Wygant et al. v. Jackson Board of Education*, 54 U.S.L.W. 4479 (1986).

20. *Somerset v. Stewart*, 20 How. St. tr. 1 (1772).

21. Levy et al., s.v. "Badges of Servitude," by Kenneth Karst, 1:87–88.

22. *Jones v. Mayer Co.*, 392 U.S. 409 (1968).

23. Section One of the Fourteenth Amendment provides: "nor shall any State deprive any person of life, liberty, or property, without due process of law; nor deny to any person within its jurisdiction the equal protection of the laws."

24. See *Jones v. Mayer Co.*, 392 U.S. 409 (1968).

25. Dyson, 155–85.

26. *Roe v. Wade*, 410 U.S. 113 (1973).

27. *The Catholic Virginian*, 17 January 1983, p. 1.

28. Joseph A. Califano, Jr., *Governing America* (New York: Simon and Schuster, 1981), 49–87.

29. Ibid., 57.

30. Ibid., 80.

31. Francis X. Winters, "The Cultural Context of the Pastoral Letter on Peace," in *Peace in a Nuclear Age*, ed. Charles J. Read, Jr. (Washington, D.C.: Catholic University of America Press, 1985), 336–41.

CHAPTER NINE

Ethical Theory
and Public Service

F. Neil Brady

D ESPITE their mythical aloofness, in recent years philosophers have shown a keen interest in the ethical issues facing the professional fields. Their disciplined thinking has provided significant insight into knotty problems in such fields as medicine, law, and management. As a natural consequence of their contribution, ethical theory has been imported as a practical framework for the analysis of issues. This is especially true in management, where a number of texts devote opening chapters to ethical theory[1] and essays in professional journals employ ethical theoretic categories for empirical or conceptual studies.[2]

Unfortunately, the link between the rigorous analysis displayed in examinations of issues in professional ethics and the more general discussions of ethical theory is weak. The practical rhetoric of persuasion simply is not adequately supported by any analytic framework based in theory. Although lip service is paid in management-ethics texts to the relevance of ethical theory for the practical problems of managing, seldom is an explicit connection made between theory and useful insight.

F. Neil Brady is an associate professor of management in the College of Business Administration, San Diego State University.

Ethical theory as yet provides only minimal insight into the very real processes of good thinking in ethics.

Consequently, ethical theory has come under recent criticism as being subjective and impractical. Recalling such allegations, Hosmer writes,

> The last argument that I have heard expressed against courses in business ethics is that the topic is, by its nature, non-empirical and consequently non-scientific. . . . It is alleged that business decisions are, or should be, based upon objective thought processes, and that ethical analysis has to be subjective, and therefore has no place in the business curriculum.[3]

Fritzsche and Becker echo this concern over the nonempirical nature of ethical theoretic categories and add that "ethical theories themselves are normative and consequently difficult to operationalize."[4]

Trevino is particularly critical of the impotence of ethical theory:

> Normative ethical theory was not found to be particularly helpful in explaining or predicting ethical decision making. . . . [It] is not designed for the purpose of explaining or predicting behavior. Rather, normative ethical theory represents an ideal that may not reflect accurately the processes engaged in by people in actual situations. A second problem with the philosophical/normative theory approach is its lack of face validity. Few managers are likely to think of their day-to-day decision making as following normative ethical theories of utilitarianism, justice, or rights.[5]

Finally, referring to currently fashionable speeches, essays, articles, and conferences on business ethics as so much "ethical chic," Peter Drucker laments the absence of objective standards in ethics which would apply to all individuals.[6]

So, although the philosophers have greatly contributed to the understanding of specific professional problems, they have as yet failed to convince us that the credit for good thinking in ethics is owed to their familiarity with ethical theory. Indeed, they might not even make this claim but instead fall back on vague appeals to the benefits of "rigorous disciplined thinking."

Herein lies the problem: We have a sophisticated body of theory on the one hand and evidence of clear, practical thinking in ethics on the other, but the generality of the former appears inadequate to generate the specificity of the latter. As Archie Bahm concludes, "We are teaching ethics without ethics to teach."[7]

Despite the misgivings mentioned above, this essay assumes that the grounds for good thinking in ethics *do* ultimately rest in ethical theory and that bridging the gap between theory and practice is one of the most pressing issues in management ethics today. But like a lot of studies where ambition is tempered by reality, this essay's aims are more modest than the problem which justifies its worth. Although the case could be made for management ethics in general, the need to provide examples and observations compels an analysis of narrower scope. Here, then, I examine the relevance of ethical theory for public administration and highlight the implications of that argument, especially where it bridges practical and theoretic concerns.

A Brief Synopsis of Ethical Theory

Ethical theory is basically the question of justification in ethical decision making. That is, it seeks the grounds for one's *judgments* concerning right and wrong, regardless of one's behavior. Unfortunately, there exists at least moderate disagreement in the field over even the most basic models of ethical theory. Although this paper may contribute toward the understanding of theory, it cannot solve these problems at the outset. What follows, then, is a short, "working version" of ethical theory.

The grounds upon which ethical judgments can be made are traditionally two: utilitarianism and (Kantian) formalism. Of the two, utilitarianism generally receives the clearer presentation in the literature. According to its founder, Jeremy Bentham, the utilitarian criterion in ethics consists of selecting courses of action which promise to bring about the greatest good for the greatest number.[8] In economic terminology, this is referred to as "utility maximization." On the practical level, utilitarianism relates most directly to public policy studies and cost-benefit analysis.[9] Viewed as a decision-procedure, utilitarian analysis consists of five familiar steps:

- List alternatives
- List criteria
- Rank criteria
- Assess alternatives
- Choose optimal alternative

Although the execution of these steps is fraught with well-known difficulties, the method attempts to formalize common human intuitions and judgment processes.[10]

The actual use of utilitarian analysis does not require full use of the method described above. Except in formal policy studies, utilitarian analysis seldom occurs in its full form. In actual use, utilitarian discussions usually focus in on the critical step(s) of the method. Utilitarian reasoning more commonly occurs in a more fragmented form—as a creative alternative, speculation over consequences, arguments about the relative importance of reasons, and so on.

Formalism, first formulated by Immanuel Kant, is much more abstract and therefore esoteric.[11] Unlike Bentham, Kant felt that ethical decisions relate more directly to motives than to consequences; but in trying to elicit the grounds of good motives, he appeals to complex ideas and unfamiliar jargon. He refers to the method of formalism in ethics as the "categorical imperative" and identifies the main requirement of this method as "universalizing." Kant provides several versions of universalizing, but the best known is this: "Act only according to that maxim by which you can at the same time will that it should become a universal law."[12] Recent attempts to clarify Kant's proposals remain complex and do not seem to lend themselves well to practical deliberation on current policy, managerial, or personal issues.[13]

However, I have argued elsewhere that despite the complex philosophical expositions and defenses of Kantian formalism, *practical* formalistic reasoning is no more difficult, no less used, and no harder to find in management ethics discussions than examples of utilitarian reasoning.[14] Like examples of utilitarian reasoning, formalistic reasoning in ethics often occurs in a fragmented form in the literature. When universalizing is considered from a practical (not theoretical) point of view and broken down into its constituent components, it ceases to be a holistic thought experiment and, instead, becomes a collection of examined cases. That is, if an action is to be "universalized," it must be consistent with precedent, applicable to analogical situations, reversible, and able to survive all counterexamples; and it must consider the import of extreme cases, counterfactuals, and even archetypal cases. In short, universalizing is simply the case-by-case consideration of the application of a principle until the principle has been measured against the universe of all relevant cases. Those that succeed are universalizable. Understood in this way, formalistic reasoning can be regarded as a common and familiar strategy for analyzing ethical issues.

A great deal more could be said about the details of both utilitarian and formalistic reasoning in ethics; but this brief review is sufficient for proceeding with the primary purpose of this essay—namely, showing that ethical theory is important for understanding ethics in public administration.

SUPREME COURT CASES AND ETHICAL THEORY

One of the most important contributions to understanding ethics in public administration in the last ten years is John Rohr's *Ethics for Bureaucrats: An Essay on Law and Values*.[15] The main argument of the book is that public officials are responsible under oath to uphold democratic values, as expressed in decisions of the Supreme Court, so far as they apply to the use of discretionary power and authority. He writes,

> Bureaucrats have an ethical obligation to respond to the values of the people in whose name they govern. The values in question are not popular whims of the moment but rather constitutional or regime values. This is because the bureaucrat has taken an oath to uphold the Constitution. As far as schools

of public administration are concerned, the best educational means for preparing bureaucrats to fulfill this obligation is to use Supreme Court opinions on salient regime values to encourage them to reflect on how those values might best influence their decision making as one who governs.[16]

The majority of the book is then spent reviewing majority and dissenting opinions of Supreme Court justices regarding landmark cases concerning equality, freedom, and property and elucidating the kind of reasoning that forms the basis of their deliberations and that lies at the root of constitutional law. I believe that this is a very helpful way to proceed in studying ethics in programs of public administration, but I do so for reasons that are perhaps more generic than Professor Rohr's. My contention is that the best ethical reasoning, whether it relates to public sector or business matters, is always either utilitarian or formalistic. This is particularly true for majority and dissenting opinions of the Supreme Court. And a brief review of the major outlines of thought in those decisions that relate to the general problems of equality, freedom, and property will provide a concrete elaboration of ethical theory in use, illustrating how ethical theory applies in broad strokes to the fundamental issues of public administration. Contrary to traditional assumptions, it will also show that the use of an ethical method is conditional: relevance of a method depends on the issue to be examined.

Equality

Over the decades, the Supreme Court has tended to promote equality through refusing to recognize racial and sexual classifications of an invidious nature as constitutional. In *Brown v. Board of Education*[17] the Court cut down the "separate but equal" doctrine as it applied to public education. Chief Justice Warren delivered the unanimous decision of the Court. His reasoning is formalistic in that the central issue is whether the institution of segregated schools is universalizable. The issue is not utilitarian, since the question of the overall effect on educa-

230

tion is not raised. Arguing against segregation, the Court cited the differences in educational opportunity and the stigma necessarily attached to segregated education as reasons compelling the integration of the public schools.

In the more recent cases concerning reverse discrimination, the question is again formalistic: Is discrimination in favor of minorities more universalizable ("generally acceptable") than equal opportunity based on universal standards for such criteria as admission, hiring, and promotion? The Court has generally upheld reverse discrimination activities on the grounds that equality is more readily achieved through at least some reverse discrimination activities than through none at all. Although six different opinions were handed down, in *Regents of the U. of Cal. v. Bakke*[18] the Court again upheld reverse discrimination in education. One of the most interesting opinions is that of Justice Blackmun, who argues that preferential treatment is acceptable partly because it is consistent with a variety of traditional and accepted behaviors. He writes,

> It is somewhat ironic to have us so deeply disturbed over a program where race is an element of consciousness, and yet to be aware of the fact, as we are, that institutions of higher learning . . . have given conceded preferences up to a point to those possessed of athletic skills, to the children of alumni, to the affluent who may bestow their largess on the institutions, and to those having connections with celebrities, the famous, and the powerful. . . . It is worth noting, perhaps, that governmental preference has not been a stranger to our legal life. We see it in veterans' preferences. We see it in the aid-to-the-handicapped programs. We see it in the progressive income tax. We see it in the Indian programs. We may excuse some of these on the ground that they have specific constitutional protection or, as with Indians, that those benefited are wards of the Government. Nevertheless, these preferences exist and may not be ignored.[19]

Justice Blackmun's argument is an interesting illustration of formalistic ethical thinking in practice. For an action to be universalizable one must intuitively accept all actions that are *like* the action in question in the ethically relevant ways. Here, he is not arguing that reverse discrimination is "universalizable," but he is saying that failing to grant constitutionality to special admission programs which prefer minority candidates is inconsistent with a number of other traditional or accepted activities.

The development of the notion of sexual equality also is dominantly formalistic. In *Weinberger v. Wiesenfeld,* for example, the Court held that widows and widowers need not be treated alike so far as systems of taxation and social security benefits are concerned.[20] The arguments focused on the fact that women had historically suffered economic discrimination; therefore, like other practices of "reverse discrimination," taxation systems designed to alter this unfair situation are constitutional. Failing to design such systems to recognize the plight of widows actually sanctions the inequalities in place, ignores the history of accumulated injustices and produces situations that are far less "universalizable" than the practice of "equal" treatment or opportunity. Reverse discrimination has thus been referred to as a "benign" form of discrimination.

Freedom

Supreme Court cases which have focused on the question of freedom also provide a good illustration of ethical theory in practice. However, unlike the equality cases, the dominant ethical approach is *utilitarian.* In general, the issue is how far the nation can go in granting legitimacy and power to personal preference without reaping greater harm than benefit.

In cases concerning freedom of speech, the Court wrestled with a criterion for restraining free speech. In *Gitlow v. New York* the Supreme Court adopted the "bad tendency test."[21] However, Justice Holmes's dissenting opinion voiced a more liberal standard which has supplanted the "bad tendency test." He argued that actions must present a "clear and present danger" in order to warrant governmental prohibition.

Cases that have tested the freedom of religion are also essentially utilitarian. In *Minersville School District v. Gobitis* the Court upheld the school board's power to require a compulsory flag salute. In delivering the Court's opinion, Justice Frank-furter called attention to the *utility* of such ceremonial functions:

> We are dealing with an interest inferior to none in the hierarchy of legal values. National unity is the basis of national secu-rity. . . . The ultimate foundation of a free society is the binding tie of a cohesive sentiment. Such sentiment is fostered by all those agencies of the mind and spirit which may serve to gather up the traditions of a people, transmit them from generation to generation, and thereby create that continuity of a treasured common life which constitutes a civilization. "We live by sym-bols." The flag is the symbol of our national unity, transcending all internal differences, however large, within the framework of the constitution. [22]

Just three years later, however, in *Board of Education v. Bar-nette* the Supreme Court reversed itself. This time the court appealed to the "clear and present danger criterion":

> But here the power of compulsion is invoked without any allega-tion that remaining passive during a flag salute ritual creates a clear and present danger that would justify an effort even to muffle expression. . . . To believe that patriotism will not flour-ish if patriotic ceremonies are voluntary and spontaneous in-stead of a compulsory routine is to make an unflattering estimate of the appeal of our institutions to free minds. [23]

The difference between the two cases is the greater value attrib-uted to freedom by comparison with national unity and cohe-sion. This is not to say that utilitarian ends are not served if national unity and cohesion are subordinated to the principle of liberty. On the contrary, preference for liberty over cohesion signifies a greater good in the minds of the people.

So, these brief illustrations help to show that Supreme Court cases which have defined the limits of freedom are historically utilitarian. They may not be exclusively utilitarian since free-doms and constraints often result in discriminatory behavior which might not be justified under the canons of formalism. But typically, questions of freedom have asked the simple utilitarian question, "Does restraint or exercise of freedom bring about greater value to the people of the nation?" And an adequate understanding of such issues can only proceed along traditional utilitarian lines.

Property

By contrast with the issues of equality and freedom, the history of the notion of property in the United States is "Janus-headed."[24] That is, its development takes two simultaneous and sometimes conflicting ethical directions, displaying both utilitarian and formalistic orientations. In the first sense, the issue is utilitarian: "What claims to property promote the national interest?" In the second, the issue is formalistic: "What kinds of things can persons claim as property?"

In *Home Building & Loan Association v. Blaisdell* the conflict of the two views is apparent.[25] Minnesota's Mortgage Moratorium Law of 1933 provided that, under emergency circumstances (the Depression) the state courts could authorize a limited moratorium on the payment of mortgages. The Supreme Court found the law to be constitutional for utilitarian reasons in that the government has the authority to secure the "peace and good order of society" and to "safeguard the vital interests of the people." In later cases involving water rights, bankruptcy, bridges, ferries, and railroads, the Court consistently held in favor of arrangements that promised a general increase in wealth and prosperity despite the violation of traditional property rights. Such utilitarian decisions clearly discriminate at least temporarily against more traditional relationships, even endangering the universally recognized practices surrounding contracts. A temporary moratorium on mortgage payments is a utilitarian exception under emergency circumstances to what is otherwise an accepted formalistic practice of honoring contracts.

Conversely, the Court has also demonstrated that exceptions can be made to securing the general welfare when the competing value of equal citizenship can be enhanced. As "new" forms of wealth have appeared, such as Social Security benefits, government contracts, occupational licenses, business franchises, public service employment, and welfare payments, the Supreme

Court has increasingly recognized the right of individuals to lay claim to this wealth, as opposed to regarding them, for example, as governmental gratuities or charity. And in spite of administrative inefficiencies and moderate costs, the Court has increasingly recognized the entitlement of citizens to such wealth.

The primary reason for ignoring utility and granting entitlements is the actual or potential unfairnesses that result from failing to do so. In *Goldberg v. Kelly* the Supreme Court held that welfare payments could not be discontinued without due process.[26] In delivering the opinion of the Court, Justice Brennan cited the necessity for administrative fairness in spite of increased costs which would limit the amount of money available for distribution to the needy. And Reich reminds us that the poor tend to be discriminated against without such safeguards:

> Society today is built around entitlement. . . . Many of the most important of these entitlements now flow from government: subsidies to farmers and businessmen; routes for airlines and channels for television stations; long term contracts for defense, space, and education; social security pensions for individuals. Such sources of security, whether private or public, are no longer regarded as luxuries or gratuities; to the recipients they are essentials, fully deserved, and in no sense a form of charity. It is only the poor whose entitlements, although recognized by public policy, have not been effectively enforced.[27]

So, although the provision of wealth is generally a utilitarian issue, a formalistic approach is required when deciding what kinds of wealth citizens can claim as property. This is clearly seen in Supreme Court reasoning relating to "new property," as opposed to the utilitarian analyses required in cases focused on "old property."

The Essential Duality of Ethical Theory

There are several things that can be inferred from this brief examination of the role of ethical theory in Supreme Court decisions. One is that ethical theory is grounded in the stubborn fact of argument. Although its reputation among nonphilosophers generally is that it is impractical, pie-in-the-sky thinking, the basic categories of ethical theory do at least refer to actual modes of reasoning in some of our nation's most important documents. Ethical theory is the "language" of administrative justification.

A second major point is recognizing that the ethical theoretic character of Supreme Court cases gives us an enhanced appreciation for judicial decisions and for the role of public servants whose duty is based in upholding constitutional values and ideals. Seeing that Supreme Court decisions represent progress toward the consistent application of two ethical theoretic paradigms dissuades us from regarding judicial history as merely reflecting changing social norms or "moods." This realization promotes trust in the Constitution and its interpretation through the Court and justifies our allegiance through more universal categories than mere nationalism or ideology.

But perhaps the most important point is the observation that ethical theory is not unitary. An assumption that has been hard for the philosophers to give up is the notion of a single decision procedure or ground of justification in ethics. Without citing a lengthy philosophical history, I believe that scholarship prefers a single account of ethics, not two. And in the professional journals, with some regularity, there are still essays providing a new argument for the dominance of one theory over the other. This preference is partly founded in the fear that multiple approaches may lead to inconsistent prescriptions and partly in the examples of methodological singularity provided by such disciplines as chemistry, biology, or mathematics.

However, given insights into the practical application of ethical theory, such as those relating to the Supreme Court decisions discussed above, a more realistic approach to ethical theory might recognize the legitimacy and usefulness of *both* utilitarianism and formalism. That is, there is an essential duality in ethical theory. This should be apparent from the hundred-year-old unresolved battle between proponents of the two views. As E. F. Schumaker suggests, some problems are "divergent" in that "the more they are clarified and logically developed, the more they *diverge*."[28] Like the classic balancing of freedom and discipline in education, or Okun's famous governmental trade-off between equality and efficiency, the requirements of utilitarian and formalistic ethics represent diverging but legitimate requirements for ethical behavior.[29]

What seems clear from this quick survey of Supreme Court decisions is that the application of utilitarian or formalistic thinking *depends on the issue*. That is, the general question of equality requires primarily formalistic reasoning, while the issue of freedom has dominantly been utilitarian. For some issues, like property, both utilitarian and formalistic approaches are helpful, and the issue becomes "Janus-headed"; that is, one issue splits into two. Numerous other issues in management ethics illustrate this "Janus-headed" model of ethical theory.[30]

These insights are still rather theoretical. They become somewhat more practical, however, when we consider the possibility that *persons*, as well as issues, might exhibit similar divergent preferences for the two ethical approaches. Based on recent research, Fritzsche and Becker have found that business executives rely almost totally on utilitarian methods for reasoning about ethical issues of various types.[31] This suggests that occupations might generally prefer one kind of ethical thinking rather than another. We might point to judges, for example, as formalists or to legislators as utilitarians. My own research and thinking further suggests that *individuals* can be classified as utilitarians and formalists in terms of their psychological propensities to adopt one approach rather than the other.[32]

This hypothesized tension might account for a number of practical conflicts. For example, the psychological differences between formalists and utilitarians might explain useless debates where persons find themselves talking past each other. The deep stereotypical differences between elected officials on a city council and career public servants in city administration, for example, may in part be accounted for in terms of the diverging (but legitimate) ethical orientations of each group. Such differences can also explain some interpersonal disagreements or "personality conflicts," mismatches of persons to issues, and so on. Definitive research yet remains to be done in this area, but such studies certainly promise to illuminate a wide array of practical concerns in administration.

The Use of Discretionary Power

So, the prime values of public administration in the United States, the present "regime values," are of worth ultimately because they reflect a history of compliance with objective, ethical theoretic categories. And such categories may be applicable to understanding occupational or even interpersonal differences in orientation on many kinds of issues. Therefore, utilitarianism and formalism clearly promise to be useful categories for the *classification* of issues, activities, and orientations.

But the origins of both utilitarianism and formalism imply that their main functions are not classificatory, but *procedural*. That is, ethical theory traditionally was meant to describe specific processes of decision making and not just general types of issues. Both Kant and Bentham intended people to act according to the specific recommendations of their theories.

The procedural use of ethical theory is most clearly seen where people have both the time and the resources to commit to the job. Utilitarian analyses are illustrated well by cost-benefit analyses, policy studies, environmental impact statements, and other detailed and extensive studies that try to assess the consequences of alternative actions or policies. Similarly, formalistic ethics is best illustrated by close analyses of policy issues that turn on conceptual themes, such as many difficult issues in medicine, law, and management.

But ethical theory is also relevant for most day-to-day operational decisions as well. Consider briefly the case of an administrator's needing to decide how to distribute personal computers in a department whose requests for computers far outnumber the computers available for distribution. The administrator can make a rational, utilitarian distribution (by need, talent, training, politics, etc.) or a universal distribution (rotate use, centralized computer services office, etc.). In theory, the two positions are conceptually discrete; and in practice the intuitive "pull" of each is strong.

The diverging claims of utilitarian and formalistic ethics are most extreme in "lifeboat ethics" cases. Either the resource of the lifeboat is made available to all (and therefore is useful to no one) or its use is maximized by discriminating among individuals for poor or no reasons (it's better to save someone—anyone—than no one). In such cases, the only ethical "solutions"—if there are any—seem intensely personal; they defy our needs to manage. This suggests that the domain of ethical behavior transcends present theory—especially where such behaviors as altruism and service are concerned.

This tension between utility and universality is particularly sensitive to the public administrator whose codes of ethics and administrative regulations consistently require promoting the general welfare, which is utilitarian, while at the same time being impartial, which is formalistic. There are many occasions where the natural tension present in the two requirements becomes unnervingly real, such as when one's personal or private preferences appear to conflict with official duties to remain impartial. The usual response in such dilemmas is to make an exception to one set of requirements or the other. One might reason, "It doesn't compromise my ability to remain impartial if I pursue personal interests here; my personal life is just as important as anyone else's." Or alternatively one might say, "A little inconvenience to me is not worth risking accusations of favoritism."

In theoretical terms, the practical options open to the public administrator might be formulated as exceptions to both requirements:

1. Be impartial except when partiality results in the good for *all*, not just greater cumulative good. (This is an administrative version of John Rawls's "difference principle."[33])
2. Pursue the general welfare except when efficiencies of experience, role, or position reduce impartiality to a mere economic judgment. (Impartiality is a larger concept than an

economic one; it relates to the nature of citizenship and may not be reduced to a mere impartial judgment of general utility.)

These two interrelated principles begin to express the delicate, practical balance possible between utilitarian and formalistic ethical requirements. Proper explication would require another essay, but at least we can sense the beginnings of an account of administrative discretion based on ethical theory.

CONCLUSION

Ethical theory can be brought down out of the clouds of abstraction for use on the cold, hard ground of administrative decision making. At least two facts seem stubborn. One, the canons of ethical theory are observed in the best thinking. Decisions of the Supreme Court are one example of both utilitarian and formalistic thinking at their best. And two, both utilitarian and formalistic reasoning make their demands on decision makers, depending on the issue. Such requirements sometimes are simultaneously satisfied, at other times result in necessary adjustments to administrative practices or rules, and at still other times result in genuine dilemmas of the "lifeboat ethics" sort.

Although the relevance of ethical theory for administrative decision making seems secure, the development of theory has not kept pace with managerial abilities or needs. In the case of formalistic ethics, theory does a very poor job of describing forms of thinking that people routinely employ. As I have suggested earlier, if universalizing consists of the examination of the interplay between case and principle, a great deal yet needs to be done to understand how people reasonably accept rules on the basis of examined cases.

Some texts suggest that the way to evaluate rules is to test them against counterexamples.[34] But counterexamples are not the only cases that have a bearing on the evaluation of rules. Consider this rule: "We should continue to use up depletable

natural resources at the current rates." How would any counterexample help here? We might consider extreme cases, such
as the gluttonous use or the miserly use of oil—both of which
seem intuitively unacceptable. Or we might conclude that at the
present rates the world's reserves will be exhausted in one
hundred years. But does that count as a counterexample? I
suggest that good formalistic reasoning considers a wide variety
of real and imaginary cases in seeking to "universalize" a rule:
extreme cases, precedent, counterfactuals, reverse cases, analogies, counterexamples, archetypal cases, and so on. But to my
knowledge the logical interrelation of these considerations has
not been studied—not even by the legal profession, which is
probably more deeply involved in formalistic reasoning than any
other. In the case of formalistic reasoning, our abilities to reason
simply exceed our understanding of those abilities; and although
I suspect such an awareness would be very complex, an explicit
study of formalistic reasoning would provide standards for thinking beyond the currently fashionable formal logic texts or texts
on informal fallacies. Before formalistic ethics can *prescribe*, it
must learn to *describe*.

Second, although utilitarian reasoning has profited from close
attention to its procedures, the practical use of utilitarianism
requires some usable standards that can be quickly applied in
day-to-day operational decision situations. Managers simply
cannot perform the cost-benefit calculations explicitly required
by the method; instead, intuitive judgments must be made
which compare alternatives and their consequences. But little or
nothing has been done to provide such practical utilitarian
guidelines for administrators. And doing so might relieve some
of the burden of hypocrisy from the shoulders of analysts who
(aggregating data for policy studies) routinely require individuals to make the kind of comparisons of incommensurable variables they themselves are unprepared to make or to justify.

Notes

1. Tom L. Beauchamp and Norman E. Bowie, eds., *Ethical Theory and Business* (Englewood Cliffs, N.J.: Prentice-Hall, 1979); Vincent Barry, *Moral Issues in Business*, 3d ed. (Belmont, Calif.: Wadsworth, 1986), 33–74; Richard T. DeGeorge, *Business Ethics*, 2d ed. (New York: Macmillan, 1986), 39–70; Manuel G. Velasquez, *Business Ethics: Concepts and Cases* (Englewood Cliffs, N.J.: Prentice-Hall, 1982), 44–106.

2. David J. Fritzsche and Helmut Becker, "Linking Management Behavior to Ethical Philosophy—An Empirical Investigation," *Academy of Management Journal* 27 (March 1984): 166–75; Gerald Cavanagh, Dennis Moberg, and Manuel Velasquez, "The Ethics of Organizational Politics," *Academy of Management Review* 6 (July 1981): 363–74; Neil Brady, "A Janus-Headed Model of Ethical Theory: Looking Two Ways at Business/Society Issues," *Academy of Management Review* 10 (July 1985): 568–76.

3. LaRue T. Hosmer, "The Other 338: Why a Majority of Our Schools of Business Administration Do Not Offer a Course in Business Ethics," *Journal of Business Ethics* 4 (1985): 21.

4. Fritzsche and Becker, "Linking Management Behavior," 166.

5. Linda Klebe Trevino, "Ethical Decision Making in Organizations: A Person-Situation Interactionist Model," *Academy of Management Review* 11 (July 1986): 604.

6. Peter Drucker, "Ethical Chic," *Forbes*, 14 September 1981, 160.

7. Archie J. Bahm, "Teaching Ethics without Ethics to Teach," *Journal of Business Ethics* 1 (1982): 43–47.

8. Jeremy Bentham, *An Introduction to the Principles of Morals and Legislation* (1789; reprint, Oxford: Clarendon Press, 1897), 3.

9. Alisdair MacIntyre, "Utilitarianism and Cost-Benefit Analysis: An Essay on the Relevance of Moral Philosophy to Bureaucratic Theory," in *Values in the Electric Power Industry*, ed. Kenneth Sayre (Notre Dame: University of Notre Dame Press, 1977), 217–37.

10. Ibid.

11. Immanuel Kant, *Foundations of the Metaphysics of Morals*, trans. Lewis White Beck (1785; reprint, New York: Bobs-Merrill, 1959).

12. Ibid., 39.

13. R. M. Hare, *Freedom and Reason* (London: Oxford at the Clarendon

Press, 1963); Onora Nell, *Acting on Principles: An Essay on Kantian Ethics* (New York: Columbia University Press, 1975).

14. Neil Brady, "Practical Formalism: A New Methodological Proposal for Business Ethics," *Journal of Business Ethics* 7 (March 1988): 163–70.

15. John A. Rohr, *Ethics for Bureaucrats: An Essay on Law and Values* (New York: Marcel Dekker, 1978).

16. Ibid., 4.

17. *Brown v. Board of Education*, 347 U.S. 483 (1954) and 349 U.S. 294 (1955).

18. *Regents of the University of California v. Bakke*, 438 U.S. 265 (1978).

19. Ibid.

20. *Weinberger v. Wiesenfeld*, 420 U.S. 636 (1975).

21. *Gitlow v. New York*, 268 U.S. 652 (1925).

22. *Minersville School District v. Gobitis*, 310 U.S. 595 (1940).

23. *Board of Education v. Barnette*, 319 U.S. 633–34, 641 (1943).

24. Brady, "A Janus-Headed Model," 569–72.

25. *Home Building & Loan Association v. Blaisdell*, 290 U.S. 398 (1934).

26. *Goldberg v. Kelly*, 397 U.S. 254 (1970).

27. Charles A. Reich, "Individual Rights and Social Welfare: The Emerging Legal Issues," *Yale Law Journal* 74 (June 1965): 1255.

28. E. F. Schumacher, *A Guide for the Perplexed* (New York: Harper and Row, 1977), 122.

29. Arthur Okun, *Equality and Efficiency: The Big Tradeoff* (Washington, D.C.: Brookings Institution, 1975).

30. Brady, "A Janus-Headed Model," 571–72.

31. Fritzsche and Becker, "Linking Management Behavior," 175.

32. Neil Brady and Penny Wright, "An Exploratory Study Testing the Empirical Strength of the Ethical Distinction between Utilitarians and Formalists," unpublished paper delivered at the Western division meetings of the Academy of Management, March 1986.

33. John Rawls, *A Theory of Justice* (Cambridge: Harvard University Press, Belknap Press, 1971), 60.

34. Barry, *Moral Issues in Business*, 25.

Index